PLAYING

AN INTRODUCTION TO ACTING

5/3/83

Paul Kuritz

Paul Kuritz

BATES COLLEGE

PRENTICE-HALL, INC. Englewood Cliffs, New Jersey   07632

Library of Congress Cataloging in Publication Data

KURITZ, PAUL.
   Playing : an introduction to acting.

   Bibliography: p.
   Includes index.
   1. Acting. I. Title.
PZ2061.K787   792'.028   81-19220
ISBN 0-13-682906-6   AACR2

For My Playmates: Deborah, Nathaniel, and Ethan

Editorial/production supervision and interior design: Richard Kilmartin
Cover design: Miriam Recio
Manufacturing buyer: Edmund W. Leone

Printed in the United States of America

10 9 8 7 6 5 4 3 2 1

ISBN 0-13-682906-6

Prentice-Hall International, Inc., *London*
Prentice-Hall of Australia Pty. Limited, *Sydney*
Prentice-Hall of Canada, Ltd., *Toronto*
Prentice-Hall of India Private Limited, *New Delhi*
Prentice-Hall of Japan, Inc., *Tokyo*
Prentice-Hall of Southeast Asia Pte. Ltd., *Singapore*
Whitehall Books Limited, Wellington, *New Zealand*

Contents

Foreword

Race Memories Recorded in the Mirror held up to life: MUSIC REMEMBERED

Coming out of the cloud
the Actor became formal
had messages from the gods had masks borrowed dramatically
    from the wavering and passing gods

Coming out of the crowd
the Actor became necessary, active, Representative
    of all emotions, of all fears, of
    all desires,
dramatically he carried on their Ceremonies, initiated their
    holidays and everyone was surprised
    always by his rituals

Coming out of the woods
the Actor carried a small branch of a tree and said
    Shinto and priests appeared and danced in
    the mist, said
Prospero and more than 37 Plays were written
    which shook Shakespeare and
    their lovers

Coming out of the darkness and light and music and seasons
    which were always changing
    the Actor
who was also the dreamer and philosopher and choreographer,
    the priest and constituent
    of Mystery
the magic from inside the green fuse, the inner voice
    of the Poem Itself
    assuming on
the Stage before the Moon or before the Sun and before the
    children of the world with their
    changing needs and masks
the Pronunciation of the Soul, its dance, its exits and
    entrances, its terrifying or gentle
    memories and words,
the Actor multiplied before our magical and dramatic
    eyes, embodied death and resurrection,
    was Apollo and Medea and Miraculous
    Child, capable of all
heroism, of all dread, of all religions and their colors
    and toys and whistles and drums,
THE ACTOR AROSE
    CHANGING HIS COSTUMES
    as if from the evening's dew and
    the MOON'S WORD
or as if from the clashing of the SUN'S BRILLIANCE
    CHANGING HIS COSTUMES AS THE
    COSMOS MOVED IN THE
MIRROR OF THE HANDS OF THE WORSHIPPING AND MOVING
AUDIENCE.

                                   John Tagliabue

Preface

When we were children we could create situations of tremendous joy, fear, and grief with imaginary friends, enemies, and families. We exhausted ourselves "playing." Play introduced us to the situations we would actually face in "real" life. Play was hard work and great fun.

The use of the word "playing" to describe both the frolic of young children and the serious professional work of mature adults suggests, I think, a fundamental link between "play" in everyday life and the process of "acting" on the stage. Both activities are distinct from what we refer to as "ordinary life," but both use the actions of everyday life as their material. Both also result in fun. Anthropologist Johan Huizinga has noted that "only the drama, because of its intrinsically fictional character, its quality of being an action, remains permanently linked to play."[1] This is the fundamental premise and basic point of view underlying this introduction to acting.

The acting student should try to recapture the spirit and process which let him "play" so effectively and joyfully many years ago. This introduction to acting encourages such an open, natural, and vulnerable frame of mind. With this outlook, a student can relearn how to "play"—psychologically, physically, and vocally.

Since the effectiveness of a particular playing technique can vary from student to student and from actor to actor, this book presents an organized, yet fervently eclectic approach to the skill of playing in the theatre.

The organization of this text is four-part: first, an introduction to yourself as your playing instrument; second, an introduction to your text as the framework for your play; third, an introduction to your character; and, finally, an introduction to the theatre as the arena for your playing.

In Part One you are asked to begin to understand how you play yourself in everyday life. Part Two presents you with four ways to think about play texts. Part Three shows you how to use the technique learned in Part One in understanding a character in a play. And in Part Four, you are placed in the larger framework of the theatre and asked to consider acting as part of a collaborative process.

This book is an *introduction* to acting. The exercises within should be viewed and *re*viewed throughout an actor's career. Each review can provide new insights into yourself and your craft. A good actor never stops growing, learning, and introducing himself to acting. The exercises in this book are diverse: some have specific goals; others expect the experience to generate its own "lessons." Some exercises are basic, some more complicated. Play those which suit your immediate needs. *The Glass Menagerie* is used as a reference play because it is a play familiar to many students, and it is easily accessible from most libraries and bookstores.

No book can teach acting. No theoretical statement, exercise, or arrangement of topics can satisfy every acting teacher, student, or training program. Diversity of educational philosophy constitutes a great strength in our theatre. So, if you are so inclined, argue with the statements made in this book. If you think some exercises are inappropriate, don't use them. Enough material in this book can suit most beginning acting courses to make this a helpful text. Use this book as a sounding board for your own ideas about acting, so that everyone can learn that there are no "right" answers to questions of art—only ardent attempts to confront the questions.

Acting is a very personal and subjective matter. Some actors place particular emphasis on internal rather than external technique; others prefer the opposite approach. Some stress improvisational technique while others prefer the craft of acting. The organization of this book allows a teacher to teach from his strengths without ignoring other approaches to acting. Feel free to dwell on those chapters or exercises most suited to your own disposition, to move quickly through or to ignore those areas you feel should be left to others. The most important element in a successful introduction to acting is not that a book be used in its entirety, but that what is used, effectively aids teacher and student.

This introduction to acting does not claim to replace, nor should anyone try to make it replace, specialized classes in voice, movement, improvisation, script analysis, and period style. These areas are merely introduced in this book as part of the whole sphere of an actor's life-long work. Let this book suggest to the student areas for further study and training.

Many people have helped in the writing of this book:
Prentice-Hall; The Lincoln Center Library for the Performing Arts; Steuben Glass; The Gorki Museum of the Moscow Art Theater; the Boston Museum of Art; my students; my parents; my teachers—Anthony Zappella, David Weiss, Roger Boyle, Hubert Heffner, Oscar Brockett, Keith Michael,

Howard Jensen, Sam Smiley, Pierre Lefevre, Albert Bermel, and my good friend and mentor, Harold Clurman. I am especially indebted to Kathryn Tracy for her wonderful illustrations. Acknowledgment is made to the International Transactional Analysis Association for permission to paraphrase from the article by Stephen B. Karpman, M.D., entitled "Fairy Tales and Script Drama Analysis," (*Transactional Analysis Bulletin* 7:26, April 1968, pp. 38–43).

Paul Kuritz

NOTE TO PREFACE

[1]Johan Huizinga, *Homo Ludens.* (Boston: Beacon Press.)

PART ONE

UNDERSTANDING YOURSELF

First, you must learn who you are. You must find your own sense of identity.

—Uta Hagen[1]

INTERNAL TECHNIQUE

Playing Qualities

That actors are often childlike is certainly true, but that is not to be counted against them: the child in all of us is to be cherished.

—Harold Clurman[2]

When I was in college I happened to tune in to a television broadcast of J. M. Barrie's *Peter Pan*. The play was one of my childhood favorites and this musical version starring Cyril Ritchard and Mary Martin had been absolutely committed to memory. With anticipation I sat alone in my room to relive the happiness. All progressed well until Peter led the initiates in "I Won't Grow Up." I had loved that song and had vowed with Peter never to wear a necktie! I'd forsworn the trappings of the adult "enemy" for a lifetime in never-never land.

Suddenly I noticed the school book open beside me. My tie and moustache likewise betrayed me. Behind my back I'd become an adult! I'd let Peter down! I'd broken my vows of years ago.

But I felt no different today than I did then. What had happened? Had my outsides matured while my spirit remained a child? Was I abnormal? I couldn't let anyone know of this! As Hedda Gabler's friend would say, "What would people think!"

My worries disappeared years later when I heard psychologist Claude Steiner say that a Child exists in each of us. Eric Berne, Steiner's friend and noted psychologist, found in his studies in intuition that the Child aspect is very important to the healthy functioning of the individual. In fact, this secret Child gives a young actor the initial basis for successful "playing." So I discovered that rather than being atypical, I was normal for an aspiring actor!

As I started to teach and direct young acting students, I discovered that the Child part had trouble manifesting itself. Pressures on young people to grow up or to act their age are tremendous. All around us rewards are bestowed on those who age before their years, those who put aside childlike behavior early. Playing, pretending, dreaming, and imagining are discounted as wastes of time or as the activities of social deviants. Only when engaged in as sport, as a means to social advancement, as a tool for treating the psychologically maladjusted, or as a motivational tool in the pursuit of the American Dream, are these human activities applauded.

Yet these very qualities are the *sine qua non* of the creative actor. The acting student's return to or rediscovery of that frame of mind allows earnest playing—pretending that the most fantastic impossibility has come to pass, dreaming of worlds and possibilities beyond earthly limitations, imagining all kinds of circumstances and traits. Unless one acts—mentally, physically and verbally—as a child, until one embraces the child within, the enjoyment and thrill of the actor are beyond one's grasp.

This does not mean that an actor should embark upon a life of selfish indulgence, narcissism or egocentricity. To act child*like* and to act child*ishly* are two different matters. One need not disorganize one's life, follow impulses blindly, explode in fits of temper, and throw up hands in utter dependency to be an actor. Understand yourself and your Child. Each of the Child's aspects can be accepted and controlled. You can liberate "him" when you choose and harness "her" when you choose. The Child within is *yours* and unless you control him or her, he or she will control you.

Everyone wants to be creative. You should develop those qualities of your personality most conducive to the creative process. You will find it more rewarding to see yourself as both the creator and the thing created. You are both the artist and the art. Just as a musician or painter must understand the tools and materials of the art, you must know, understand, accept or change the qualities of your personality. You cannot get a new instrument as the pianist can get a new piano or the painter a new canvas. You cannot run away from or ignore your acting instrument and still hope to be able to play creatively and compellingly. Your individual mind, body, and voice must be perfected and mastered. If the prospect is frightening or overwhelming, so be it. You must discipline yourself just as other artists. The Romantic notion of inspired brilliance ought to be dismissed in favor of one consisting of gruelling and often frustrating self-exploration in trial and error.

REVELATION OF SELF

Every stroke of acting is a revelation of self. Every stroke may not be effective or appropriate. Consequently, when you reject an aspect of your art you are rejecting an aspect of yourself. This can devastate the young actor. Often the young actor tries to protect himself by revealing less or by relying on old acceptable aspects of self. This results in dead acting and dead art. Every act must be bold and potentially devastating. Only by risking much is much ever achieved. You may have to experience embarrassment and rejection before achieving creativity and acceptance. Always act with boldness, courage, freedom, intelligence, and confidence. Timid and safe actors are boring and unenlightening actors.

Acting is essentially the public doing of private actions—mental, verbal, and physical actions. You would do well to understand the personality from which the actions emanate before you perform the actions. The audience, on the other hand, perceives your actions first and from them infers your personality. Taken together, thought, deeds, and words constitute your personality in life and your character on stage. To understand character or personality, actions must be identified and comprehended as part of a whole.

An investigation of the actor's personality reveals three sources for action. Every action is a manifestation of a Child, a Parent, or an Adult's needs, desires, or wants. In a sense each of us is three distinct personalities. Your Child is one of three parts of your personality. Everything you do or say in life and on the stage originates in one of three main qualities of your personality. Since your Child is the first stage to develop in your personality we will examine it first.

THE PSYCHOLOGICAL INSTRUMENT

Each of us arrives in the world uninhibited, untrained and, for the most part, carefree. This *Natural Child* deals with immediate wants and objectives such as food, drink, air, and sleep. Biologically satisfied, the Natural Child can turn his attention to security, stability, consistency, structure and freedom from fear and chaos. In pursuing these objectives a young child can manifest characteristic behavior ranging from affectionate, cute, sensuous, and fun-loving to aggressive and selfish.

The Natural Child soon comes into contact with parents and circumstances seeking to influence either the objectives he is pursuing or the manner by which they are pursued. Parents have their own desires and goals. Drama—the conflict of objectives—soon arises. And so do tensions. Since parents are bigger, their objectives are victorious as they succeed in "socializing" or censoring the Natural Child's behavior through a system of rewards and punishments. Those actions which comply with parental wishes or avoid them through withdrawal create the second aspect of your young personality, the *Adapted Child*. The Adapted Child learns to differentiate between "good" and "bad" behavior. The Adapted Child may even learn new objectives such as the sense of belonging, love, acceptance, and approval.

When the child tries to reconcile the objectives of his Natural Child aspect with the needs of his Adapted Child aspect and to relieve tension, a third aspect develops, the *Little Professor*. The Little Professor tries to satisfy, discover, explore, or manipulate ways and means to get both objectives. The Little Professor intuits the best course of action through calculation, imagination, and pretense.

Consequently, a child has a three-part personality composed of the Natural aspect, the Adapted aspect and the Little Professor aspect. These three aspects remain within a person throughout life. Each of us continues to act from them under the right circumstances. A "right" circumstance is one which activates one of these behavioral packages. We act from our Child when we conclude, consciously or unconsciously, that it offers the best means to achieve our desires. Sometimes we move into our Child automatically even though it not only hinders achievement of our objectives but also prevents the attainment of our goals! You should discover the Child in each of its three manifestations so that you can use it in the creation of character and in the pursuit of character goals or objectives. The Child also contains your potential for successful "playing" through *relaxation*. The Natural Child is free from the pressures to conform or to please. But another factor works against your desire to relax your playing instrument.

I can't remember ever leaving my parents' house to go off to play without hearing one of them say, "Be careful." And today when my wife goes to work or to shop I automatically say, "Be careful!" Once I asked my grandmother what she remembered her husband telling my father when he went out and she replied, "Oh nothing much; just to be careful." My family has transmitted this injunction from generation to generation just as surely as if it were genetic. I fear that I already know what two words will fill my sons' ears as they go to play. Our parents live on in us and we in our children. And both affect relaxation in playing and acting.

Perhaps the first "character" we play is that of our parent. The character is in the popular children's play of "house." This drama is performed on playgrounds and in backyards throughout the world. Tiny voices repeat familiar injunctions as if miniature tape machines played the words heard at home the previous day or week. Thousands of children act this drama daily in hundreds of dialects, reflecting the social mores and values of their culture. This drama reveals the development of the second quality of our personality, the *Parent*.

Imitation leads us to tighten certain of our muscles and relax others to conform to the vocal and physical modeling of our parents. Mannerisms, walks, vocal qualities, and even word choices are copied from our parents. The tensions of our parents are likewise learned along with their inhibitions, fears, and anxieties. Your Parent is essentially a copy of parental actions—verbal, mental and physical. It contains the advice, warnings, prejudices, attitudes, and feelings which your parents or parent figures gave you. A parental figure could be a biological or adopted parent, a grandparent, a clergyman, a teacher, a television personality, or a fictional personage. Any source of wisdom or advice could contribute to the Parent. Astrological signs, advice for the lovelorn columns, and even personal names and nicknames hold expectations and associations which can govern the way you express yourself to others and guide your behavior. The Parent demonstrates your first successful attempt to imitate another person.

Most parent behavior can be considered either nurturing or critical in quality. For centuries sexist societies have assigned the nurturing functions of parenthood to the mother and the critical faculties to the father. Consequently children acquire the personality of their sexual model—girls are encouraged by father to nurture like mother and boys are encouraged by mother to criticize like father. Girls can practice on dolls; boys with the ultimate criticizer, guns. So deep-seated are these behavior patterns that unnurturing women may be considered unfeminine, uncritical men unmasculine! Remember your parents' reactions to your interest in theater and acting? Some parents immediately question their sons' masculinity and their daughters' morality! Actors have been plagued for centuries by prejudicial Parents. Recently (and fortunately) the movement for human rights has challenged such stereotyping. However, the residue of centuries of sexist role models remains in many of us and in most of the drama. Men still tend to have a larger critical aspect and women a larger nurturing aspect in their Parents. Attempt to redress the sexist bias in your own personality. A well-rounded Parent should be your goal. Care, concern, consideration, protection, permission, sympathy, love and nursing, should not remain the exclusive resource of women; nor should punishment, evaluation, prejudice, condescension, authoritarianism, dictation, closed-mindedness and ridicule remain the exclusive "right" of men. Laurence Olivier remarked that the feminine nature inside each of us can provide a great source of inspiration for male actors while the masculine nature can equally stimulate female actors.

Fortunately you have the potential to ward off detrimental Parent and Adapted Child qualities which could thwart your natural urges and abilities to play and act by creating unwanted tensions. The eternal conflict between parent and child exists in every personality. The Parent wants you to follow the injunctions your parents have placed within you. Your Parent finds a natural ally in your Adapted Child. The Adapted Child will gladly follow any piece of advice and accept any prejudice without question since it desires approval and fears parental punishment. Against these forces for conformity fights your Natural Child, still trying to liberate its basic genuine feelings and impulses. Your Little Professor is trying to outsmart the Parent to aid the Natural Child. How are these warring factions ever to be reconciled? How can relaxation occur?

Time and experience provide us with a mediating force in our personality, the Adult. Experience occasionally reveals that a parental opinion has no basis, that a too-adapting child may be abused and used by others, that a too-active natural child causes social ostracism, that particular tensions affect voice and movement. Your Adult allows you to examine objectively the demands put upon you by your Parent and Child. It functions for the whole human being as the *Little Professor* functions within the Child. Your Adult gives you the potential for self-knowledge, self-control, autonomy, and creativity. Your Adult is computer-like in the gathering, storing, and processing of information for decisions, estimates, and probabilities. When you exhibit emotionless behavior dealing with facts, you operate from your Adult.

Unfortunately, sexist tendencies in our society affect the Adult's development. For centuries women have been denied access to the kinds of information, schools, and jobs which could allow for the full development of the *Adult* aspect of their personality. Instead women have had to rely on what was smugly referred to by condescending males as women's intuition, the functioning of the female's Little Professor, in lieu of Adult capability. Even today the male-dominated society may consider a woman with a developed Adult aggressive or unfeminine.

As an actor you will be involved in doing actions. That's what an actor does. Actions reveal character. Only a certain type of character is capable of doing certain kinds of actions. Thus the doing of actions reveals character. Pope John Paul II has written that a person is seen through his actions. You are what you do. Your personality, your character, is the end rather than the means of your work; it is the sum of all your doings and sayings.

In order to effectively use your psychological instrument in playing actions which will reveal your personality, you need to develop certain *playing qualities. Relaxation, concentration, justification,* and *imagination* are essential to effective play.

Relaxation

Relaxation is essential if you are to explore the possibilities of human action. Relaxation rests, for the actor, in the effective functioning of the Adult, Little Professor and Natural Child. The Adapted Child hinders relaxation and thus creativity since it seeks to please at any cost and will do anything to avoid failure or embarrassment. The Parent is full of untested advice and warnings regarding actions yet untaken. Directors interested in fast results and fellow actors interested in boosting their own egos at others' expense often function from their Parents and pose perhaps the greatest obstacle to the creative actor's relaxation. The temptation to resort to Adapted Child activities is extremely great in this atmosphere. As game analyst W. Timothy Gallwey writes, "perhaps the most important step a person can take to increase awareness of the events in his experience . . . is to try to rid himself of the concepts of 'good' and 'bad'. . . . When we see ourselves as bad, we attempt to improve and consequently lose all touch with natural growing. . . . The player who decides that he isn't any good will soon be playing that way. . . ."³ "If the judgment process could be stopped with the naming of the event as bad, and there were no further ego reactions, then the interference would be minimal. But judgmental labels usually lead to emotional reactions and then to tightness, trying too hard, self-condemnation, etc. This process can be slowed by using descriptive but non-judgmental words to describe the events you see."⁴ Remember that compliments are criticisms in disguise! Both are used to manipulate behavior.

Gallwey suggests instead *the process of natural learning:*

> The first skill needed . . . is called "letting it happen." This means gradually building a trust in the innate ability of your own body to learn and to perform. Building this relationship of trust takes a little time but it can start immediately. Instead of telling your body what to do, let it do what it wants to, let it have its way. Don't scold it for its mistakes, but let it learn from them. Let your body control itself without any henpecking from your mind. Anyone who does this re-discovers natural learning, the beautiful process by which we learned how to walk and talk.⁵

As you play the exercises and as you watch others play, expect and welcome mistakes. Trust yourself and others to learn from them. Acting teacher Robert Benedetti states that a possible source of trouble rests in our ingrained habit of showing others our efforts rather than surrendering to the work at hand.

> This began when Mom or Dad or some teacher asked you a long time ago to do something, and you were eager to please them, even though you weren't terribly interested (or even happy) about the thing you were doing; your activity therefore became not so much real effort as a *display of effort* that said "look at me doing this." In acting class we call this "look at me" attitude *indicating;* you *indicate* by showing us that you are doing something instead of really doing it. This is to be avoided not only because it looks and feels false on stage, but also because it prevents you from having a deep and meaningful experience of your task.⁶

The following exercises can integrate your psychological instrument into a unified, functioning, relaxed personality. Be daring and bold in your playing. As you exercise rid yourself of notions of good or bad, right or wrong. Don't aim to please your teacher or your classmates. Attack your work fearlessly, searching for more honest information about yourself in action.

Your acting instrument is unique. Each personality is different. Don't try to copy another's action, but search for your own. These exercises are not designed to let you play at "being yourself" but instead to help you play. Approach these exercises with the same seriousness of purpose with which a biology student approaches laboratory experimentation. Simply because our experimentation may be enjoyable does not mean that the experiment is inconsequential or silly!

Effort produces tension. Too much effort produces too much tension. Too much tension interferes with playing and with an audience's enjoyment. As Bertolt Brecht, the German director and playwright, pointed out, "a man who strains himself on the stage is bound, if he is any good, to strain all the people in the stalls."[7] How much effort or strain is enough? A muscle should tense only enough to accomplish the task; only the muscles used in the task should be tensed. Too much tension means either too much tension in a useful muscle, or tension in an inapplicable muscle.

How do you start to eliminate irrelevant tension? Of these three choices, which requires the most tension and which the least: (1) declining to play, (2) playing, (3) trying to play? If you think trying to play requires the most tension you are correct. If you believe that declining to play needs the least effort you are right. Thus you can eliminate unnecessary tension by either declining to act or by declining *to try* to act. You simply let action happen. As Brecht said, "if you want to master something difficult, take it easy."

The following exercise distinguishes *trying* from *allowing*. Raise your arm and try as hard as you can to keep it straight while another player tries to bend it at the elbow. Count aloud while trying. Repeat this process, this time without "trying" to keep your arm straight. Just let your arm remain straight. Stand apart from your arm and observe it remaining straight. Remain disinterested yet aware that it isn't bending. Count aloud as the player exerts pressure. The second method should produce a longer count. Your voice should seem less strained. See yourself having more strength with less effort.

A major problem for a beginning actor is too many tense muscles. Unnecessary tension reduces power which causes instability and erratic playing. Unwanted tension can be seen most often in the face, neck, shoulders, arms, and legs. Actors sometimes mistakenly assume that tension increases power. The opposite is actually the case.

Having read this, you may now be interested in controlling your playing. Body control, as well as vocal control, is achieved not by tightening muscles but by relaxing them. Trying brings harmful tension. Once I told a student not to try and then observed him trying not to try! Instead of trying to control your playing, simply note which parts of your body are tense and during what circumstances.

EXERCISES

1. Make a fool of yourself. One of the greatest fears and one of the major obstacles for a beginning actor is the fear of making a fool of himself. The entire personality mobilizes to prevent this inevitability. Go before your group and do something you would never dream of doing, something you've always feared would happen, or something you only do in the privacy and security of your own room. If you are ashamed of your voice, belt out a song. If you are reserved about your body, throw yourself into a strip-tease. Experience embarrassment now so that you can overcome the eventuality. Let your instructor and classmates signal to you when they think you have succeeded. Remember not to create a character to hide behind and not to embarrass the audience. You should embarrass yourself!

2. To experience the feelings, demeanor, gestures, voice, and vocabulary of your Child, play the group games you played as a child. Don't play *a* child but allow your *own* Child to emerge! The resultant behavior will not be childish but childlike. Play games like Farmer in the Dell, Did You Ever See a Laddie/Lassie, Tag, Hide & Seek, Follow the Leader, Musical Chairs. Even Simon Says, which reinforces one's Adapted aspect, is a valuable game. Observe your own and others' actions—what you do, what you say, what you think. Afterward, discuss these actions, voices, vocabulary, gestures, and demeanors. Which aspects of your Child seem strongest?

DRAW YOUR CHILD EGOGRAM

| Adapted Child | Little Professor | Natural Child | or | Adapted Child | Little Professor | Natural Child |

FIGURE 1-1:   The child with you has three aspects—Natural, Adaptive, and Intuitive.

3. Experience action as it currently exists; do actions which you consider too tense. Repeat the actions, noting aloud the degree of tension on a one to ten scale, ten being the most tense. Awareness will reduce tension. Use this technique whenever unnecessary tension appears.

4. Refuse to do actions. Don't walk, stand, sit, hop, or skip. By refusing to act you eliminate unnecessary tension, especially in the neck and shoulders. This preliminary tension is evident, for example, when you lift a full suitcase which turns out to be empty and your arm flies up and out. Unnecessary preliminary tension is the result of mobilizing more muscle power than the task actually requires.

5. Let another player stand you from a seated position and walk you around before seating you in a chair. As he leads you, keep your neck and shoulders relaxed. Let the other player tense the muscles as you remain relaxed.

6. Walk in a circle. Tense each muscle gradually moving downward—face, neck, shoulders, chest, arms, hands, stomach, pelvis, upper legs, lower legs, feet, and toes. Increase the tension until almost unbearable. Relax gradually, beginning with the toes and moving up. Any part of your body you could not tense was (and is) already tense!

7.   a. Stretch your chest and neck as far up as possible. Hold them there and then relax.

b. Push your neck into your chest until it strains. Hold it there and then relax.

c. Move your head in as large a circle as you can.

d. Close your eyes and jaw. Tighten them. Hold, and then relax them.

e. Extend each arm to stretch your fingers and arms as much as possible. Hold them and then relax.

f. Rotate your hands and stretch your fingers as much as possible.

g. Stretch your arms as far as possible while rotating them in the largest circles you can.

h. Put your hands into fists and place them on your shoulders. Bend your arms toward your head as far as possible. Strain to touch your head. Hold them and then relax.

i. Push your shoulders as far forward as possible. Hold them there and then relax. Pull them back as far as possible, hold, and relax. Move your shoulders forward in as large a circle as possible. Repeat, moving your shoulders backwards.

j. Bend forward as far as you can; hold, then relax.

k. Lean back as far as you can; hold, then relax.

l. Lean left/right as far as you can; hold, then relax.

m. Rotate your torso in as wide a circle as possible.

n. Pull your stomach in as hard as you can; hold, then relax.

o. Straighten your left/right leg and lift your pointed foot forward/backward as far as possible. Hold, then relax.

8. Walk in a circle while another player calls numbers. Tense or relax the appropriate muscles when the number is called:

#1   Neck
#2   Shoulders
#3   Arms
#4   Torso

#5   Hands
#6   Legs
#7   Feet

9. Return to childhood body positions to recapture an awareness of natural movement:

a. In a fetal ball, roll around in all directions—forward, sideways, backwards—occasionally stopping to balance yourself in a precarious position.

b. Open from the fetal ball but keep your arms and back curved in toward your center. Roll about in all directions. Crawl around, occasionally rising to return to the squat position.

10. Sit in a chair. Take the seat in your hands at the sides of your hips. Pull the seat upwards, driving your shoulders downwards. Strain while slowly pushing your torso up between your arms. Feel your head lift upward until you feel like an ostrich. Let the tension out of your elbows and arms to allow your arms to hang at your sides.

11. Stand and rise on your toes. Slowly let yourself down to the floor. Bounce easily without taking your toes off the floor. Think of your back widening as your head moves forward and up.

12. Let your hands become as loose as possible. Let your head fall on your chest. Watch your breathing for a few seconds. Gradually increase the length of each inhalation by one second while letting the exhalations happen naturally. Your body will move into the rhythm of sleep, relaxing both mind and body. This is a good exercise prior to performance. Welcome yawns; they relax your throat and neck muscles.

13. Lie on the floor. Let another player lift your hand and arm. Do not help. Let your hand drop when the player drops it. Any hesitation is a sign of tension. Let the player push your knees to your chest after testing your legs for tension. Let him put them through a bicycling motion. The player should push your knees to your chin to raise your rear end from the floor. Straighten your legs, roll to your stomach, and let the player massage you.

14. Yawn, stretch, and move, over and over again. Yawn and shake every part of your body over and over again. Yawn and laugh hysterically.

15. Memorize a brief poem. Deliver it as heroically as you can. Exaggerate everything. Overact. Emote! Ham it up! Pretend you are the most bombastic actor ever as you declaim the poem. Repeat the poem doubling the exaggerated manner of the first reading. Extend your body and voice to their limits—past their limits. You cannot overdo this exercise.

Concentration

When your mind is relaxed you can direct your attention to your immediate tasks. With a relaxed body and voice you can rely on total psychophysical commitment from your acting instrument. Concentration, conversely, helps relaxation; putting the mind on a specific target frees the body and voice from the tension that purposelessness can create. *To concentrate is to fulfill a purpose, to pursue a goal, to do a deed.*

Concentration is not *trying* to concentrate, nor is it concentrating on concentration. Concentration in acting means *action*. Trying to act makes you think about how well or poorly you are acting; you monitor your action to judge it. Action exists in the present; your mind must remain in the present rather than on past missteps or on future obstacles. True concentration is a state in which you are unaware that you are concentrating.

Concentration has various levels, ranging from simple *noticing* to complete *identification*. In between these two conditions of concentration are *attraction* and *absorption*. When attracted, you are fascinated; when absorbed, you are oblivious to everything but the object of your focus. Identification unites actor and focal point into one.

According to the great Russian director Meyerhold, "only via the sports arena can we approach the theatrical arena."[8] Consequently, you would do well to develop concentration through play.

EXERCISES

1. Bounce a sponge ball on the floor so that it will hit a wall and carom back toward you. Attend to the flight of the ball as it returns toward you from the wall. Don't try to catch the ball or even move toward or away from it. Just watch the ball. Repeat this experience with a desire to get a better view of the ball than you had before. So great should your desire to view the ball become, that you will feel compelled to move into the ball's trajectory. The ball will hit you. Repeat this experience, following the ball into your hands. Keep your eye on nothing but the ball!

2. Draw or tape a two to three foot square or circle on the wall. Stand back from this target to concentrate on the space within the tape or drawing. Without trying to hit the target, concentrating only on perceiving the target's space, bounce the ball on the floor to rebound it on the wall. Repeat this action. Do not try to adapt your toss to hit the target. Neither should you try not to hit the target. Just let the ball bounce as you let yourself throw the ball. Keep your eye not on the ball, but on the space within the target, even after the ball has left your hand.

3. With your fellow players, stand in a circle. All begin to walk to the circle's center and all stop together. All bend down together and straighten up together. All walk to their starting places together. The unison movements should have no leader and no follower. Attend on the space the group occupies at all times. An effective exercise occurs when no leading is apparent.

4. Invent unison movements as in the previous exercise. To draw attention to oneself by initiating a movement is as inappropriate as being last to follow the group's dynamics. No one should know who is leading and who is following. This is an exercise in democracy and *ensemble*—a unified and balanced group performance.

5. With a fellow player, decide who will play a mirror. One player faces the actor–mirror and begins to move *very slowly*. The actor–mirror reflects the actions. Do not try to confound or outsmart the mirror. On signal, reverse roles without stopping the action. On signal, both players become mirrors, neither and both leading and

following. On signal, the players close their eyes while continuing the slow motion actions. On signal, the players freeze, open their eyes, and compare positions. Communion between players results in close approximation of final poses.

6. Repeat the previous exercise with a distorting carnival mirror reflecting a grotesque image.

7. Play children's games involving physical action such as Tag, Red Rover, Flag Football, Relay Races, Hopscotch, Leap Frog, and Blindman's Bluff. Attention should be placed on economy of movement and level of concentration.

8. Stand with your arms hanging at your sides. With the count of 1–2–3 the right arm moves forward and out, straight up, and back to the side. With the count of 1–2–3–4 the left arm moves forward and out, straight up, sideways and out, and back to the side. Perform both counts simultaneously until both arms eventually come together at your sides. (When the right arm is at position 3, the left arm is at position 3; when the right arm moves back to position 1 the left arm moves to position 4, and so on.)

9. Repeat the previous exercise while walking.

10. Stand in a circle with your fellow actors. One player begins by making a physical action. The next actor in the circle repeats that action and adds one of his own. The next actor repeats the first two actions and adds one of his own. This process continues for as long as the movements are remembered and repeated in the proper order. Go around the circle several times before error.

11. Wrestle in slow motion with a fellow player. Attention should be paid to the give and take necessary to keep the actions slow and smooth. Cooperation rather than competition is the key to a successful slow motion match.

12. One actor begins a rhythmic movement. Another actor invents a rhythmic movement and adapts it to the rhythmic movement of the first actor. Movements are added and adapted to create a living machine.

13. Sit for one, then two, and finally three minutes without moving anything, not even your eyes. Only breathing is permitted.

14. Take a single sentence from a poem of your choice. Each player should utter one of the words as the group coordinates their voices to sound the sentence as if a single voice utters it. Stacatto delivery signifies inadequate concentration. Tone should flow as natural utterance.

15. Use the same sentence as in the previous exercise and with a partner divide the consonant sounds from the vowel sounds. One player utters the consonants and the other the vowels to sound a believable natural utterance as a single voice.

16. Tongue twisters provide excellent opportunities to develop concentration. Say each three times.

    a.   Red rubber baby buggy bumpers.

    b.   The sinking steamer sunk.

    c.   Strange strategic statistics.

    d.   Toy boat.

    e.   Six thick thistle sticks.

    f.   The sixth sheik's sixth sheep's sick.

    g.   How much wood could a woodchuck chuck if a woodchuck could chuck wood?

    h.   Vicious fishes.

    i. Sixty-six sick chicks.

    j. Lemon liniment.

    k. She sells seashells by the seashore.

17. Speak a memorized poem as other players try to make you laugh without making physical contact.

18. This exercise requires two players and a third player who serves as an arbiter, a role as taxing as player. The arbiter scores the play of the two sitting face to face. The players cannot break eye contact, laugh, or pause. Every violation of this injunction results in a point for the other player. On signal, both players begin to talk about anything they like. A player scores a point each time he changes to the topic of his opponent. A player also scores a point each time he realizes his opponent is taking up his topic and changes the topic to a new one. On signal, the talking stops and the points are tabulated. The winner plays the arbiter; the loser arbitrates.

19. With a group of players, walk in a circle singing "Row, Row, Row Your Boat." A player in the center of the circle will ask each singing player individually to answer a mathematical problem without ceasing the song. For example, "8 × 17 =" or "74 − 19 =." The player may not pause to calculate; vocal utterance must be as continuous as the walk.

20. Develop your ability to observe sounds by bringing objects to class which make distinct sounds, such as eggbeaters, electric razors, noisemakers and smoke alarms. Imitate exactly the sounds they make with your own voice.

21. All players in the group simultaneously begin to hum or whistle an unnamed familiar tune. Each player walks about, writing down the name of each tune he hears. A player may not stop his own tune to listen to another's tune. At the end of a fixed time period, read the titles to see if all were identified.

22. In a circle of players, one player states a noun. The player to the right repeats the noun and adds one of his own. The next player repeats the two previous nouns and adds another. This process continues until a noun is forgotten or uttered out of order. Repeat the exercise adding a gesture for each noun. The circle should be encompassed several times in each round.

Justification

Concentration provides a *target* for action; *justification* supplies a *reason* for action. Concentration looks forward and is directed to the future; justification lies behind and propels the action onward. When you know where your action is going (concentrate) and why it's going there (justify) you find yourself in a state of relaxation. Psychological play thus precedes physical and vocal action. Valentina Litvinoff, the renowned dance instructor, isolates the value of physical play in conveying psychological motivations:

> A physical action is easier to grasp than a psychological attitude; it is more accessible than an elusive inner feeling. It is easier to capture, is more concrete, more readily perceived. A physical action is connected with all other elements. Truly there is no physical action without a will towards it, a direction, a use of the imagination.[9]

On the other hand, physical actions can both communicate preceding psychological actions and motivate subsequent physical actions. To a psychologically oriented spectator who assumes motivation for everything, an action, movement, gesture, or facial expression which comes *before* another action, movement, gesture, or facial expression, is assumed to have motivated the latter action. Likewise, the second of the two actions is emphatic in the eye of the spectator since it is perceived to be the result of the first or motivating action. Motivation is expected and imagined whenever one action precedes another.

EXERCISES

1. Toss around an imaginary ball to a group of fellow players. Invent and communicate through your actions a motivation for throwing the ball.
2. Erect a statue out of two fellow players. The statue should reveal the players in a relationship. When complete, the statue should justify its position by inventing circumstances which resulted in the pose.
3. Justify the following activities and communicate them physically:

    a. picking flowers
    b. listening to a humorous story
    c. watching someone cry
    d. sensing the wind on your body
    e. sensing the sun on your body
    f. taking a cold shower
    g. taking a hot shower

Invent specific circumstances so that, if asked, you could provide immediately any detail surrounding your actions.
4. Taking random words and gestures, invent circumstances which justify the simultaneity of gesture and utterance.
5. Justify the following phrases and communicate them only physically:

    a. "No, you can't."
    b. "No, I won't."
    c. "Please come with me."
    d. "Help, I'm lost."
    e. "What do you want?"
    f. "I can't help you."
    g. "Shut up!"
    h. "Great!"
    i. "Come over here."
    j. "Bring that here."

 k. "I love you."

 l. "I like you."

 m. "Here comes the parade."

 n. "Here comes the bride."

6. Distribute random words, sounds, or phrases clipped out of a newspaper or magazine. The players should invent circumstances to motivate or justify the utterances. Repeat this exercise considering random wordings as consecutive lines of dialogue.

Imagination

Concentration gives the action direction. Justification provides the action with motivation. *Imagination* gives the action shape, substance, and particular *manner. To imagine is to picture.* To act with imagination is to behave as if the picture in your mind were real and you were actually in the picture. Blaise Pascal, the French philosopher, seems to be speaking of the power of the actor's imagination when he wrote: "It is imagining . . . that makes people happy, unhappy, healthy, sick, rich, poor . . . mad or wise. . . ."

EXERCISES

1. Use sounds rather than distinct words to communicate the following ideas to another player. Listeners should face away from the player who is "sounding."

 a. Fire

 b. Water

 c. Rose

 d. Rattlesnake

 e. Blue

 f. War

 g. Freedom

 h. Bubbles

 i. Ice

 j. Now

2. Using sounds rather than words, speak to an audience of players on the merits and uses of an object, a garment, or an idea.

3. Using sounds rather than words, demonstrate something to an audience of players. Answer whatever questions the audience may have with sounds.

4. A group of players lies with toes touching in a circle on the floor. On signal, one player makes a vocal sound, the player on his right imitates it, and the imitation proceeds around the circle.

5. Sitting with a group of players in a circle, one player begins a story. After a sentence or two of narration, the player stops in mid-sentence. The player to his right completes the sentence and adds one or two sentences before stopping in mid-sentence. The story continues this way to the final player who ends the narrative.

6. Repeat the previous exercise with all imaginary objects beginning with the same letter of the alphabet.

7. Repeat the previous exercise with each new object larger/smaller than the preceding one.

8. In a circle of players, one player begins to enact while narrating an invented story. Each action should be motivated. In mid-action and mid-sentence the player freezes and allows the next player to continue to invent, enact, and narrate the story. Each player must introduce a new imaginary object to the tale. The final player ends the story and wraps up all loose imaginary ends.

9. Walk in a circle as if:

a. free, open, and carefree

b. walking barefooted through mud

c. walking barefooted through burning sand

d. walking barefooted through sand at the ocean's edge

e. wading through snow drifts

f. walking along an icy pavement

g. walking through dried grass

h. walking barefooted through dew-covered green grass

i. walking barefooted over slippery rocks in a brook

j. walking through ocean waves

k. walking through autumn leaves

l. walking in outer space

m. walking slow motion in a dream, trying to reach someone

n. walking slow motion in a nightmare, trying to escape from someone

10. Make a list of locations and invent actions to communicate them.

11. Make a list of moods and invent circumstances and actions to communicate them.

12. Collect objects of various sizes, weights, colors, odors, and tastes. Experience each physically and sensuously. Recreate the experience physically using imaginary substitutes.

13. In a circle of players, bat a balloon from person to person. When each player has hit the balloon, recreate the actions exactly as they occurred with an imaginary balloon.

14. Choose an everyday activity featuring a single object—for example, smoking a cigarette or eating an apple. Play the activity first with the actual object and then with an imaginary substitute. Attend to recreating the identical actions and sensory experiences.

15. Repeat the previous exercise after inventing specific circumstances. Invent actions to communicate the circumstances. Repeat the performance after changing one or two of the circumstances.

ACTION AS RESPONSE

Whenever actors gather, one of them will inevitably resurrect the old saw, "Acting is reacting." This adage underlines the fact that actions are responses first and stimuli later. From the moment of conception our biological and physical activities respond to previous stimuli. Our pursuit of basic physiological needs reacts to biological insufficiencies. Every action is really a reaction. Try to accomplish an action which is not in response to something else. Even that attempt is in response to my request! All of this means that you must stay alert to the ever-changing circumstances so that you can respond spontaneously.

The importance of reaction should again suggest to you the importance of action in defining your personality or character. The psychologist Gordon W. Allport defines personality as "the dynamic organization within the individual of those psychophysical systems that determine his unique adjustments to his environment."[10] Allport's definition serves our understanding by stressing key concepts. *Dynamic* emphasizes the constantly changing elements facing the actor as he continuously adapts to new phenomena in his environment. *Psychophysical* underlines the relationship between self and the world by stressing the relationship between body and mind—what we do affects what we think, and what we think affects what we do.

To what does the actor react in his environment or circumstances? You react to the stimulation of place, time, persons, and self. All sensory aspects of a situation can cause a response. You should open yourself to your surroundings.

The Need to Act

Your actions are responses to other people as you pursue various needs. Psychologist Abraham Maslow considers human needs hierarchically. According to him, our basic needs are *physiological* drives for food, drink, sleep, sex, and relaxation. When these needs are satisfied, we may pursue *safety* needs such as security, protection, and structured time. Next, safety needs quenched, we could turn to our need to belong by trying to find *love and affection*. Finally, after all other needs are satisfied, we can fulfill our need for *esteem*. Fulfilling any of these needs brings us into contact with other people. And contact brings reacting.

To summarize our discussion of action:

1. Action occurs as a response to the context or circumstances in which you exist.
2. Action seeks to fulfill a need within you; action is therefore purposeful.
3. Fulfillment of the need is helped or hindered by the circumstances.

4. Purposeful action within a stimulating environment defines your personality and character. Therefore, you would do well to analyze the circumstances of the moment to understand the nature and direction of your actions.

Analysis of Circumstance

The analysis of circumstance should answer the following questions:

What do I want? This question implies that satisfaction lies in the future. To reach the desired future you must do certain things. Consequently, the phrasing of the goal as an active or transitive verb shows activity rather than passivity. State what you want, not what you don't want. *This is your object of concentration.*

Why do I want it? This question suggests that motivation for the goal lies in the past. *This is your action's justification.*

How will I get it? This question brings the future goal and the past motivation to the present moment, to the here and now. The answer to this question could be a chronological list of actions you plan to perform to reach your goal. *The imagination shapes this action.*

What stands in my way? This question forces you to look for obstacles in the path toward your goal. Struggle and conflict are more interesting to watch and more compelling to perform, so find or invent an obstacle for each goal. Obstacles will force you to plan alternate answers to the previous question.

What leverage do I have?[11] This question searches for the particular advantages you have over other people in your battle to overcome the obstacle.

Where am I? This question concentrates on the influence of place on your actions. How does location affect your actions? Is it an obstacle or an element of leverage?

When is it? How does the time affect your actions? Is it helpful or detrimental to your striving?

After your analysis is complete, concentrate on reaching your goal while allowing the dynamic circumstances to affect the specifics of your pursuit.

Actors and Circumstances

You will find that most circumstances for action contain other actors. They transmit verbal and nonverbal stimuli which affect the pursuit of your goal. Their very presence helps or hinders your striving. In reacting to them, you direct your actions from your specific personality aspects to their specific personality aspects. In return, their actions are directed from specific aspects to specific aspects in you. However, the aspect sought and the one activated are not always the same. For example, if you send a parental message to another actor's Child the transactions would look like this:

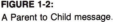
FIGURE 1-2:
A Parent to Child message.

If the other actor responds from the aspect you sought (Child) the transaction is *complementary*.

FIGURE 1-3: The Parent to Child message elicits a complementary Child to Parent response.

Four decisions are manifest in this brief transaction: (1) to send stimulation from the Parent, (2) to aim at the other's Child, (3) to return the message from the Child, (4) to aim at the other's Parent. In actual occurrence the decisions would probably occur instantaneously and automatically.

Four other possible complementary transactions exist—Adult to Adult, Parent to Parent, Child to Child, and Child to Parent.

Figure 1-4a

Whereas complementary transactions provide continuity, *crossed transactions* bring conflict—unexpected responses that break the flow of action. (See Figure 1-5.)

A third kind of transaction is the *ulterior transaction,* a transaction occurring on two levels. On the *overt level* are the words themselves; on the psychological, *subtextual level* are tone of voice and facial expression. The subtextual level reveals your real reason for acting, not apparent through the words themselves. *The subtext contains the momentary object of your attention, your intention, your purpose for action.* (See Figure 1-6.)

Figure 1-4b

FIGURE 1-4a, b, c, d: Complementary transactions all involve responses from the aspect toward which the original message was sent: **(a)** Adult to Adult from Adult, **(b)** Parent to Parent from Parent, **(c)** Child to Child from Child, **(d)** Child to Parent from Parent.

Figure 1-4c

Often actors hear directors tell them to "play the subtext." This means that the actor should make the ulterior levels of the transactions more overt. As critic Ronald Hayman tells us, "The actors who make us watch them are the actors who tell us something with their movements that we

Figure 1-4d

FIGURE 1-5: Crossed transactions feature unexpected or unwanted responses.

FIGURE 1-6: Ulterior transactions operate on two levels. The covert level contains the subtext.

do not get simply from listening to the lines."[12] In ulterior transactions verbs define your real actions on the psychological rather than on the overt social level.

Verbs

Verbs define the means you use to pursue your goal. Every line is an action; every action is an active verb. As Russian acting coach Richard Boleslavsky states, "a verb is action itself. First you want something, it is your artist's will; then you define it in a verb, it is your artist's technique; and then you actually do it, it is your artist's expression."[13] Acting, then, could be considered "verbing." The skill and art of acting comes in part from the choice, arrangement, and conviction of playing verbs. Verbs embody how you will pursue your goal. Consequently a verb must be able to be acted compellingly and in detail.

As you exercise, keep in mind Gallwey's "Six Guidelines for Effective Play":[14]

1. Increase awareness of where you are—that is, your situation.
2. Increase awareness of where you want to go—that is, of achieving your goal.
3. Let go of internal interferences—fears, self-doubts, conceits.
4. Give up unnecessary objectives.
5. Seek active inspiration from those of like commitment.
6. Practice frequently and with awareness.

EXERCISES

1. Using the verb list in Appendix B, play various verbs from different aspects of your personality. Do some seem more closely associated with your Parent, your Child, or your Adult?

2. Deliver each of the following statements from your Parent, Adult, and Child. Use a different verb each time in playing the subtext.

"I love you"
"Get out of here"
"Mother, please"
"Today is Tuesday"
"It doesn't matter"
"Hello"
"So it is"
"You have my number"

3. Think of important transactions you had today. Diagram them. Which personality aspects were most frequently used? Were the transactions complementary, crossed, or ulterior?

4. Sit facing another actor. Alternately comment on each other's actions or behavior. Let the comments trigger spontaneous reactions and comments. The rest of the group can note aspects and diagram the transactions.

5. Choose an Open Scene from Appendix A. Arbitrarily assign a personality aspect to each character and read the scenes aloud. Change aspects and repeat. How do the transactions change as aspects change? How does the change affect the nature of the scene?

6. Play a simple action based on one intention. For example, you want to wrap a birthday present. List the actions you would do to accomplish this task in the order you would do them. Think of an obstacle which could occur to alter your behavior. Adjust your action to accommodate that obstacle.

7. With another actor, invent circumstances which could include both of your actions from the previous exercise. Use dialogue only when necessary or spontaneous. Repeat the scene several times switching combinations of personality aspects. Change the circumstances of the scene to involve conflicting objectives and play it again.

8. Listen to a piece of music. Let the music suggest circumstances for action. Detail the circumstances in writing by answering the questions. Play the actions. The class can note and diagram key transactions.

9. Observe a painting. Let your imagination put you in the place of a character in the picture. Detail the circumstances in writing and play the actions. The group can note and diagram key transactions.

10. Choose an object with a distinct taste or odor. Examine the object utilizing your entire sensory apparatus. Let the stimulation free your imagination to invent specific circumstances for action. Play the actions while the class notes and diagrams key transactions.

11. Choose one of the statements in Exercise 2. Imagine circumstances involving two characters for which the statement can be the first line of dialogue. Detail the circumstances in writing. Prepare to play the action. Let someone now assign you another of the statements from Exercise 2. This statement will conclude the scene. As you play the action, you and your partner should move the action to a logical conclusion with that sentence. The class can note and diagram key transactions.

12. Select a simple, ordinary activity and prepare to pantomime it for the class. Detail in writing the circumstances. Your actions should communicate all important elements of the circumstances without indicating. Repeat the pantomime with a different motivation; in a different location; at a different time; with a different obstacle; with different leverage. How does the change in circumstance affect the manner in which the actions are performed?

13. Select three random verbs from the verb list in Appendix B. Imagine circumstances in which these actions could occur. Detail the circumstances in writing and play the action. Repeat with a different motivation; with a different location; at a different time; with a different obstacle; with different leverage. Note how the changes affect the manner by which the verbs are played. The group can diagram key transactions.

14. Choose one of Maslow's needs and formulate a specific goal which satisfies that need. Detail circumstances in writing and play the action leading to the goal. Repeat the exercise after a change in goal. The group can diagram key transactions.

15. Choose one of the Open Scenes in Appendix A. Detail the invented circumstances in writing. Justify and motivate every line without altering, omitting or adding lines. Use properties when needed to clarify the action. Give each of your lines and actions a compelling verb. Play the scene while the class diagrams key transactions. (Do not fall prey to the easy way out of the Open Scene's challenge by making the characters either crazy or secret agents!)

Units of Action

Children often tug at their parents asking, "What shall I do now?" Adolescents "hang out" in pinball arcades or at fast food restaurants to "kill time." The aged sometimes sit alone replaying past actions in their minds' eyes. As the novelist Tom Robbins writes, "And time brought along its secretary memory, and space its brat, loneliness."[15] We all need a purpose for our actions and structure to our time.

When exploring transactions, you may have noticed how action achieved a structure when it existed within a particular set of circumstances. When your action was directed toward one goal, it had a basic temporal structure—it was a unit of action. Whenever your goal changed (the "what" of the circumstances) you moved into a new unit of action or *beat,* as it is sometimes called. Charles Marowitz, the British director, defines a beat more completely as "a section of time confined to a specific set of continuous actions, or perhaps the duration of a mood or an internal state. As soon as our actions graduate to the next unit of activity, we can be said to be in the next beat of the scene. Some beats last for moments. Some go on for the entire scene. A beat, in our usage, is a unit of time bounded by a common pre-occupation with related actions."[16] In other words, a unit of action ends and a new one begins when the answer to the circumstantial question "What do I want?" changes.

Eric Berne, the psychologist, found six types of units of action—*withdrawal, ritual, activity, pastime, game,* and *intimacy.* Each kind of unit may be directed toward the same goal; the goal does not determine the kind of beat. The kind of beat chosen to pursue a goal is more a function of the "how" of the circumstances of action than of the "what." Berne believed, however, that *all* goals had, at their base, a desire for love. Thus, each kind of beat may be seen as an attempt to deal with love or lovelessness.

Withdrawal involves aloneness or loneliness, depending upon whether the physical or psychological departure from others is voluntary or forced. In withdrawal, you transact with memory. You may withdraw to satisfy any of Maslow's needs. Regardless of the reason, withdrawal brings a recall of memories—to relive past satisfactions of needs, to review past strategies of satisfying needs, to avoid present need by retreating into more pleasant times recorded in the mind.

Rituals are social or cultural transactions with predictable outcomes. Rituals fix action in a set manner of passing time. Nods, smiles, pats on the back, handshakes, greetings and farewells, cast party rituals, eating rituals, vacation rituals, audition rituals, coffee breaks, and religious worship display the variety of ritualized action used to structure time. Rituals in no way dictate your goals or motivation; rituals describe the manner upon which the motivation or goal is acted.

Activities include work and hobbies. They are actions involving projects or materials. Writing this book is an activity; reading this sentence is an activity. Attending class is an activity; acting is an activity. Most of your life is comprised of activities. Like rituals, activities can involve all motivations and goals.

Pastimes pass time. Actions designed to fill a void between two other units of action are pastimes. "Small talk," "shooting the breeze," or "passing the time of day" are other ways of describing pastime. Pastimes may occur at bus stops, on line at a movie, in a theatre lobby, in the green room. Topics include any innocuous subject such as automobiles, sports, fashion, the weather, politics, or children.

Games take pastimes and add an ulterior level of transaction toward a defined, yet concealed, outcome. Players of games engage in these actions to reinforce existing views of themselves and others. Reinforcement is the goal of the game. Games begin with an opening move designed to hook another player. If the other player responds appropriately he is hooked. The game initiator then pulls a switch which confuses the hooked player and produces the payoff for both players. Eric Berne's *Games People Play* catalogues this type of beat.[17]

Unfortunately, games are sometimes played in the theatre. For example, the game "I'm Only Trying to Help" presents Actor A offering unsolicited advice (the response to the hook) to Actor B. Actor B, who until now appeared to welcome constructive suggestions, explodes in anger (switch), giving hurt feelings (payoff) to Actor A who thought he was "only trying to help." Player A collects a reconfirmation of his belief that no one ever listens to him and that people are ungrateful. Actor B collects a reconfirmation of his belief that people butt into other people's business and that Actor B is a know-it-all. In the game of "Yes But" Actor A announces that he has a problem (the hook). Actor B responds with "Why don't you. . . ." Actor A discounts each of Actor B's suggestions with a "Yes But. . . .", confusing (the switch) Actor B. Eventually Actor B gives up (payoff), reassuring Actor A that he can find fault with any solution and that everyone wants to dominate him.

Intimacy differs from the other time-structuring devices by being unstructured. Intimacy is spontaneous. Neither person in intimacy fears the other. Consequently, actions are uncalculated, egos are undefended. Maslow defines intimate love as "a feeling of tenderness and affection with great enjoyment, happiness, satisfaction, elation, and even ecstacy."[18] Intimacy lets the Natural Child freely interact with another Natural Child.

Actions are free, spontaneous, uncensored, and pure delight. Together two partners experience Shelley's love—"a communion not merely of the senses, but of our whole nature, intellectual, imaginative and sensitive." Unfortunately, intimacy is as rare and brief in the drama and on the stage as it is in life. The attainment of intimacy satisfies one of our most compelling needs. Intimacy is the most desirable way of spending time, yet it is the most feared. Five other techniques for structuring action and time exist to aid your struggle toward or away from this state.

Improvisation: A Tool for Exploration

Whether you know it or not, many of your previous exercises have involved you in what is known as *improvisation*. Improvisation is playing actions invented through the imaginative analysis of invented momentary circumstances. Improvisation consequently involves some prior planning in the determination of the circumstances. Improvisation also leaves much to chance by allowing you to invent the specific means or "how" of the circumstances based upon the unforeseen developments in the actual playing. In planning the circumstances for improvisation, invent circumstances which lead *to* action, rather than *away from* action, and to *deeds* rather than to *words*. When playing an improvisation, remember that you depend upon your partner; do your actions to see how they affect your partner, and listen purposefully to use whatever is said to further your intention. Listening is a continuation of your goal, not a pause to refresh!

EXERCISES

1. List your day's activities. Divide the activities into *units of action,* each unit pursuing a specific goal. Label each goal. Choose one or two of the units and list the specific actions you performed to accomplish the goals. Assign a verb to each action. Note all obstacles met and leverages used. Choose one unit and perform it for the group. The class should note and diagram significant transactions.

2. Log the time you spend in a single day in each of six kinds of beat.

3. Using one of the *rituals* uncovered in the previous exercise, invent and detail in writing the circumstances of that action. Play the beat for the group.

4. Invent circumstances based upon an *activity* of the previous day. Detail the circumstances in writing and play the beat for the class.

5. Invent circumstances surrounding a *pastime* you engaged in the previous day. Detail the circumstances in writing and play the beat for the class.

6. Using one of the *games* you played yesterday, invent and detail in writing specific circumstances for action. Play the beat for the class.

7. This is an exercise based on an experiment developed by Eric Berne.[19] Two actors sit facing each other with their faces no more than thirty-six inches apart. They

must keep eye contact throughout the exercise. Each player must interact with the other avoiding withdrawal, rituals, pastimes, activities, games, or any ulterior trans-actions. A third person should interrupt if this stipulation is violated. Let the exercise continue for fifteen to twenty minutes. The exercise should diminish Parent or Adult responses, expose the Natural Child, and lead to a relationship of intimacy between the players.

8. Invent circumstances with another actor in which one player makes a demand and the other refuses. Do not collaborate on the strategy each will use in playing the improvisation.

9. Invent circumstances with another actor in which you have conflicting ob-jectives. For example, in Dreiser's *American Tragedy* Clyde Griffiths wants to break up with his girlfriend, Roberta Alden; Roberta, on the other hand, must convince Clyde to marry her since she is pregnant. It can help if one actor tells the other of his objective and allows the other actor to invent a secret one which conflicts. Play the improvisation.

NOTES

[1]Uta Hagen with Haskel Frankel, *Respect for Acting* (New York: Macmillan, 1973), p. 22. Copyright © 1973 by Uta Hagen.

[2]Harold Clurman, *All People Are Famous (Instead of An Autobiography)* (New York: Harcourt Brace Jovanovich, 1974), p. 206.

[3]W. Timothy Gallwey, *Inner Tennis: Playing the Game* (New York: Random House, 1976), pp. 24–25. Copyright © 1976 by W. Timothy Gallwey.

[4]W. Timothy Gallwey, *The Inner Game of Tennis* (New York: Random House, 1974), p. 43. Copyright © 1974 by W. Timothy Gallwey.

[5]Gallwey, *Inner Tennis*, p. 10.

[6]Robert Benedetti, *The Actor at Work*, rev. ed. (Englewood Cliffs, N.J.: Prentice-Hall, 1976) p. xvii.

[7]From *Brecht On Theatre*, ed. and trans. by John Willett. Copyright © 1957, 1963, and 1964 by Suhrkamp Verlag, Frankfurt am Main. This translation and notes © 1964 by John Willett. Reprinted by permission of Hill and Wang (a division of Farrar, Straus & Giroux) and Methuen and Co. Ltd. Original title "Schriften zum Theater" published by Suhrkamp Verlag, Frankfurt am Main. All rights reserved. Copyright © 1957 by Suhrkamp Verlag.

[8]From *Meyerhold on Theatre*, ed. and trans. by Edward Braun. Copyright © 1957 by Edward Braun. Reprinted by permission of Hill and Wang (a division of Farrar, Straus & Giroux) and Methuen Co. Ltd.

[9]Valentina Litvinoff, *The Use of Stanislavsky within Modern Dance* (New York: American Dance Guild, 1972), p. 3.

[10]From *Personality: A Psychological Interpretation* by Gordon W. Allport. Copyright, 1937, by Henry Holt and Company. Copyright © 1965 by Gordon W. Allport. Reprinted by permission of Holt, Rinehart & Winston.

[11]This and the preceding question acknowledge the concept of "press" developed by Henry A. Murray in *Explorations in Personality,* (New York: Oxford University Press, 1938), pp. 40–41. Press is "a temporal gestalt of stimuli which usually appears in the guise of a threat of harm or benefit to the organism."

[12]Ronald Hayman, *Techniques of Acting.* (New York: Holt, Rinehart & Winston, 1969), p. 2.

[13]Richard Boleslavsky, *Acting: The First Six Lessons* (New York: Theatre Arts Books, 1966), p. 60. Used by permission of the publisher, Theatre Arts Books, 153 Waverly Place, New York, N.Y. 10014.

[14]Gallwey, *Inner Tennis,* p. 161.

[15]Tom Robbins, *Even Cowgirls Get the Blues.* Copyright © 1976 by Thomas Robbins. By permission of Bantam Books. All rights reserved.

[16]Charles Marowitz, *The Act of Being: Towards a Theory of Acting.* (New York: Taplinger Publishing Company, 1978), p. 29.

[17]Eric Berne, *Games People Play* (New York: Grove Press, 1964)

[18]Abraham Maslow, *Motivation and Personality* (New York: Harper and Row Pubs., 1954), p. 236.

[19]Eric Berne, "Social Dynamics: The Intimacy Experiment," *T.A. Bulletin,* 3 (January 1964), p. 113, and "Research: More About Intimacy," *T.A. Bulletin,* 3 (April 1964), p. 125.

2

The Psychological Player

*The mind of man is capable of anything—because everything
is in it, all the past as well as all the future.*

—Joseph Conrad

Often crossword puzzles ask for a seven-letter word for bad or hammy acting. The answer is *emoting*. Many young students believe that acting is emoting. They cry at the drop of a hat or else plan strategies to wring emotion out of their bodies. The simple fact is that if you do everything else effectively—play the action in a relaxed, concentrated, justified and imaginative manner—emotion will take care of itself. *Emotion is the sweat of action*.

Emotion can cause action and emotion can result from action. It is like the chicken-or-the-egg question: Which comes first? Either. If the circumstances create a genuine emotional feeling within you, actions will result from it. On the other hand, doing certain actions can produce an emotional reaction to the deeds. *Emotion can be the cause or the effect of action*. Fear can cause retreat, love advance. The effect of retreat can be fear; the effect of advance can be love. If you are sensitive to the surroundings certain emotions may be triggered within you which prompt certain actions. At the same time, doing definite actions in pursuit of a particular goal can generate certain emotions. However, play must move along through action; you cannot wait for or wallow in the circumstances until an emotional feeling overtakes you. You must do actions which can produce emotion on the way to the goal while remaining open to the dynamics of the circumstances. *Emotion may be the cause or emotion may be the effect, but emotion is never the goal of action*. The function and status of emotion becomes clearer if its nature is understood. Psychologist Magda Arnold provides a definition of emotion suited to our consideration. Emotion is "the felt tendency toward anything intuitively appraised as good (beneficial) or away from anything intuitively appraised as bad (harmful). This attraction or aversion is accomplished by a pattern of physiological changes organized toward approach or withdrawal."[1] Keep your senses open to stimulation from the circumstances. Your *Child* intuits the stimuli and automatically perceives a sense of attraction or repulsion. These feelings result in either advancing action or retreating action.

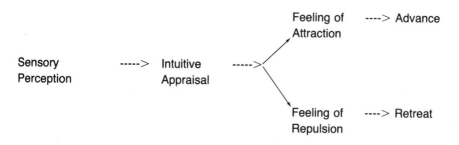

Each of us automatically and intuitively appraises everything we perceive as it relates to us. Dispassionate, objective appraisal is a function learned by the *Adult*, a personality aspect not concerned in the emotive processes.

See Knife ----> Intuit ----> Sense Fear ----> Run Away
                Danger

Hear Weeping ----> Intuit ----> Sense Compassion ----> Comfort
                   Sorrow

Certain verbs can be grouped according to whether they are in response to a feeling of attraction or to a feeling of repulsion. These verbs are preferable in your work since they embody advancing or retreating action. From the doing of compelling verbs certain feelings may result.

Emotion and the means of its expression (action) are stimulated subconsciously, spontaneously through executing actions toward a goal. Come on stage not to feel or experience emotion, but to do or act toward your objective. Eugene Vakhtangov, the Russian director, elaborates on this need for action:

> An actor must not simply stay upon the stage, but act. Every action differs from feeling by the presence of the will element. To persuade, to comfort, to ask, to reproach, to forgive, to wait, to chase away—these are verbs expressing will action. These verbs denote the task which the actor places before

himself when working upon a character, while the verbs to become irritated, to pity, to weep, to laugh, to be impatient, to hate, to love—express feeling and therefore cannot and must not figure as a task in the analysis of a role. Feelings denoted by these verbs must be born spontaneously and subconsciously as a result of the actions executed by the first series of verbs."[2]

Conflict—acting against an obstacle to a goal—generates emotion spontaneously. Often conflict is internal and involves a psychological obstacle. For example, a young boy wants to meet Reggie Jackson but fears he won't be able to think of the right words to say. Or a man wishes to declare his love for his girlfriend but fears her refusal or laughter. In these cases emotion—love—prompts the goal while another, conflicting emotion—fear—serves as the obstacle. In playing these actions, both actors would try not to display fear; on the contrary, they might wish to persuade the other party that they are not afraid. *Playing the opposite* is a term sometimes used to describe this technique. If the tendency is to advance in accordance with a favorable emotion (love), counteract it by playing a tendency to retreat generated by the other emotion (indifference or hate).

MEMORY: A STOREHOUSE OF STIMULI

All action has an emotive element. Even thinking—mental play—can produce an emotional response. Moving various thoughts through our minds gives our mind's eye and ear something with which to relate. Your mind contains detailed recordings of everything you have experienced. Psychologist Wilder Penfield experimented with a stimulating electrode in his patients' brains and found that he could produce a recollective hallucination:

> Under the compelling influence of the stimulating electrode, a familiar experience appears in a patient's consciousness whether he desires to focus his attention upon it or not. A song goes through his mind, probably as he heard it on a certain occasion; he finds himself a part of a specific situation, which progresses and evolves just as in the original situation. It is, to him, the act of a familiar play, and he is himself both an actor and the audience.
>
> The subject feels again the emotion which the situation originally produced in him, and he is aware of the same interpretation, true or false, which he himself gave to the experience in the first place. Thus, evoked recollection is not the exact photographic or phonographic reproduction of past scenes and events. It is reproduction of what the patient saw and heard and understood.[3]

The implications of Penfield's experimentation hold important information for an actor:

1. Stimuli can tap your memory to recall past experiences.
2. Past experiences are recorded in your brain with the emotion associated with the event.
3. Your brain retains *sensory* data in the recording process. If artificial stimulation can tap the memory, so too can the natural stimuli of circumstance tap the recollection of past experiences. A fleeting thought, word, odor, sound or color can release a stream of memories and emotions. By making yourself open to the stimuli of circumstance you grant yourself the possibility of having memories and emotions liberated. By developing the sensory apparatus you increase the ability to stimulate the stored material in the brain.

However, more important to our consideration of memory and emotion is the fact that emotion is a by-product, a result of action. You need not strive for emotion; emotion will result from other pursuits. In fact, memory and emotion may lead automatically and instantaneously to an impulse to act:

> Psychologically speaking, the recall of memories represents an action impulse: when something seen or heard or touched has to be dealt with in some way, it becomes imperative to discover how it has affected us in the past. During waking hours, each sense impression will automatically arouse an impulse to recall similar situations, which will help us to decide upon action.[4]

Thus, if you are awake and alert to your circumstances you do not need to consciously work to recall past, analogous experiences to generate emotion; action comes automatically from sensory awareness of the *present* circumstances.

We should review our discussion of emotion and the actor:

1. You should not concern yourself with emotion while playing.
2. Emotion comes as a result of pursuing a specific goal in specific circumstances. To increase the probability of emotion, increase the desirability of the goal or the dynamics of the circumstances.
3. You need only remain open to the changing stimuli in your environment while vigorously pursuing your goal.
4. Problems with emotion can arise if you are not sensitive to the dynamics of your environment, if the environment does not contain sufficient stimulation, if you merely wait for the environment to affect your emotional status, or if your goal does not elicit zestful pursuit.
5. Remembering brings emotion. Remember *what* the character remembers *as* the character remembers it; you need not substitute personal memories however analogous they may be. The reason? You cannot visualize in detail anything you haven't experienced in fact, fantasy, or dream. By trying to visualize the character's recollection you automatically remember things you have experienced. Conscious substitution unnecessarily duplicates subconscious substitution and burdens you with unnecessary actions. As French actor-director Jean-Louis Barrault tells us:

... emotion is a state which the actor must never be conscious of. One can only become conscious of an emotion which has already passed, for the act of consciousness dissipates the actual emotion.

Thus the actor need no more concern himself with emotion as such, than he concerns himself with his perspiration in the course of performance. But he must, on the contrary, attach importance to emotions viewed as means of behavior and actions, and that will lead him to realize that characters never pause for one moment in the middle of their actions in order to offer gratuitous displays of feeling. They are involved in continuous actions and reactions; they argue, they plead, they discuss, they fight against others or against themselves, they delude themselves and others, sometimes in good faith, sometimes in bad faith, but they never stop. The spectator might try to analyze their behavior, feelings, and emotions, but for the actor who is caught in the middle of the dramatic game, there is nothing else but action.[5]

EXERCISES

1. Choose a very emotional moment from your past, one which you have told someone about before. Sit in a chair, close your eyes and relax. To relax, each time you exhale think the word *one.* Remember the environment in which this event took place—the specific objects, colors, textures, sounds, smells, in great detail. Then rise, still with your eyes closed, and imagine that you are now in that environment. Place the important people and objects around you in your mind's eye. Begin to re-enact the event, doing what you did, saying what you said, hearing what you heard, and thinking what you thought while giving time to see and hear in your mind's eye the words and actions of the other people in the event. Take your time. Your goal is not to entertain an audience but to discover for yourself your past actions. Emotions are on tap in our sense memory.

2. In a group discuss the results of the previous exercise. What gestures, demeanors, voices, or words seemed significant? Which remembered sensory objects seemed most adept at triggering an emotional response?

3. With randomly assigned emotions, discover under which circumstances and by performing what actions you feel the assigned emotions. *Remember that action precedes feeling.* Which personality aspects are involved?

4. Stand before the class and play "A Day in the Life of (Your Name)." Begin the sololiquy with the words "What a day!" Unburden your mind and heart to the audience. Explore the feelings the day's events produced in you. Discuss how everything has contributed to your present mood. Discuss your present mood and use recollections to define the mood. Avoid exaggeration and dramatization.[6]

5. Memorize a brief descriptive poem and talk it to the class as if it were a personal recollection. See, hear, smell, touch each thing described. Detail the image before you as specifically as possible. Take time to visualize each sensory image before you utter it.

6. List the emotions you experienced today in approximate chronological order. Label each emotion as either positive or negative. Toward what goal were you acting

when you experienced each? What motivated each goal? What was the effect of the circumstances on your sensory perception and on your action?

7. Using the verb list in Appendix B, select the "feeling" verbs (as Barrault calls them). Invent actions and choose other verbs which could produce the "feeling" verbs as "perspiration."

8. Invent and detail in writing circumstances which would cause you to generate or stimulate one of the following emotions in another actor in improvisation.

hate
anger
sorrow
laughter
affection
fear
alarm
terror

The other actor should be open to the circumstances and to your actions. He should not fake anything; you should actually generate the emotion within him. Often a note in a play text describing the emotion a character feels is really a note for the other actors in the scene. It can suggest to them actions to produce the desired emotion in the actor with the note.

9. Invent and detail in writing circumstances with the potential to generate great emotion in the players. Play the improvisation only relying on words when absolutely necessary.

10. Invent and detail in writing circumstances involving a conflict of emotions. Play the improvisation relying on words only when necessary.

11. Invent and detail in writing circumstances involving conflict between two people. Play the improvisation using objects or properties to further the action.

12. Sit in a relaxed position and recall the sensory details of an emotional experience in your past. Recall the physical actions you performed. Recall the words you heard. Recall the thoughts you had. Talk aloud each remembrance as you recall it.

Now invent and detail in writing circumstances which *could* evoke the same emotion. Play the improvisation incorporating some of the physical actions and words recalled in the first half of this exercise. As Stanislavski said, "make use of everything that will stimulate your feelings."7

13. Choose one of the following words or phrases or invent a "charged" phrase of your own. Repeat the phrase over and over, increasing volume, rate, or intensity each time. Become more and more involved with your phrase each time you utter it. Gradually add physical movement to the repetition. Repeat the words over and over with growing involvement.

"Die"
"I love you"
"Kiss me"
"Don't go"

"Please don't"
"Just you wait"
"No"
"Yes"

Let the repetition suggest circumstances. Detail the circumstances in writing. Play the improvisation.

14. Observe people who are emotional. Note their actions. Detail in writing the circumstances of the actions, inventing when necessary. Play the improvisation for the group not as the other person but as yourself. Was the same emotion generated? Another? None? Discuss possible reasons for the emotional effects generated by the exercise.

15. Observe yourself carefully the next time you laugh or cry. Pay particular attention to your breathing pattern. Repeat the breathing pattern later, tensing and relaxing the appropriate muscles. Gradually let a sound emerge from the breathing. Force the sound as you concentrate on the breathing. Increase volume, intensity and involvement with each repetition. Notice what occurs.

16. Choose one of the Open Scenes from Appendix A. Invent and detail in writing circumstances which *could* produce strong emotions. Play the scene. Afterward, discuss whatever emotions the scene generated. Were they the same as the ones you anticipated when you invented the improvisation?

Music, Light, and Emotion

The exercises you have been performing have, hopefully, stimulated your emotions. This experience confirms Stanislavski's belief that external aids stimulate an inner process. Unfortunately, often a novice actor gets so caught up in his emotions that he has no idea what his body and voice are doing. Even worse, some actors fear to know what their body and voice are doing, lest the knowledge stifle their inspiration or dampen the fire of their emotions!

Music has been called pure emotion. Consequently if you will allow music to affect your emotions while remaining aware of your play, you will be on the road to sensible and sensitive playing. Remain open and sensitive to the dynamics of your circumstances even with planned playing. Let the surroundings affect your emotional attitude; respond to changes in mood. Explore the relationship between mood, emotion, and action.

EXERCISES

1. Play various records (classical, jazz, popular, ethnic, electronic, sound effects) and let the music inhabit your body and soul. Let the music move you about the room.

2. Invent and play an improvisation on an everyday activity centered on an imaginary object to two emotionally distinct pieces of music. Allow the music to affect the manner of your movement. Attend to the effect the music is having, without letting the awareness interfere with your ability to execute the action. Allow the music to influence *how* you execute your action.

3. Play an Open Pantomime to two emotionally distinct pieces of music. Attend to the same experiences as in the previous exercise. (An Open Pantomime is a scene for which no circumstances are provided. The actor must invent circumstances and communicate them through action alone.)

4. Alter the quality, intensity, or color of the light available in your playing space and repeat the previous exercise. Note the effect light has on your emotions and mood.

5. Choose a poem. Find music which produces in you the same emotions the text's speaker undergoes in the piece. Play the recording as you play the selection. Listen to the music as you speak. Allow the music to affect your rate, volume, and pitch. Play the piece two more times, each time to completely different mood music. Let the music stimulate your rate, volume, and pitch.

6. Play the selection from the previous exercise in approximate mood lighting. Candlelight, firelight, moonlight, sunlight, or flashlight can create definite moods in players. Repeat your selection twice, each time in completely different mood lighting. Let the atmosphere affect rate, pitch, and volume.

Relationships

Rarely are you alone on the stage. Other characters populate the stage, pursuing their goals and satisfying their needs. When you connect your actions with those of another character a relationship is formed. You should understand the nature of relationships—the factors influencing their formation, and the dynamics of their operation.

Why should you concern yourself with why relationships are formed? What does this have to do with acting? The answer is that every circumstance of action can involve other actors—as obstacles, as allies, as tools for leverage, as means to an objective. The analysis of circumstances must include a consideration of other characters.

Why are relationships formed? If we act to satisfy our needs, we quickly realize that our needs may be satisfied more effectively and efficiently in cooperation with others. Think of how much you depend upon others to satisfy Maslow's needs. When we encounter people, we respond intuitively as we do toward any stimuli—favorably, toward those we like, or unfavorably, away from those we dislike. If we continue with these people a relationship forms which is either favorable or unfavorable. Most favorable relationships lead to friendships; least favorable relationships produce animosities.

Relationships which further our objectives and bring us closer to our goals exist among friends or allies. Three factors seem to characterize those who are friends or allies:

1. *Nearness.* The adage "absence makes the heart grow fonder" belies the psychological studies. People favor people who are physically close.
2. *Similarity.* Opposites do *not* attract. At least one common element must exist as a bond between the one liked and the one doing the liking.
3. *Reward.* People like people who "reward" them, that is, who give them something desirable they would not ordinarily have. This can be anything from aesthetic pleasure to money, security, flattery, or intellectual stimulation. On the contrary, those who are distant, dissimilar, and unrewarding hold a least-favored relationship.

You would do well to analyze the circumstances of your action with attention to the friends or allies who can aid you in attaining your goals. As Gallwey tells us:

> Once a player has decided on his goal and dedicated himself to it, his will to reach it can be strengthened by keeping the company of people of like commitment. Our will needs to be inspired to stay constantly strong, and that inspiration comes best from those who are genuinely committed to the same objective.[8]

Favorable relationships can give you leverage; unfavorable ones can pose obstacles. Power results from the former and is required to overcome the latter.

Power and Love Emerson wrote, "You shall have joy, or you shall have power, said God; you shall not have both." As power is amassed, the relationship most desired—love—moves farther away. Power demands inequality. Allies and friends working together have more power to attain goals and satisfy needs than individuals working alone. However, within a relationship power is rarely equally distributed among the parties. As distinguished actress Uta Hagen tells us, "in almost all human relationships—or at least in certain areas of a relationship—one person dominates and the other submits; one person leads and the other follows."[9] Power remains a basic human need since the satisfaction of other needs can depend upon it. For our purposes, power may be defined as "the ability of one person to move another through a wide range of outcomes."[10]

A simple example demonstrates power and relationships. Suppose you need food and your goal is money to buy food. You need either (a) power to obtain money, or (b) a favorable relationship with someone with the money (power) to buy food. If you agree to chop a cord of wood for ten dollars, you exert muscle power and are rewarded with money. If you take a gun (firepower) to a bank and demand money, you may also satisfy your need. If you pawn the gun, you have traded firepower for money. These three scenarios reveal individual action from a position of power. On the other hand, if you ask a parent for money or take out a bank loan, you are using a favorable relationship to attain your goal. Asking a parent or signing a loan contract are dependent and powerless acts.

Almost every act within a relationship comes from a position of either power or powerlessness. Low-powered people usually comply with the wishes of high-powered people to reach their goals. For example, a parent may require extra work for the money as the bank requires an interest payment for the money given for food. Psychologist Edward Jones describes the relationship between the dependent and the powerful:

> If one person has more to gain and more to lose in the relationship than the other, he has greater dependence in the other and the other therefore has greater power over him. The person who has greater power in this sense can get the other person to do things for him—he can call forth certain responses out of the other's repertory because of his superior capacity to reward and punish.[11]

Eric Berne nominated intimacy as the most desirable but difficult relationship to achieve. Free, open, spontaneous, child-like love between two people remains an ideal for almost all people. To one degree or another everyone's goal is love—a Natural Child to Natural Child relationship. Intimacy satisfies most needs while demanding no power. In fact, power more often thwarts intimacy; *when you have some power, someone else has less.* A powerful person needs someone else to confirm that power through a dependent position. True intimacy exists between equals. Consequently, as we try to reach love by amassing power, intimacy becomes more unlikely. As Emerson reminds us, you can have the joy of intimacy or the domination of power, but you cannot have both.

Characters strive to accomplish their goals. A *power play* occurs when one player in a relationship demands certain actions from the other player. Claude Steiner, in *Scripts People Live* defines a *power play* as a "technique used to get people to do something they don't want to do."[12] Our lives and our theatre teem with power plays. The powerful player and the dependent player alike may initiate these exertions of will. For example, Steiner suggests a power play initiated by high-powered Player A:

> Player A makes a decision without consulting Player B.
> Player B objects.
> Player A reminds Player B of B's dependent position.
> Player B continues to object to A's decision.
> Player A suggests their relationship end if B is not happy.
> Player B still objects to A's decision.
> Player A can:
> (a) terminate the relationship with B.
> (b) physically force B to acquiesce to the decision.

Powerful players exert strength in increasing intensity to a climax. Dependent players, on the other hand, exert power defensively:

> Player A makes a decision without consulting Player B.
> Player B acquiesces but may:
> (a) arouse A's guilt.
> (b) hurt A by retaliation.
> (c) waste A's time.

All in all, Player B interferes with Player A's actions, probably making A angry.[13]

Power plays result when people try to satisfy their needs through relationships. The dynamics of power playing provide a source of the actor's power over an audience. As the great Russian teacher, actor, and director, Constantin Stanislavski tells us, "if actors really mean to hold the attention of a large audience they must make every effort to maintain an uninterrupted exchange of feelings, thoughts, and actions among themselves."[14] *In fact, your partner in a relationship is your primary audience.* Through your partner's genuine reactions, the audience forms its impression of your character's power. Michael Chekhov, the Russian actor, elaborates on this phenomenon:

> The only satisfactory performance comes with the right relationship with one's fellow actors. If the actor, like a human being, makes himself clear and understood by his stage partner, the audience will understand him, the performance will become real. Suppose a character has to beg from another. If the actress plays for the audience she will be trying to prove to them how much it means to her. If she is playing for herself she will churn up desperation inside herself, and end by feeling sorry for her. All she needs to do is actually to beg favor from the other actor, to concentrate upon convincing him of her need—then the audience can be convinced.[15]

This principle of first establishing the relationship between *actors* before moving into the realm of character is extended by acting teacher Robert Cohen. Cohen would have you *"actually use the tactics on the other actor."* "If you, Tybalt, are designated to threaten John–Romeo, you must *actually threaten John.* If you Romeo, are designated to seduce Jane–Juliet, you must *actually seduce Jane. . . . The actor should play tactics strongly enough to create visible changes in the other actor's autonomic system."*[16] Both parties in the relationship may forget that the tactics of the character often become those of the actor. If you follow Cohen's suggestion you can observe the reactions of the other actor to monitor your success in playing.

Adaptation and Change   As you try to reach your goal and satisfy your need, relationships develop. Power may move you closer to some goals, farther away from others. Relationships can increase or decrease power, sometimes both. Relationships change as the circumstances of action change. You *adapt* to the transforming situation. Stanislavski defines *adaptation* as "the inner and outer human means that people use in adjusting to one another in a variety of relationships and also as an aid in effecting an object."[17]

Changes in relationship constitute a significant change in action and produce drama. Will change occur? Does change satisfy each party in the relationship? Is there a shift in power? Is anyone hurt in the change? Relationships exist between personality aspects; consequently, six possible changing relationships may exist:

> Parent to Parent
> Adult to Adult
> Child to Child
> Parent to Child (or Child to Parent)
> Parent to Adult (or Adult to Parent)
> Child to Adult (or Adult to Child)

One person may change a relationship quite often, utilizing each possible type. Another person may hold only one kind of relationship with everyone. For example, in an hour my wife and I go through each of the six relationships many times. On the other hand, until I became a parent, the number of possible relationships I could have with my parents was limited. Now all relationships are possible, although not all preferable to both parties! And I have known people so fixed in objective scholarship that they never could engage in anything but Adult to Adult relationships!

ROLE-PLAYING

The number of roles you can play is impossible to estimate. You play many each day. Father, husband, teacher, actor, scholar, friend, customer, son, audience, brother, and writer are but a few I have played today. Role is independent of personality aspect; any role can be played from any personality aspect. Certain roles, however, are usually associated with particular aspects—father with Parent, son with Child, teacher with Adult. Yet even these roles are probably played just as frequently from other aspects— childlike father, dispassionate son, authoritarian teacher.

Though the number of roles is uncountable, psychoanalyst Stephen Karpman maintains that "only three roles are necessary in drama analysis to depict the emotional reversals that are drama." The three necessary roles are Persecutor, Rescuer, and Victim. "Drama begins when these roles are established, or are anticipated by the audience. There is no drama unless there is a switch in the roles."[18]

This *drama triangle* is important to the actor because it combines the features of a unit of action with the dynamics of relationships. The *drama triangle exchange* is a frequent component in many dramas. The switching of roles in the basic drama triangle exchange is diagrammed:

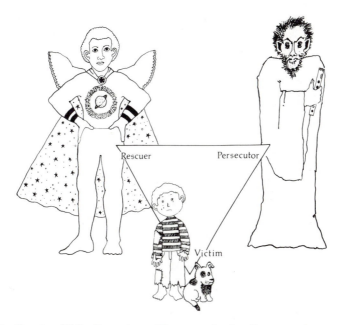

FIGURE 2-1:   The roles of Victim, Persecutor, and Rescuer can be played by anyone of any age or sex. The Drama Triangle reveals the dynamics of changing relationships.

This fundamental relationship exists under many costumes and many characters' names.

The fairy tale *Cinderella* lets Karpman demonstrate how the exchange exists in that context. If actors were to play *Cinderella,* an understanding of the triangular nature of the character relationships would help their playing. Cinderella is a Victim double-Persecuted by her two stepsisters. She is triple-Rescued by her fairy godmother, the mice, and the prince. After midnight, she is Persecuted again, only to be finally Rescued by the prince. So the character of Cinderella plays Victim-persecuted, Victim-rescued, Victim-persecuted and finally, Victim-rescued.

Victims are powerless. Persecutors and Rescuers have power. When roles switch, power is redistributed. If, for example, Cinderella (now the wife of the prince) wanted to use her new power, she could either rescue or persecute her stepsisters. Either move would push the stepsisters into Victim roles. Suppose Cinderella decided to rescue them by sending money. Her husband, the prince, might play Persecutor by scolding Cinderella for wasting his power. The stepsisters might then try to rescue Cinderella from the Victim role into which her abusive husband forced her. Thus drama and the role-switching would continue.

Not only do fairy tales illustrate the drama triangle operation, but they also can provide you with the basic source of your character's action and relationships. The analysis of fairy tales and the fairy tale elements of a particular situation can provide an interesting and often definitive insight into character role-playing and relationships. Educator Bruno Bettelheim believes that fairy tales help us define our roles:

> Then the child has a basis for understanding that there are great differences between people, and that therefore one has to make choices about who one wants to be. This basic decision, on which all later personality development will build, is facilitated by the polarization of the fairy tale.[19]

The fairy tale scenario may indeed hold a key to the roles you play and the relationships you establish. I mentioned my fondness for *Peter Pan*. As you remember, Peter wanted to rescue boys and girls from reality by taking them to the magical world of never-never land where they could remain as children. Twice in the Barrie play Peter says, "I want always to be a little boy and to have fun."[20] Perhaps my fondness for this tale explains my role as teacher of theatre—leading students to the magical world of the theatre, reintroducing them to their ever-young Child personality aspects. The theatre is where I am always a little boy and have fun. Favorite fables can often give us insights into our actions and relationships.

In reviewing the relationships which affect actions, consider the following:

1. the needs the relationship satisfies or frustrates.
2. the factors which create friendships or antagonisms.
3. the degree of power the relationship provides or withdraws.
4. the manner by which power is exerted.
5. the roles played and exchanged.
6. the influence of fairy tales on role, relationship, and action.

EXERCISES

1. Outline the drama triangles and roles you engaged in today. Which roles do you play most frequently? What usually causes you to switch roles? Play one of your dramas after detailing the circumstances in writing.

2. Invent and detail in writing circumstances which force you to put your partner into a predetermined personality aspect. Play the invention.

3. Choose an Open Scene from Appendix A and play it, trying to force your partner into a predetermined relationship (role). Invent and detail in writing the circumstances for action.

4. Invent and detail in writing circumstances in which you try to establish a relationship in the drama triangle. Adapt to each other's actions. Repeat in silence.

5. With a partner, repeat the Mirror Exercise. Facing each other one of you is the mirror, the other himself. Slowly the mirror follows the leader on signal; exchange roles without stopping action. On signal, both play mirror, both play leader without stopping. On signal, close your eyes and continue slow motion action. On signal, freeze. Open your eyes to see how close your relationship has become.

6. Invent and detail in writing circumstances in which you try to elicit a specific response from your partner. You should have some common elements of circumstance (where and when) and some secret elements (what, why, and how). Play the improvisation.

7. Invent and detail in writing circumstances in which you attempt to establish a relationship to satisfy one of Maslow's needs. Play the improvisation.

8. Play an Open Scene from Appendix A in which you hold a distinct attitude toward your partner. Invent and detail the circumstances. The attitude should remain a secret from your partner until performance. How does attitude affect action?

9. Choose a partner and listen to music. Let the music suggest a relationship. Follow the music as it changes, physicalizing the attitudes as the relationship changes.

10. With a partner start a rhythmic movement. Never lose touch with your partner. Alter the contact point and repeat.

11. Mold your face into a rigid mask of a definite attitude. Reveal it to your partner who reacts immediately with a mask of his own. Carry on this dialogue gradually adding sounds. Incorporate large movements. Everything must be in reaction to the other player.

12. Tie a rope of at least ten feet around your waist and your partner's. Play an Open Scene using the rope to imaginatively reveal role switches, relationship changes and power plays.

13. Play a simple action six times with a partner. Each time play in a different personality relationship.

14. Invent and detail in writing circumstances involving the handling of many objects. Use the objects to reveal changes in the relationship. Play the improvisation.

15. Actor A sits at a table knowing nothing. Actor B enters after inventing and detailing in writing the circumstances of action. Actor B includes A in his action in a definite relationship. A adapts to B's actions, assimilating the circumstances. Before the scene ends Actor C enters with new circumstances. Actor A invents a logical exit while B adapts as quickly as possible to the new circumstances and relationship.

16. Sell or demonstrate something to the group. You must make both eye and physical contact with each member of your audience.

17. Choose an Open Scene from Appendix A and invent and detail in writing circumstances for action. Play the scene making direct physical contact with each new phrase or thought. Use variety as you react to changing relationships. Actions should be natural and spontaneous.

18. Invent, detail in writing, and play circumstances for action involving a relationship so tense that each player is unable to speak. (The scene must, therefore, be played in silence!)

19. Invent and detail in writing circumstances for action. Play the improvisation using pauses to heighten communication and to reveal relationship. Use pauses to strengthen relationship, change relationship, or to build tension in the existing relationship.

20. Choose an Open Scene from Appendix A. Invent circumstances and begin to play it in these physical relationships:[21]

standing side by side
standing face to face
standing back to back
seated side by side
seated face to face
seated back to back
one seated, one standing: face to face
one seated, one standing: side by side
one seated, one standing: back to back
one kneeling, one standing
both kneeling
one lying down, one standing
one lying down, one sitting
one lying down, one kneeling
both lying down

How does physical relationship affect the nature of the psychological relationship?

21. Invent circumstances for an Open Scene chosen from Appendix A. Play the scene three times: once touching your partner when you speak, once speaking when not touching, and once touching to interrupt or silence your partner.[22]

22. Invent circumstances for an Open Scene chosen from Appendix A. Play it with eye contact throughout. Repeat, looking only at your partner's hands; neck; feet; ears. Repeat the scene never looking at your partner. Repeat the scene looking only at the floor. Repeat the scene looking only at the ceiling.[23]

23. Recall you favorite fairy tale. Cast and play it. Invent circumstances placing the relationships of the tale in your contemporary life. Play this improvisation as your favorite character of the fairy tale. Did you discover any familiar roles or relationships in the playing?

UNITY OF CHARACTER

In *Alice's Adventures in Wonderland* the Caterpillar asks Alice who she is. Alice replies, "I—I hardly know, Sir, just at present—at least I know who I was when I got up this morning, but I think I must have been changed several times since then."[24] Identity concerns each of us. With all of the different roles played, how does an actor achieve unity and thus identity in his playing? We are the product of our actions; who we are is the sum of what we did. Nobel prize-winning author I. B. Singer tells a discerning story:

> Once a boy came over to the *cheder* where I studied, and he said, "Do you know that my father wanted to box my ears?" So the teacher said, "How do

you know that he wanted to box your ears?" And the boy said, "He did it."
A man may sit for hours and talk to you about what he thinks. But what he
really is, you can judge best by what he did.[25]

Action is the actor's art. Action reveals character—personality, relationship,
motivation, goal, and circumstance. To act is to do; to do is to create oneself.

But how do actions create a person? How do the individual units of
action add up to a whole—a unified artistic creation with a beginning, a
middle, and an end? If we use the musician as an analogous performer,
an answer may appear. Each note played is part of a measure. Each measure
is a unit of action. Each measure may be part of a subject or theme. Each
unit—measure, subject or theme—has a goal, circumstance, and motivation.
A measure follows a previous measure and leads to the next measure.
Together measures form the musical score. The score leads the musician's
playing to the logical ending of the piece of music. The score achieves unity
since all of the parts together fulfill a purpose larger than itself. The larger
purpose determines the shape and content of the individual measures,
themes, and subjects. To an actor this larger purpose is the *superobjective*.

Superobjective and Script

Stanislavski defined the *superobjective* as "the main foundation of an
actor's life and part, and all minor objectives are corollaries to it, the in-
evitable consequence and reflection of the basic one."[26] All actions, to Stanislavski, lead to one ultimate goal. The playwright's script provides you with
your character's actions and superobjective; your *personal script* provides
you with your own actions and superobjective. Your script details a drama
of which you may be unaware, but which you may follow compulsively until
your death. A script governs at least a part of each of our lives. By understanding your script you can choose to retain all of it, some of it, or
none of it.

You need to understand your personal script. You should realize how
some of your actions are prescribed so that you may choose to liberate
yourself from them. A large part of actor training involves freeing the
actor from learned vocal, physical, and mental behavior. You should be
free to play alien actions as you characterize various roles. Analysis allows
you to understand why you may prefer to act from certain personality
aspects, to initiate certain games, to choose certain people as friends and
others as enemies. Analysis reveals a blueprint for a life course written to
a large extent by parents or parent figures. Analysis begins to supply you
with material for revelation on stage. For as Marowitz warns:

> The theatre is as harshly revealing as psychoanalysis. The art of acting is the
> ultimate exposure. An actor is in the constant state of revealing his true
> character, and so he must suffer the consequences of his paucity just as he
> reaps the rewards of his abundance.[27]

Every life is directed toward some overriding goal, something in the future which lures one onward. J. M. Barrie notes this in dedicating the play version of *Peter Pan:*

> Perhaps we do change; except a little something in us which is no larger than a mote in the eye and that, like it, dances in front of us beguiling us all our days.[28]

This goal or "want" mobilizes all actions. This is the *superobjective.* The most effective and compelling means of stating the superobjective is "I want" or "I must" plus a transitive verb infinitive with an object. For example, "I want to succeed in the business world" or "I want to develop my skill as an actor." Avoid using verbs which are static or express states of being rather than action, such as "I want *to be* successful" or "I want *to be* an actor." The transitive verb encourages action whereas the "to be" verb results in passivity and indicating.

Beginning actors sometimes have difficulty phrasing their intentions so as to maximize the opportunity for compelling action. Your action will be as compelling as the verb you choose, so avoid verbs like, *tells, asks, inquires, states,* or *explains.* Also, make sure that the phrasing of your objective includes a verb after the "I want." Often students write, "I want money" or "I want security" as objectives without including verbs which give them specific means to attain their goals. More stimulating statements might be, "I want to wheedle ten dollars out of my boyfriend" or "I want to implore my girlfriend to take me back."

The superobjective creates a characteristic disposition. At birth we have positive feelings about ourselves and others, sometimes expressed as "I'm OK—You're OK." This is a healthy disposition in which a person can hope to solve problems constructively. Frequently, we change our estimations of ourself and others based on circumstances and on what we have come to believe. Other dispositions can be called, "I'm OK—You're Not OK," "I'm Not OK—You're OK," "I'm Not OK—You're Not OK." A person will move in and out of these positions often in a single day. Yet he will favor generally one position summarizing his life's position or outlook.

As an actor you need to have positive feelings about yourself and your fellow actors. As Uta Hagen says, "to seem to want or need a mask behind which to bury one's self often comes, not only from an incorrect concept, but from a distrust in ourselves. We harbor suspicion that we ourselves are boring and that only the character in the play is sufficiently interesting to hold an audience."[29]

As children we often search for others who have a similar superobjective or disposition on whom to model our strategy for achieving our goals. Fairy tale heroes sometimes serve as models or heroes. Often a hero's physical, vocal, and mental characteristics are copied. We seem to put ourselves in situations and relationships analogous to those of our heroes.

Physical manifestations of this hero-worship can serve as the basis for your use of Michael Chekhov's *psychological gesture* or PG. The PG helps you physicalize your character's superobjective:

> Ask yourself what the *main* desire of the character might be, and when you get an answer, even if it is only a hint, start to build your PG step by step, using at first your *hand* and *arm* only. . . . Having once started this way, you will no longer find it difficult (in fact, it will happen by itself) to extend and adjust your particular gesture to your shoulders, your neck, the position of your head and torso, legs and feet, until your *entire* body is thus occupied.[30]

The Psychological Circumstances of Action

The messages parents give their children as they grow up construct the parameters for subsequent action. Many of these still exist in your Parent and surface from time to time as you advise and criticize others. An *injunction* is a negative command given by parents to prevent certain behavior. An injunction usually begins with the word *don't*. (Don't slouch. Don't talk to strangers. Don't be funny. Don't shout.) *Attributions* give us positive qualities for action. (Be quiet. Be seen and not heard. Respect your elders. Be nice. Be a good little girl. Behave. Act your age. You're just like your father.) Names and nicknames can act as attributions as well. We may be named after people our parents liked and hoped we would either consciously or unconsciously emulate. Even if our parents knew no one with our name, they associated certain traits with the name when they gave it. Attempts to follow these messages can result in the adoption of a script *objective* or *counterobjective*.

The Counterobjective Sometimes people and characters do things which do not seem directed toward the single superobjective. Indeed, many actions seem to lead in the opposite direction. These actions may constitute a *counterscript,* an optional path programmed along with the script but leading toward another objective. Contrary parent messages build this weaker script. For example, a parent could give the injunction, "Be careful," while very easily encouraging the child to have a good time. This would account for a person taking a skiing vacation while still functioning under the "Be careful" attribution; the person would ski warily and thereby not really enjoy himself. The counterscript can influence an actor's actions. For if a counterscript exists, then all actions do not lead to a single, dominant superobjective. Some actions lead to a counter-superobjective or counterobjective. Dramatic actions often result from the tension between the superobjective and the counterobjective. Tension between goals can result in inner tension. Investigate your acting instrument as it relates to your personal script. Use the following exercises to understand your psycho-physical and psycho-verbal mechanism.

EXERCISES

1. List all of your wants or desires or goals. Number them in order of preference. You should have at least ten. Place a plus (+) by those toward which a parent figure expressed a positive view and a minus (−) by those for which a parent expressed a negative view. A zero (0) notes those for which no opinion was expressed. If the wants at the top of your list are mostly pluses, your parents have succeeded in scripting your life to their desires. If most of your top desires are minuses, you are still scripted but in direct opposition to your parents' desires. A fair distribution of pluses and minuses indicates an adult view of your life course. Number one could be your superobjective and number two your counterobjective.

2. How does your superobjective satisfy Maslow's needs? How does your counterobjective satisfy Maslow's needs? Does your personality advance or hinder your super- and counter-objectives? Do your characteristic units of action bring you closer to your super- or counter-objectives? Invent and play an improvisation in which your superobjective clashes with your counterobjective. Do your relationships advance either goal? What power do you have to attain these goals? Which roles do you need to play to reach your two dominant goals?

3. Face another person and repeat this dialogue with deeper and deeper levels of conviction: A: "You are OK" B: "I am OK" Switch roles and repeat. Make sure that you believe what you are saying and that the other person knows you mean it.

4. Determine your favorite childhood fairy tale, the one with which you could most identify. Read the story again. Cast the fable and play it with you in your favorite role. If you had a favorite television personality or real-life hero, play him in a characteristic improvisation. What aspects of your hero do you see operating in your own interpersonal relationships? What are the dominant verbal and physical manifestations?

5. Invent one psychological gesture for your superobjective and another for your counterobjective. Assume a bodily attitude which conveys your basic disposition. Incorporate one or two of your hero's typical poses. Repeat your number one want with deeper and deeper conviction. Now alternate superobjective and counterobjective utterance and pose.

6. Make a mask of yourself. The mask should communicate your superobjective, disposition, and key feature of your hero. If you can't incorporate all of these factors in one mask make a mask for each one. With a full-length mirror communicate with yourself physically. Walk to your image. Run to your image. Laugh with your image. Cry with your image. Let the mask take over your whole body. Create another mask for your counterobjective.

7. Repeat your encounter with the mirror wearing another's mask. What does it feel like to assume another's identity? What do you feel as you see another as you? Do you see new aspects of yourself?

8. What messages—verbal and nonverbal—did your Parent give you about your body? About your voice? About playing? About your superobjective? Your worth?

Your abilities? Your looks? Often the psychological circumstances which govern our lives are passed on from our Parent as advice. Be alert for these instances.

   9. Improvise the final scene of your life. Who are the other characters? Where will it take place? Play yourself. Note your last words. Compare this scene with the last scene of your mythic hero.

NOTES

[1]Magda Arnold, *Emotion and Personality* (New York: Columbia University Press, 1960), vol. 1, p. 182.

[2]Eugene Vaktangov, "Preparing for the Role," in *Acting: A Handbook of the Stanislavski Method,* rev. ed., Toby Cole, ed. (New York: Crown Publishers, 1971), p. 118. Used by permission.

[3]Wilder Penfield, "Memory Mechanism," *Archives of Neurology and Psychiatry,* 67 (1952), p. 181. Copyright 1952, American Medical Association.

[4]Arnold, vol. 2, p. 125.

[5]From *The Theatre of Jean-Louis Barrault,* trans. by Joseph Chiardi. Reprinted by permission of Hill and Wang (a division of Farrar, Straus & Giroux). English translation copyright © 1961 by Barrie and Rockliff (Barrie Books).

[6]This exercise is based on an exercise in Marowitz's *The Act of Being.*

[7]Constantin Stanislavski, *An Actor Prepares* (New York: Theatre Arts Books, 1966), p. 173. Used by permission of the publisher, Theatre Arts Books, 153 Waverly Place, New York, N.Y. 10014.

[8]Gallwey, *Inner Tennis,* p. 168.

[9]Hagen, *Respect for Acting,* p. 166.

[10]Edward E. Jones, *Ingratiation.* (New York: Irvington Publishers, 1964), p. 119. Used with permission.

[11]Ibid., p. 9.

[12]Claude Steiner, *Scripts People Live* (New York: Grove Press, 1974), p. 2.

[13]Ibid., pp. 218–220.

[14]Stanislavski, *An Actor Prepares,* p. 186.

[15]Michael Chekhov, "Stanislavski's Method of Acting," in *Acting: A Handbook of the Stanislavski Method,* rev. ed., Toby Cole, ed. (New York: Crown Publishers, 1971), p. 109. Used by permission.

[16]Robert Cohen, *Acting Power* (Palo Alto, Calif.: Mayfield Publishing Co., 1978), pp. 79–80.

[17]Stanislavski, *An Actor Prepares,* p. 211.

[18]Stephen Karpman, "Fairy Tales and Script Drama Analysis," *T.A. Bulletin,* 7 (April 1968), pp. 38–43. Copyright 1968, The International Transactional Analysis Association, Inc. Reprinted by permission.

[19]Bruno Bettelheim, *The Uses of Enchantment: The Meaning and Importance of Fairy Tales* (New York: Knopf, 1977), p. 9. Copyright © 1975, 1976 by Bruno Bettelheim.

[20]J. M. Barrie, *The Plays of J. M. Barrie* (New York: Charles Scribner's Sons; London: Hodder and Stoughton, 1928), p. 32.

[21]Adapted from an exercise in Derek Bowskill's *Acting: An Introduction* (Englewood Cliffs, N.J.: Prentice-Hall, 1977), p. 256.

[22]Ibid.

[23]Ibid.

[24]Lewis Carroll, *The Complete Works* (New York: Knopf, 1976), p. 53.

[25]*New York Times Magazine,* November 26, 1978, p. 36. Copyright © 1979 by The New York Times Company. Reprinted by permission.

[26]Constantin Stanislavski, *Creating a Role* (New York: Theatre Arts Books, 1961), p. 78. Used by permission of the publisher, Theatre Arts Books, 153 Waverly Place, New York, N.Y. 10014.

[27]Charles Marowitz, *Stanislavsky and the Method* (New York: The Citadel Press, 1964), p. 44. Published by arrangement with Lyle Stuart. Copyright © 1961 by Charles Marowitz.

[28]Barrie, *The Plays,* p. 8.

[29]Hagen, *Respect for Acting,* p. 27.

[30]Michael Chekhov, *To the Actor on the Technique of Acting* (New York: Harper & Row Pubs., 1953), pp. 73–74.

EXTERNAL TECHNIQUE

3

The Physical Player

Movement is the most powerful means of theatrical expression. The role of movement is more important than that of any other theatrical element. Deprived of dialogue, costume, footlights, wings, and auditorium, and left only with the actor and his mastery of movement, the theatre remains theatre.

—Vsevelod Meyerhold[1]

Chapter 2 introduced you to the process and problems of acting by beginning with the mind's inventive play. Success meant that your actions were lifelike. Truthfulness to everyday life and the ability to do private actions publicly are highly desirable goals. Many would-be actors never reach them. But *honesty* in playing is just the first step for the actor. Believable, logical, genuine, and truthful actions in specific circumstances which generate sincere emotion must have two other qualities.

To be believable, logical, genuine, and truthful can also be boring. Look around you. You see people doing honest actions. Not very exciting. Playing must fulfill its second function—to elicit an action which is *compelling*. A compelling action is what Stanislavski sought when he discussed the "unexpected adaptation," what Serge Diaghilev, the great Russian impressario, wanted when he insisted, "Astonish me." You must not only be honest but you must also make us sit up, lean forward, drop our jaw, forget about time and space, be thrown back into our seat. Honest action, of course. But also, compelling. If your playing is not compelling we may as well stay home and wallow in our own honesty. The presence of the actor, even in the most mundane situation, must arouse, electrify, thrill or perturb us—in an honest manner!

For great playing the great actor must have actions which are honest and compelling. But life, too, can provide us with honest and compelling actions. If someone were to slam the door unexpectedly, your actions or reactions could be honest and compelling. What makes the theatrical action different from the everyday action is embodied in the third function of theatrical playing—the production of an action which is *beautiful*. Not only must your action be honest and compelling, it must be beautiful. The beautiful action is controlled, restrained, selected, ordered, disciplined, arranged, simplified, and economized. In short, you do what Stanislavski urged—remove the "dirt" of life. Honest, compelling, and beautiful action must be your goal in every play situation. Compelling and beautiful is hollow; beautiful and honest is boring; honest and compelling is still part of life. Without all three qualities life and art begin to overlap. But life is not art. Acting, as an art, must possess its fundamental constituent element—beauty. Probably you didn't consider the beauty of your actions!

How do lifelike actions become beautiful expressions of the actor-as-artist? The answer to this question emerges in the next two chapters. In a nutshell, the answer is *by doing less*. Whereas the laws of everyday behavior reveal compound, random actions blurring into one another in spontaneous bursts of effort, the laws of art dictate control, restraint, selectivity, order, discipline, arrangement, simplicity, and economy. If ordinary (or even extraordinary) private behavior placed in the public eye constituted art, then everyone would be an actor, and theatre would surround our every action. *The art of acting is the art of doing less.*

Less is More

The poet Robert Browning's observation that "less is more" has been echoed by the great practitioners and observers of theatrical art. Constantin Stanislavski noted that "unrestrained movements, natural though they may be to the actor himself, only blur the design of his part, make his performance unclear, monotonous, and uncontrolled."[2] And British director Tyrone Guthrie remarked: "If there is no good reason to move, KEEP STILL. Inexperienced actors are apt to feel self-conscious if they are doing nothing. Painfully conscious of large, red things on the ends of their arms, they make gestures. WATCH people in real situations analogous to those in which you find yourself on stage. See how very little they actually do."[3] And finally, the pioneering French master acting teacher, Francois Delsarte, realized that if "an audience is asleep, logic demands more warmth, more fire. Not at all. Keep silent and the sleeper will awaken."[4]

The demand for less may indeed go against your impulse to entertain, to please, to succeed at all cost. In fact, the notion that less is more flies in the very face of most of our cultural values. Nevertheless, the fact remains that you achieve greater artistry and power not by piling on more and more traits and actions, but by reducing your actions to the necessary, the essential, the archetypal. An audience appreciates and responds more to the details projected by its own imagination onto a clean, clear performance than by any "realistic" touch you may add.

Discipline

Since the notion of subtraction may be, at first, alien to your tendencies, discipline must be introduced into your work. To some the notion of discipline seems antithetical to creativity—how can one create if restricted? To flourish creativity needs a stimulating problem to channel imaginative energy. Discipline provides that stimulation and channel. As Jean-Louis Barrault points out *"there should be deep in every actor, an element of the robot.* The function of art is to lead this robot towards the natural."[5] Perhaps the notion of discipline and the prospect of automation would seem less fearful if defined. Basketball coach Bobby Knight provides a valuable interpretation of discipline:

1. Doing what has to be done
2. When it has to be done
3. As well as it can be done
4. Doing it that way all the time.

This chapter applies Coach Knight's definition to the subject of physical play; the following chapter applies the definition to vocal play. Only practice can enable you to master the fourth phase of Knight's definition. The ideas of discipline and practice are as old-fashioned and essential as are the ideas of theatre as a significant art and acting as a creative act.

QUALITIES OF EFFECTIVE
STAGE MOVEMENT

Before proceeding, we should state our goals regarding physical play. An eloquent summary of desirable physical playing qualities was issued in the sixteenth century by theatre producer Leone di Somi:

> I can say only that the actor ought in general to have a lithe body with free-moving limbs, not stiff and awkward. He must place his feet on the ground naturally when he speaks, move them easily when occasion demands, turn his head without artificiality—not as though it were fastened to his neck by rivets. His arms and hands, too, when there is no need to make gestures with them, ought to hang naturally at his sides. The actor should avoid the manner of those many persons who introduce inappropriate gestures and seem to know not what they are doing.[6]

Di Somi's standards require you to engage in the minimum amount of work with the minimum expenditure of energy, to move easily without unnecessary preliminary bodily adjustment, and to allow your internal organs space for proper functioning. But any improvement of your present physical play depends upon *body awareness*.

Awareness and Observation

Awareness differs from thinking. Thinking about your body diminishes your awareness of your body's condition and actions. Thinking also interferes with your body's natural functioning; if you think about what your body just did (or didn't!) do, you will not be able to perceive what your body is doing *now*. For example, I had a student who would preface many of his gestures by wiping his fingers on the seat of his pants. When I pointed this out to him he was flabbergasted; he was unaware of what his body was doing. You should sense your body's actions at all times.

To experience physical awareness, slowly take a single step forward. Experience the movement, focusing on how it feels to take a step. *Awareness is noting how it feels*. What sensations do you feel? Repeat this simple exercise to become aware of awareness. Awareness attends to some muscles tightening while other muscles relax. Movement requires some tension and some relaxation. Too much of either interferes with movement. Take a backward step; take a side step. Raise and lower your arm. Experience the act of moving.

One of the great obstacles to both awareness and effective movement is the concern for correctness within an idea of right and wrong. If you think about correctness or rightness while moving, you aren't experiencing the movement. Attend to what you are doing, not to what you should be doing. "Should" and "ought" merely increase tension and, thereby, hamper effective movement. Whenever you are corrected, smile and delight in it. Trying to be correct causes tension and defies the realization of your goal.

Alignment and Breathing

Freeing the moving body from unnecessary tension can cause the realignment of your skeletal system if it has been forced into an unnatural order by needless muscular action. An *aligned body* has a natural posture, giving the lungs freedom to inhale and exhale as needed. Body alignment is often referred to as *correct posture* or *body balance*. Moving from an aligned position conserves energy since the body is always poised for action. If your body allows you to stand well, you can breathe well. Practice alignment in all of your work until it becomes habitual before and beside a mirror.

EXERCISES

1. An aligned posture slightly curves the spine so you stand tall as a concave vertical. Place your back against a wall with your heels, pelvis, lower back, shoulders

FIGURE 3-1: An aligned position is sometimes referred to as "good pos- ture." The body has lift to it without tension or rigidity.

and head touching the wall. Stretch your arms downward while your entire body stretches upward. Sense the position of your body; practice this posture away from a wall while doing the following:

a. Extend your arms one at a time over your head, stretching from leg to finger tip.
b. With both arms extended upwards, twist your torso from side to side as far as you can.
c. Grab the backs of your ankles and pull towards your knees.
d. With your hands, turn your head as far left and as far right as you can.
e. Stand facing a wall. Place your palms flat against the wall, lean toward it and do standing "push aways."
f. Sit on the floor and ease yourself into a prone position. Repeat several times.
g. Bounce on both feet; bounce from foot to foot; bounce on your left foot; bounce on your right foot.

2. Stand with your arms stretched above your head. Slowly bring your arms down while dropping your head and shoulders. As your arms lower, bend at the waist. Relax your knees to hang like a rag doll or an unused marionette. Dangle and bob. Attach an imaginary wire to your breastbone and imagine being raised very slowly from above by a master puppeteer. First your waist will straighten, then your shoulders, and finally, your head. Think of piling your spinal links on top of one another. Exert no effort in this process. Arms hang loosely at your sides as the wire raises you to your toes. You are lowered slowly from your tiptoes to stand erect and relaxed.

3. Repeat the previous exercise inhaling at each slight rise from the collapsed position. Think of your back as moving into a concave rather than a ramrod or convex posture. *A prerequisite to effective movement is the lengthening of the spine.* Con- sequently, keep your neck free, your head extended, and your spine unarched.

4. Each part of your body is responsible for the support of another part. Often instability is due to a lack of trust between parts of the body. Your spine should

support your neck; your torso, your shoulders; and your pelvis, your torso. Unless trusting support is maintained, the body can unalign through misapplied muscular tension. Free each part to support only its share by lying on the floor and letting another player control your hinges. Let go of your urge to control. Stand and let the player swing and shake various parts of your body.

Reconditioning

As we discovered in the first two chapters, the attitudes toward and uses of our bodies are conditioned by environmental factors. I once had a student who moved stiffly with a broomstick-straight posture. When I made him aware of this condition he recalled that his father had always told him to put his shoulders back. Consequently, the student *always* pulled his shoulders back, over-tensing them, his neck, his chest, and his back. The acting class gave him permission to slouch; he did. We told him to slouch, skip, and sing; he did. Slowly the stiffness began to leave as he enjoyed the childlike nature of his actions and situation. When asked to walk the student displayed a marked improvement in his gait. He began to sense and experience tension-free walking. He would gradually fall back into his old pattern of moving but now he had an experience to use as a point of reference. The student was aware of his problem, experienced in the solution, and responsible for his own further improvement.

F. Matthais Alexander, the brilliant movement therapist, correctly observed that "change involves carrying out an activity against the habit of life."[7] Learning is, to a large extent, a process of unlearning. The distinguished acting teacher Maxine Klein comments:

> Notice how a baby can find almost infinite delight in his/her toes. We adults forget we have toes unless they hurt us from too-tight shoes. How dreadful to think about our body only when it is in pain or need! As actors, as people, we must regain touch with our bodies. We must recognize them for what they are—our SELVES. If we neglect, overlook, become dissociated from our bodies, we become dissociated from our selves. One reason we have become dissociated from our bodies is that we don't know our bodies.[8]

Explore what you have, how it moves, and the space in which it can move.

EXERCISES

1. Energize your body by shaking your hands from the wrist as hard as you can. Make them insensate. Suddenly reach for the sky, stretching as hard as you can with every part of your body. Make your stretch inch up higher than you thought possible. Slowly bring your body down into a relaxed, aligned position. You should

feel a tingling in your fingers. Use this exercise to energize your body before every play situation.

2. Begin to discover what parts of your body you can move, beginning at the top of your head. Continue to explore your body down to the soles of your feet—eyebrows, ears, nose, tongue, teeth, jaw, neck, chest, wrists, waist, spine, hips, toes, etc. Move one part at a time. Move everything at once.

3. Have a fellow player explore your body to discover parts which need someone else to move them.

4. Observe how others move their parts. Recreate their manner of moving, walking, sitting, running, and eating.

5. Visit a daycare center to observe ways of moving. Recreate a walk, a run, a jump, a manner of sitting and rising observed there.

6. Visit a senior citizens center to observe ways of moving. Recreate a walk, a run, a jump, a manner of sitting and rising observed there.

7. Fear of injury sometimes inhibits movement. Falling is often a major fear. To begin to overcome this fear, learn to fall. Children fall effortlessly and painlessly. Sit on the floor and fall in all directions, going as slowly as you need at first. Your eventual goal is to throw yourself in any direction without restraint. Move to a kneeling position and fall after the seated fall is mastered. Gradually move to a squatting position and then to a standing position. Fall in all directions from each. Inhale and lift your torso as you make each fall.

8. The free fall into a group is another type of fall. Four pairs of players should lock arms, stand side by side, and form a net of arms into which another player can fall from a medium height. The falling player can fall forward, sideways, or backward with arms at the side. Fall, do not jump! After being caught, replace one of the players as part of the net. Experience in catching is as valuable as experience in falling.

Space

You should utilize the space available to you. Many beginning actors do not "fill their spaces." They restrict the scope of their movements either by habit or unconscious design. Discover the space available to you and begin to occupy all of it. Become familiar with and comfortable when using the space available to you.

EXERCISES

1. Let each part of your body touch all of the space surrounding you as you stand in an aligned position. Imagine you form the diameter of a clear sphere. Fill every radius of the sphere with movement. Fill the sphere from a lying position and then from a sitting position. Move about, filling the sphere.

2. As you move about, attend to how your body feels as it fills space and how the air around you is displaced by movement. Imagine that your sphere of action

contains not air, but jello; not jello, but butter; not butter, but foam rubber. Move through these environments.

3. Examine Chapter 13 to discover the meaning of the following terms:

a. upstage
b. downstage
c. stage right
d. stage left
e. above
f. below
g. center line
h. full-front position
i. one-quarter position
j. profile
k. full back position
l. three-quarters position
m. upstaging
n. steal
o. taking stage
p. stealing the scene
q. sharing
r. open
s. close in
t. cross
u. countercross
v. cover
w. cheating
x. faking
y. freezing

Invent improvisations or repeat improvisations from the previous chapter to utilize these concepts.

4. Choose an Open Pantomime for two players from Appendix C and play the scene after inventing circumstances. Try to *upstage, cover* and *steal the scene* from the other player.

5. Repeat the Open Pantomime from the previous exercise incorporating these concepts: *stealing, sharing, countercross, downstage turn, cheating, faking,* and *freezing.* Do not include the harmful practices explored in the previous exercise.

6. Repeat the Open Pantomime utilizing as many stage areas and body positions as possible.

Grace and Balance

Grace is, as British Prime Minister Disraeli once said, beauty in action. All of your play, even that of chaos and vulgarity, must have a sense of artistry and design. Litvinoff believes that eloquent movement "happens when movement contains only that which belongs to it at the moment and nothing extraneous."⁹

Movement can be either simultaneous or sequential. Physical movements in life are simultaneous—we often move our arms when speaking, our legs when gesturing, our faces when turning, and so on. Actions on the stage, however, need a more successive arrangement to create a line—an unbroken line—of action. Tyrone Guthrie wrote:

> You learn how to do only one important thing at a time. Beginners are forever trying to run to the door, open it and react to what they see, with gesture, facial expression and audible sounds, all at the same time. You must plan a *sequence* of impressions for the audience . . . . ¹⁰

You need to develop flexibility for grace and selectivity for sequential action. Sequential action, when effective, does not *appear* to be sequential; it just looks clean and beautiful.

EXERCISES

1. Bend backward and then forward as far as you can. Try to touch the floor as you bend.

2. Hopscotch on one foot and then on the other through an obstacle course.

3. Balance a tray on your head while walking. Keep your neck and shoulders free of unnecessary tension.

4. Raise and hold a leg in front of you. Sit on the supporting leg and then rise, still holding the leg before you. Repeat with the other leg.

5. Assume an aligned position and jump to make a complete turn in the air. Repeat, turning in the opposite direction.

6. Run, leap, and land gracefully on one foot. Repeat, landing on the other foot.

7. Stand a book on end on the floor. Stand to one side of the book with your hands on your hips. Jump over the book and back. Jump sideways, forward, and backward.

8. Stand a cane or broomstick on the bridge of your nose while walking. Keep your arms extended at your sides.

9. Practice leading with your eyes. Turn your eyes alone toward the focus of your attention before turning your head. When your face turns to follow your eyes, think of pivoting from the chin rather than from the nose or neck.

10. Practice leading from your chest as you walk.

11. Practice leading your gestures from the wrist. Let your wrist lead your hand.

12. Imagine that a bead of mercury runs through your arms. Slowly move the bead from your shoulder down through your arm and wrist into each finger, and then back to the shoulder and arms to the other shoulder where the movement is repeated.

13. Stretch your right/left arm from your body and then fold it back toward your chest. Make sure each part is stretched. Move your hand first, then your wrist, then

your elbow and finally your shoulder. Repeat this with your legs, moving your hip first, then your knee, then your ankle, and finally your toes. Reverse this order to return your leg.

14. Stand before a mirror and move only one part of your body at a time. In gestures, isolate hand, fingers, and wrist. In facial expression, isolate eye, brow, nose, mouth, and ears.

15. Repeat your improvisation of an everyday activity featuring an imaginary object, this time with movements planned sequentially. Move only one part of your body at a time. Avoid simultaneous action.

Thus far we have investigated physical play with regard to selectivity, control, discipline, awareness, relaxation, alignment, conditioning, space, and balance. These are desirable qualities in all physical expression. Our next area of consideration introduces the variables of physical play—*tempo, rhythm,* and *timing.*

Tempo-Rhythm

Constantin Stanislavski is said to have criticized an actor for standing in the wrong rhythm. Life itself is based upon rhythms. Life begins during the rhythmic coupling of man and woman and is thought to end with the cessation of the pulse or brain rhythm. The rhythm of your action reflects your soul's rhythm as part of the rhythm of your life.

Little can be written about tempo and rhythm which could reveal its nature as well as first-hand experience with tempo and rhythm. Suffice it to say that *rhythm may be defined as the recurrence of a unit of time distinguished by a pattern of accent or stress. Tempo, on the other hand, is simply the speed of those accented units.* These definitions become clearer when you exercise to develop a sensitivity to rhythm and tempo.

EXERCISES

1. Feel your pulse in your wrist. Note each beat as an accent in the pulse's characteristic rhythm. Run in place as fast as you can for a minute. Recheck the pulse. The faster speed notes a change in tempo rather than in rhythm. Feel your pulse again and begin to move to its beat. Involve your whole body.

2. Tempos are notches on a metronome. You can create a rhythm by starting the metronome and counting three (or four or five or six, or so on) ticks over and over to create a time unit of three. On every "three" ring a bell (accent). Count to four over and over ringing the bell on every fourth tick. You now have a new rhythm within the same tempo. Maintain the four-count rhythm while another player maintains the three-count rhythm. Two rhythm's can exist within the same tempo. By adjusting the metronome the tempo of the three- and four-beat rhythms is increased or decreased.

3. Rhythms and tempos may be played with like toys. Establish a four-beat rhythm with a metronome and play the following:

(X = clap, + = "and", — = rest)
"1" "2" "3" "4"
X "2" "3" "4"
X "2" X "4"
"1" X "3" "4"
X X "3" "4"
"1" "2" "3" "4" +
"1" + "2" + "3" + "4" +
— "2" — "4" +

Invent your own rhythmic variations on this four beat unit. Let each player have his own variation. Move to your rhythm. Play with three, five, and six beat combinations. Try various rhythms simultaneously. Explore the rhythms with your whole body.

4. Create a metronome rhythm and invent movements or gestures or facial expressions to occupy the time between the beats (ticks). Set another metronome establishing two beats (ticks) for each single beat of the first metronome. Invent movements for the intervals between those ticks. Continue to set metronomes in relationship to the first metronome with four, eight and sixteen beats per first metronome beat. Each repeated series of actions should suggest circumstances for action. Rhythm is a powerful tool for stimulating the imagination.

5. Tap out the rhythms of familiar pieces of music. Let the other players discuss the mood each rhythm suggests. Imagine circumstances appropriate to the rhythm. Move to the rhythms as you formulate your imaginings. Reveal the identity of the tune whose rhythm you tapped.

6. Tap out a very irregular rhythm for another player. Let him move to it trying to invent circumstances for the rhythm.

7. Set a metronome and move each part of your body to that tempo. Adjust the tempo and move individual parts of your body to the new tempo.

8. Stand with a group of players in a circle. Establish a four beat count with a metronome. The first player does a four count action. The next player repeats the action without missing a beat and adds a four beat action of his own without missing a beat. Each player repeats the preceding actions and adds another four beat action.

9. Establish a four-beat rhythm for a group in a circle. The first player claps the first unit, walks the next unit, moves his entire body for the next unit, and moves a single body part for the next. The next player repeats the sequence inventing his own actions. Repeat this exercise with three, six, and twelve-beat rhythms.

10. Choose two contrasting vocal music recordings. Lip sing each, mobilizing the entire body in the different emotional rhythms.

11. Invent a silent improvisation in which your Parent, Adult, and Child ego aspects debate how to perform a particular physical activity. Give each ego aspect a characteristic rhythm.

12. Play an everyday activity focused on a single imaginary object to a metronome. Vary the tempo and repeat.

13. Repeat the previous exercise with two metronomes, one for an inner, concealed tempo-rhythm, and the other for the outer, apparent tempo-rhythm. The improvisation should reveal a conflict of tempo-rhythms.

14. Play your everyday activity simultaneously with another player's everyday activity. Give each player a different rhythm within the same tempo.

15. Repeat the previous exercise with each actor playing at a different tempo-rhythm. Use two metronomes.

16. Play an Open Pantomime from Appendix C for one player with a metronome. Repeat at different tempos.

17. Play an Open Pantomime from Appendix C for two players with a metronome. Each player acts in the same tempo. Repeat the Open Pantomime with each player performing with a different tempo-rhythm. Use a metronome for each player.

18. Repeat all of the exercises which utilized a metronome *without* the aid of a metronome. Internalize the tempo-rhythms.

Timing

The relationship between two movements, two vocal utterances, or between a movement and a vocal utterance requires timing. *Timing is the temporal relationship between movements and/or words.* Timing can involve one actor or several actors. In any case, timing requires planning.

Timing has nothing to do with tempo. Instead, timing involves the relationship of the beginning, duration, and end of one action to the beginning, duration, and end of another action. If each action has a beginning, a middle, and an end—as all actions do—then these parts of an action must be arranged. The point at which the action will start, the length of its duration, and the point at which it will cease must all be calculated in rehearsal.

Between two actions, three relationships may exist—before, during, and after. For example, if you have the line "I love you" and invent the gesture of an arm extended, you can do one of the following:

1. Say "I love you" *and then raise* your arm.
2. Say "I love you" *while* raising your arm.
3. Raise your arm *and then say* "I love you."

If we consider your gesture to have a beginning (raising the arm), duration (the extended arm), and an end (lowering the arm) even more possibilities exist:

B = raise arm (begin gesture)
E = lower arm (end gesture)

1. B E "I love you"
2. B "I" E "love you"
3. B "I love" E "you"
4. B "I love you" E
5. "I" B E "love you"
6. "I" B "love" E "you"
7. "I" B "love you" E
8. "I love" B E "you"
9. "I love" B "you" E
10. "I love you" B E

Each of the ten possibilities follows the *sequential* action principle. If *simultaneous* actions are considered the possibilities would be greater yet, as your gesture could begin or end during any of the three words! Each possible timing of the word to your movement brings with it a subtle shift in intent, motivation, and relationship. You should experiment in rehearsal to find the perfect timing to communicate your intention.

Adding a simple movement by another player to your "I love you" example multiplies the possibilities. Actor B could turn his back on you at six points in any one of our ten possibilities. If simultaneous actions are considered, the number of possibilities would be far greater than the sixty of sequential action, since Actor B could turn his back on you before, during, or after any single movement or word!

Time is crucial to an actor. Timing can reveal motivation; an action preceding another action *seems* to motivate the subsequent action. Timing can also emphasize a particular word or gesture; that which follows has greater emphasis than that which precedes. As a general rule of thumb (rules of thumb are always subject to the dramatic circumstances) a gesture's duration should be for the duration of the particular thought, intention, idea, or emotion which it expresses.

EXERCISES

1. Combine into one improvisation two of the everyday activities focused on imaginary objects. Work on timing your actions to your fellow player's actions.

2. Play an Open Pantomime from Appendix C for two players with attention on timing your actions to your partner's actions.

3. Choose a poem. Imagine that you are the one to whom the poem is addressed. Plan and time your reactions to what is said. Have another player read the poem to you as you play. Avoid anticipating what will be said. Remind the other player to allow time for your reactions.

THE STRUCTURE OF ACTION

When investigating timing, the notion of structure in action was mentioned. All stage action has a structure, an organization. Shape is what distinguishes stage action from everyday action. Structure moves everyday action into the realm of art.

The basic structure of a simple action requires a beginning, a middle, and an end. The beginning initiates the action through stimulation, by providing an impulse to act. The middle holds the excitement and suspense of the action by revealing the action striving toward its resolution or goal. In striving, the action may meet obstacles which produce conflict. Suspense is generated as the conflict raises questions: Will the action prevail? How will the obstacles be overcome? The end of an action resolves the conflict—either the action is completed or it is stopped. A simple breath can contain all of the elements of a structured action. Inhalation is stimulated by the body's need for oxygen (the beginning). The held breath creates suspense: Why is the breath held? Has something happened which interfered with respiration? Exhalation (the middle) resolves the questions, completes the action, and satisfies the original impulse for breathing (the end).

Complex actions contain the same structural elements. An actor walks into a restaurant to buy a hamburger to satisfy his hunger. He places his order, but when the time comes to pay, he finds he lacks six cents. Will he find the money? If not, will the restaurant let him have the hamburger? If not, how will he satisfy his hunger or handle his embarrassment? The actor finds a nickel and the next patron in line gives him a penny. He walks to a table, sits, and opens his hamburger to discover that he has forgotten to request a burger without ketsup, mustard, and relish. What will he do? Will he scrape off the unwanted condiments? Will he eat the burger as is? Will he return the hamburger for a substitute? The actor decides to scrape off the unwanted seasonings. However, in his anxiousness, he accidentally scrapes the meat patty into the trash can. Will the actor finally abandon his effort to eat? Will he plunge his arm into the trash to retrieve his hamburger? Our hero chooses the second option. He returns to his table with a clean burger only to discover another customer in his seat. Will he sit elsewhere or will he ask the lady to vacate his seat? The actor notices that no other seat remains. He begins to ask the lady to move but reconsiders. He decides to eat his hamburger while standing. He does.

The action of our story began with the decision to buy a hamburger to satisfy hunger. The beginning also communicated the circumstances of the action: Who? An actor. What? To eat a hamburger. Why? Hunger. How? Buy a hamburger. What stands in the way? Two other customers ahead in line and a lack of money. What leverage? None. Where? In a fast food restaurant. When? Lunchtime. An important function of a beginning is the communication of the circumstances.

The middle of the action posed several obstacles—lack of money, unwanted relish, loss of meat, and a stolen seat. Each obstacle created conflict and moments of suspense during which we waited for the actor to consider his various alternatives before deciding upon a course of action. The ending resolved both the final conflict and satisfied the actor's original goal.

In this compound action the actor may utilize various types of movement. Acting teacher Jerry Blunt defines three kinds of movement an actor may choose to employ:[11]

1. *Preliminary movement:* a small movement which precedes a main movement. The preliminary movement's function is to direct the audience's attention to the main action. For example, if the hungry actor shifted an armful of books and shopping bags before freeing his arm to search his pockets for coins, the shift would constitute a preliminary movement. Art Carney made the character of Ed Norton in *The Honeymooners* famous for preliminary movements such as flicking the wrists or adjusting the shoulders.
2. *Arrested movement:* freezing a movement in mid-channel before continuing the action. The actor might arrest his search through his pockets when he discovers no more money in his final pocket. This would exemplify an arrested movement.
3. *Suspended movement:* temporarily stopping an action to perform an intruding action. For example, the actor's explanation to the waitress of his lack of money could be suspended while he picks up a book he dropped.

EXERCISES

1. Repeat your improvisation of an everyday activity featuring an imaginary object giving the action a clear structure. Invent actions to communicate the circumstances. Obstacles should arise to create conflict and suspense.

2. Repeat the previous exercise incorporating preliminary, arrested, and suspended movements.

3. Combine two players' everyday activities into one structured action. Utilize preliminary, arrested, and suspended movements.

4. Play an Open Pantomime from Appendix C as a structured action. Utilize preliminary, arrested, and suspended movements.

Integration of Physical Play

This chapter concludes with an opportunity for you to assimilate the ideas presented in a unified experience. Begin to consider physical play as a prelude to vocal play. With vocal play here and in the next chapter, activate the same technique of control, restraint, discipline, and economy you found so necessary for effective physical playing.

EXERCISES

1. Choose an Open Pantomime from Appendix C. Invent circumstances and play the scene. Use properties, costumes, and actions to communicate the circumstances and to justify each of the given actions.

2. Repeat the previous exercise inventing lines to motivate each given action.

3. Repeat Exercise 1 using each given action to motivate an invented line.

4. Choose a love poem or prayer and play the piece with movement alone. Attend to the fact that a frequent fault with beginning actors is the repetition of a gesture, usually a palm-up extended hand. Play the selection again while another player reads it aloud. Finally, play the memorized poem or prayer as the vocal extension of your physical performance. Use your body, gestures, and face to express the beginnings, durations, and ends of the changing ideas, thought, emotions and intentions.

5. Play the poem *Jabberwocky* by Lewis Carroll while another player reads it aloud.

6. Select a fable to play. Use your body to physically characterize the agents of the tale. First, play the fable silently while others read it aloud. Next, divide the entire text, narrative and descriptive passages alike, among the fable's characters. Consider all words as character lines. Play the fable vocally and physically. Suitable fables may be found in Aesop's *Fables,* Chaucer's *Canterbury Tales, Taoist Tales,* edited by Raymond van Over, *Indian Tales* by Jaime De Angelo, and *American Negro Folktales,* collected by Richard M. Dorson.

7. Select and play in movement alone a Jack and Jill episode from *Knots* by R. D. Laing.

NOTES

[1]From *Meyerhold On Theatre,* p. 147.

[2]Constantin Stanislavski, *Building a Character* (New York: Theatre Arts Books, 1949), p. 69. Used by permission of the publisher, Theatre Arts Books, 153 Waverly Place, New York, N.Y. 10014.

[3]Selections from *Tyrone Guthrie On Acting.* Copyright © 1971 by Tyrone Guthrie. Used by permission of Viking Penguin Inc.

[4]John W. Zorn, ed., *The Essential Delsarte* (Metuchen, N.J.: Scarecrow Press, 1968), p. 145.

[5]Taken from *Actors On Acting* by Toby Cole and Helen Krich Chinoy. Copyright 1949, 1954, © 1970, 1977, and 1980 by Toby Cole and Helen Krich Chinoy. Used by permission of Crown Publishers.

[6]Leone di Somi, "The Dialogues of Leone Di Somi," in *The Development of the Theatre* by Allardyce Nicoll. (New York: Harcourt Brace Jovanovich, 1966), p. 268.

[7]F. Matthias Alexander, *The Alexander Technique: The Resurrection of the Body*, ed. Edward Maisel (New York: University Books, 1970), p. 3. Copyright © 1969 by Edward Maisel. (Published by arrangement with Stuart Lyle.)

[8]Maxine Klein, *Time, Space and Designs for Actors* (Boston: Houghton Mifflin, 1975), p. 21.

[9]Litvinoff, *Use of Stanislavsky within Modern Dance,* p. 38.

[10]Guthrie, *On Acting,* p. 12.

[11]Jerry Blunt, *The Composite Art of Acting* (New York: Macmillan, 1966), pp. 65–70. Copyright © 1966 by Jerry Blunt.

4

The Vocal Player

Consider your voice: first, last and always your voice. It is the beginning and the end of acting.

—Mrs. Fiske[1]

Actors with beautiful, resonant voices will claim that voice and language are the essences of acting; actors with beautiful, lithe bodies will assert that gesture and movement are the quintessences of acting. The first kind of actor prefers plays featuring poetic speech and the adroit turn of a phrase. The second kind of actor selects plays in which athleticism and the turn of a wrist dominate. Both kinds of actors prefer Shakespeare. A beginning actor should strive to master both kinds of plays by developing an equal facility in mental, physical, and vocal playing.

The voice is the last of the three playgrounds of acting. Certainly the voice is not last because least; rather, voice prospers best with well-tuned minds and bodies. Speech comes before words, as the French visionary Antonin Artaud reminds us. Man's inability to satisfy his needs physically spurred the development of his vocal expression. Thus, movement precedes speech.

Voice is the product of heredity and environment. The physical apparatus of vocalization, like that of movement, is the result of heredity; application of that instrument is a function of cultural conditioning. The opening chapters of this text found parents to be of significant importance in voice development. No less a distinguished voice teacher than Kristen Linklater acknowledges the influence of environment on voice:

> . . . the tensions acquired through living in this world, as well as defenses, inhibitions and negative reactions to environmental influences, often diminish the efficiency of the natural voice to the point of distorted communication.[2]

Often simple awareness of the causes of tension can help you begin to return to your *natural* voice. Once a student came to me complaining of severe laryngitis and vocal strain. The pain was so great that doctors had been consulted. Her condition had been going on for several years and (I suppose out of desperation) the student turned to her acting teacher as a last resort. I began to question her about her voice. What were her earliest memories of comments made about her voice? Her father told her that she had a deep and (blushing) "sexy" voice. Did that please her? No, it embarrassed her. What do her friends think of her voice? Her best friend and rival is a soprano who wins the ingenue roles, forensic contests, and soprano solos in their church choir. My student was left with character roles, runner-up awards and contralto parts in church. The girls even vied for the same boy's attention.

I suggested to the student that she may be trying to compete in her friend's soprano vocal arena when, in fact, she was really an alto. After thinking about my suggestion, she admitted that alto had always seemed to be second best, something she and her parents never wanted. I asked her to sing alto in her church for a few weeks and to report the results. Months went by and I assumed that another of my suggestions had not worked out, when one day the student appeared at my office. Happily, she reported no further throat problems and a new boyfriend who thought her new voice sexy!

Needless to say, such counsel will not always benefit all students; nor will mere awareness of cause always correct harmful effect. But this case underlines the power of environment on the psycho-vocal mechanism. Awareness and a determination to correct past errors can improve your playing skills. But what route do you follow if awareness fails to restore your natural voice?

Before beginning work on improving vocal play, you should discover what, in particular, is lacking. Once specific areas for improvement are located, exercises can improve and even correct faulty voice and speech production. But even the natural expressive voice of everyday discourse needs to be adapted for work on the stage. Acting is an unnatural activity; to stand on a platform before hundreds of people and project a characterized voice to all corners of the auditorium without seeming too loud to some or too quiet to others is not an everyday occurrence. Add to this artificiality the requirement that the voice seem appropriate, truthful, believable, and even beautiful, and you are faced with a unique set of vocal demands.

Distinguished people of the theatre question the advisability of making voice production on the stage a conscious process. Acting teacher and author Clive Barker thinks voice-consciousness diminishes the actor's ability to respond or react:

The voice mechanism corrects itself by a combination of aural feedback and physical sensation, which are mutually interactive, and part of the reflex process of the body/think. To listen to the voice with concentration brings the process into the conscious reflective front of the mind and inhibits the body reaction.[3]

Speaking on the stage is like tying your shoe. At first the mechanics of the task are learned and practiced consciously. The learning process of trial and error requires a deep level of concentration. Indeed, children often flare out if you try to speak to them while they are trying to tie a shoe. Only one process at a time can occupy the conscious mind. Eventually, the art and craft of shoe-tying and voice production become habitual and move to shallower levels of concentration, and finally to mere awareness. As an adult, you can easily carry on a conversation and react to what is being said while aware of tying your shoe. Similarly, the experienced actor can pursue intentions reactively while aware of the actions of his vocal instrument. Voice and speech for the stage begin as conscious processes in the classroom and in rehearsal rooms until concentration becomes awareness and conscious effort becomes habit. Once voice production becomes habitual, mental and physical play can respond freely to the dynamic stimulation of the dramatic circumstances.

VOICE EVALUATION

You speak the way you do for a variety of reasons. The size and shape of your larynx, throat, tongue, jaw, soft and hard palates, vocal folds, mouth, and rib cage contribute to the character of your voice and speech. Figure 4-1 shows the various components of the vocal instrument.

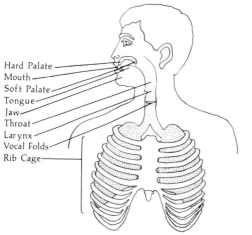

Hard Palate
Mouth
Soft Palate
Tongue
Jaw
Throat
Larynx
Vocal Folds
Rib Cage

FIGURE 4-1: Many parts of the mouth are involved in the speech act—larynx, throat, tongue, jaw, palates, vocal folds, and mouth.

Infants emit an amazing variety of sounds. Through imitation, by trial and error, they learn the sounds of the people around them. Many of an infant's free sounds will never be heard again because they are not reinforced by the language of the people in the infant's environment. For this reason, cultures have characteristic language sounds, and families have characteristic inflections, rates, articulations, volumes, and pronunciations. Friends and associates may influence the development of voice and speech as they did in the case of my student with the hoarse voice. Likeness is, as we discovered in examining relationships in Chapter 2, a factor of friendship; vocal likeness can bond friendships. School and geography likewise influence the quality and inflection of speech.

Your personality as reflected in your personal script objective and disposition can also affect the character of your voice. People who are hearty, argumentative, gushy, inhibited, or apologetic have voices to match. Voice also reinforces the attitude you have about yourself. A laughing voice, a whining voice, and a grumbling voice each reflects the person's attitude about himself and his world.

Finally, the immediate situation or *gestalt* affects your voice. Each of the factors which constitute the circumstances of action—what you want, why you want it, how you will get it, what stands in your way, what leverage you have, where you are, and when it is—can affect the character of your voice.

EXERCISES

1. Choose a poem and read it aloud. Tape or videotape the reading. After playing back the reading, discuss the following questions:

    a. Did you seem uncomfortable, slouched, or tense?

    b. Did you move your upper chest and shoulders when breathing?

    c. Were your inhalations noisy, slow, or obtrusive?

    d. Did you take in too much breath or take too much time to inhale?

    e. Did your breath leak out on *s, sh, th,* or *f* sounds?

    f. Did your breath leak out before or after sounds, or during pauses?

    g. Did you run out of breath?

    h. Did you drop or swallow the ends of sentences or phrases?

    i. Did your voice flow in an unbroken line of sound?

    j. Did your voice resonate too much in your nose, throat, or mouth?

    k. Was your voice thin or throaty?

    l. Was the quality of your voice tense, harsh, or unpleasant?

    m. Was your pitch monotonous or too inflected?

    n. Were words slurred?

o. Were all necessary consonants heard? Were unnecessary consonants added?
p. Were the vowel sounds correct?
q. Was the rate ponderous or rapid?
r. Was your voice too soft or too loud?
s. Was the phrasing unnatural or dull?
t. Were the pauses effective, logical, and sustained?
u. Were pauses frequent or infrequent?
v. Was the sense of the line intelligible?

The answers to these questions may suggest work on developing proficiency in specific areas of your voice and speech production.

2. Write a voice analysis of someone you overhear. Imagine how this voice became as it is. What kind of personality do you imagine this person has? What could be the influence of the immediate situation on this voice?

3. Write an analysis of your own voice, discussing physical, environmental, psychological, and immediate situational influences.

Tension and Relaxation

As with physical play, vocal play requires a proper balance between muscular tension and relaxation. Too much tension is a common problem. Relaxation and physical alignment exercises, as found in the preceding chapter, can prepare you for the variety of demands suggested by the circumstances of playing. A relaxed voice tenses only those muscles necessary for speech; a relaxed body produces a relaxed voice ready for speech.

EXERCISES

1. Collapse from the waist from a standing position. Raise yourself on a ten count. Repeat this three times. Raise your shoulders and screw up every facial muscle until your shoulders and face begin to hurt. Relax your face and drop your shoulders.

2. Lie with your back on the floor, feet apart and knees bent. Your feet should be flat on the floor and your arms at your sides, palms down. If another player can put a hand between your back and the floor, you are not relaxed. Relaxing all your limbs should make you dead weight. Place your hand on your diaphragm and notice the movements of breathing.

3. From a standing position, stretch your arms over your head and lower your spine into alignment. Let your stomach hang out! (Ignore messages from your Parent aspect about decorum and beautiful bodies; now you are concerned with a beautiful voice.) Sucking in your stomach can cause harmful muscular tension in voice production and alignment. Repeat the stretch upwards as if pulled from your fingertips by a master puppeteer. Relax each part of your body downward beginning with your fingers. Relax hands, arms, neck, shoulders, links in your spine, until your torso hangs from your tailbone. Rebuild your spine link by link into an aligned position.

4. *Relax your lips* by blowing raspberries (the Bronx cheer) through them. Blow air through closed, unpuckered lips to make a sound like a horse. Exaggerate *TOO-TAY-TEE* over and over.

5. *Relax your jaw* with yawns. Let a big sound accompany each yawn. Occasionally an actor finds himself yawning almost uncontrollably before going on stage. This is nature's way of relaxing your jaw for utterance. Welcome yawning. Exaggerate *TOO-TAW-TOO-TAW* over and over.

6. *Relax your tongue* by stretching it to extremes and then relaxing it. Put the tip of your tongue against your bottom teeth and push it so that the rest of your tongue goes over your bottom teeth. A relaxed tongue lies on the floor of your mouth with the tip gently touching the back of the lower teeth.

7. *Relax your soft palate* so that it will not hang unwanted, muffling sound moving from your throat to your mouth. Sound should not detour through your nose, so relax your soft palate by *KAAing* as you inhale. Exhale with a relaxed mouth by yawning. *KAA* while yawning as you inhale and exhale.

Breathing

Once relaxed and aligned, your body can experience the freedom of natural respiration. Tyrone Guthrie gave us an invaluable motto: "Before you say anything, or do anything, on the stage, TAKE A BREATH."[4] Not only does this keep you alert, but it also underlines the notion that the naturally *unconscious* process of breathing becomes a *conscious* matter in the unnatural circumstances of the theatre.

Respiration in life as on the stage is composed of two parts, a beginning and an end—inhalation and exhalation. In life, however, inhalation is an active process and exhalation a passive process; in the theatre both activities become active. Moreover, in everyday life the amount of time utilized by each half of the process is about equal; onstage, inhalation draws into the lungs a greater amount of air than in everyday life in order to project the voice to all corners of a potentially large space. Exhalation on stage takes whatever amount of time is needed to say whatever must be said. In natural offstage respiration, long inhalation is followed by short exhalation; for

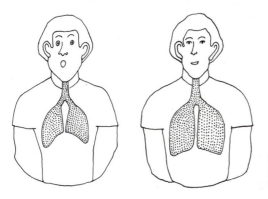

FIGURE 4-2: Inhalation contracts the diaphragm to make the chest larger. Exhalation relaxes the diaphragm to empty the lungs.

long stage utterances, short inhalations are followed by long voiced exhalations. This process necessitates conscious breath control. But before
considering the control of breath, let us examine briefly the actual process
of respiration.

During inhalation your diaphragm contracts—flattens and pushes
against your abdomen—making your chest cavity larger. Rib muscles contract as well, raising your front ribs to widen and deepen your chest. Meanwhile, air fills your lungs. Exhalation occurs automatically. Figure 4-2 shows
the operative organs of respiration during inhalation and exhalation.

EXERCISES

1. Place your hand on your lower ribs. Inhale through your nose and exhale
through your mouth twenty times, feeling the movement of the ribs. Repeat this
process with your hands on your diaphragm. Repeat this with one hand on your
diaphragm and the other hand on your lower ribs. Notice how one expands before
the other one. Inhale to expand only the lower rib cage and exhale a whispered count
to ten. Do this ten times. Inhale to expand the ribs while whispering *OO;* inhale to
expand the diaphragm with a whispered *AH* sound. Exhale each using the same
sound for a count of six. Repeat the *whispered OO/AH* respiration five times, then
intone the *OO/AH* respiration five times.

2. To activate your diaphragm, pant through your nose with a closed mouth.

3. To relax and stretch the muscles of your rib cage, stand back to back with
another player, linking hands overhead. One player—the stretcher—bends his knees
to put his buttocks under the buttocks of the stretchee. The stretcher bends forward
to make his back parallel to the floor, thus raising the other player off the ground.
Synchronize your exhalations and inhalations. The above player lets himself relax as
the lower actor dips toward the ground for inhalations and rises for exhalations. This
process stretches the rib muscles upward. To stretch your rib muscles sideways,
repeat the procedure with arms extended out to the sides. The below actor pulls his
arms toward the ground for inhalations and raises them for exhalations. **(Do not
perform this exercise if you have a history of back problems.)**

4. While inhaling, quickly lift your arms sideways to the shoulder. Lower your
arms slowly while exhaling. Respiration should be with open mouth and whispered
AH.

5. With your hands on your hips, move your elbows back while quickly inhaling.
Exhale slowly, moving your elbows forward. Respiration should be with an open
mouth and a whispered *AH.*

Breath control   To control your breath is to control the rate of your
exhalation. The traditional technique of *diaphragmatic breathing* can provide
you with a sure technique of breath control. By placing primary emphasis
on the diaphragm rather than on the ribs, you are assured of a ready
supply of "emergency" air in your rib cage cavity. Breathing diaphrag-
matically takes conscious effort at first to make the process eventually as

habitual as tying shoes. This technique of breathing is characterized by deep breathing—shoulders remain stationary instead of rising and falling with every inhalation and exhalation. Your rib cage moves horizontally rather than vertically in diaphragmatic breathing.

EXERCISES

1. a. Place your fingers on the lower sides of your rib cage, thumbs pointing toward your spine. Inhale to expand the lower rib cage. Sense your back widening, not your shoulders rising. Inhalation should be simultaneous through your nose and mouth.

b. Divide your inhalations in half. First fill the lower rib cage and then fill your diaphragm as your abdomen moves out and down. Let exhalation empty only the second half of your inhaled air; your lower rib cage remains extended as it reserves a quantity of air. Inhale again to extend the lower abdomen. Diaphragmatic breathing is sometimes called *abdominal breathing.*

2. Using diaphragmatic breathing, divide the respiration act as follows:

a. 3 counts to inhale, 3 counts to hold, 3 counts to exhale
b. 3 counts to inhale, 3 counts to hold, 6 counts to exhale
c. 3 counts to inhale, 3 counts to hold, 9 counts to exhale
d. 3 counts to inhale, 3 counts to hold, 12 counts to exhale
e. 2 counts to inhale, 2 counts to hold, 15 counts to exhale
f. 2 counts to inhale, 1 count to hold, 20 counts to exhale

Repeat these while walking.

3. Using diaphragmatic breathing, exhale *HAH* in one breath for twenty-five walking steps; *WHO* for twenty-five walking steps; *HEEH* for twenty-five walking steps.

4. Using diaphragmatic breathing, recite either "The Twelve Days of Christmas" or "The House That Jack Built."

5. Using diaphragmatic breathing, sound the following consonants 6″ from a lighted candle for as long as possible: *s, f, th, h.*

6. Choose a poem and speak it with controlled breath using diaphragmatic breathing. Breathe at the end of each phrase. If you have trouble with diaphragmatic breathing, speak the piece with hands behind your head and with shoulders down.

7. Repeat the previous exercise building from a quiet voice to a loud voice; next, start with a loud voice and decrescendo to a quiet one by the end.

8. Repeat Exercise 7 breathing at the end of each line; breathing after every two lines; breathing after every three lines.

Resonance

To resonate is to vibrate. Resonance of voice creates fullness of tone and sonority. Every musical instrument has material which vibrates and a cavity which amplifies the vibrations. The head of a drum vibrates and the bowl below amplifies the vibrations; the strings of a guitar vibrate and the hollow wooden structure amplifies the vibrations. With the human voice, the vocal cords of the larynx vibrate and the nose, mouth, and pharynx amplify the vibrations (see Figure 4-2). In full resonance each cavity contributes equally to the amplification. Too much or too little reliance on any one cavity distorts the quality of your voice. Tone is manifested in vowel sounds; consequently, vowels are responsible for resonant tone.

EXERCISES

1. For maximum resonance keep your teeth about 3/4 inch apart, lips loose, tongue flat on the floor of your mouth with its tip against the back of your lower teeth. Your jaw, lips, and tongue are relaxed. Diaphragmatic breathing expands your pharynx. Whisper *AH* in this position, then intone the vowel sound. To resonate other vowel sounds, move your tongue and lips rather than your jaw. The *AH* position is the basic position for full resonance of all vowel sounds. All vowel sounds vary from this basic position. Whisper and then intone:

   a. *HAH HOO*
   b. *HAH HEE*
   c. *HOO HEE*

Keep jaw and tongue movements separate from one another and avoid tightening the corners of your lips.

2. Yawn *AH* three times. Yawn *OO, AW, EE* three times each. *MMMMM* rapidly as if laughing. *MMMMMM* as you crescendo the volume.

3. In the maximum resonant position, *AH* or *MMMMM* your favorite tune. Lips should be relaxed, jaw open, and tongue flat.

4. Tape yourself reading a poem. Your voice sounds different on tape since you are outside of your resonators instead of inside them as with natural utterance. Other people hear your voice resonating through air to their ears; you hear it resonating through your bone structure.

5. Use Figure 4-3 to check proper tongue placement for the vowels of the Phonetic Alphabet (see Appendix D). Practice each vowel sound with full resonant voice.

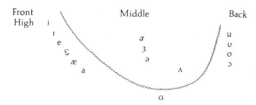

FIGURE 4-3: Proper placement of the tongue is essential for correct phonation of vowel sounds.

6. Choose a poem and whisper it, attending to maximum resonance through cavity expansion. Next, intone the selection, attending to continuity of tone; think of

an unbroken line of sound. Finally, speak the piece with full frontal voice, combining the intonation of chant with normal inflection. (You should be able to feel with your hand the bones of your face vibrating.)

Pitch

Pitch refers to the highness or lowness of tone. Each key of a piano produces a different pitch of the piano's basic tone. Singing up and down the musical scale moves your voice through many pitches of tone. The actor "sings" his feelings through words and sounds. Each person has an *habitual pitch,* a level at which most speaking is done and to which the voice returns after moving up and down the scale. Habitual pitch is not, however, necessarily the most efficient and effective level for utterance. Habitual pitch level may involve unnecessary muscular tension. For the richest, fullest, most effective, and efficient tone, you should speak from your *optimum pitch* level. Once located, the optimum pitch level should become your habitual pitch level.

EXERCISES

1. To determine your habitual pitch, read a poem, listening for the pitch most frequently used. Prolong the sound of each vowel to locate the pitch on a piano. The pitch is usually around middle C for women and below middle C for men.
2. To locate your optimum pitch sing down the scale to the lowest tone you can comfortably intone. Find that note on a piano and four notes above it will approximate your optimum pitch. Say your name and address on this note. Repeat them one note higher and one note lower. Decide which of the three gives the fullest and purest tone with the least effort. That note will be your optimum pitch.
3. Another technique to determine optimum pitch requires you to plug your ears and hum up and down the scale to find the note which rings loudest in your ears. That is your optimum pitch.
4. Use the following vowel sounds to develop a wide pitch range. Tyrone Guthrie believed that "a well-trained voice should easily cover a range of two and a half octaves."[5] First use each sound to move up the scale from your optimum pitch, then down the scale from your optimum pitch, remembering to keep the resonance forward in your mouth. The higher or lower the note, relax and open your mouth and throat more and more.

   a. *HOO*
   b. *HOH*
   c. *HAH*
   d. *HAY*
   e. *HEE*

Work to meet Mr. Guthrie's request.

5. Choose a poem and sing it.

6. Chant or intone your poem text on your optimum pitch, attending to controlled breathing. Repeat the selection one pitch above and then one pitch below optimum pitch level.

7. Start on the lowest note of your pitch range as you perform your poem. Raise your pitch one-half or one note for each word, then for each line. Often actors "over inflect" their lines by having too great a pitch variation in too short a time span. The result is a voice like a sea cruise recreation director or a daycare center supervisor. Voice teacher J. Clifford Turner suggests that you think of speech "not as a series of rising and falling patterns, but as if the voice proceeded along a straight line, rising above it or dipping below, as occasion demands."[6] Repeat your practice selection with this new attitude and discuss any differences you notice.

8. Repeat your poem first with a lower optimum pitch level and then with a higher optimum pitch level. Pitch placement is an important consideration in characterization.

Volume and Projection

Imagine your frustration if the volume of your stereo system decreased as you changed the speed of your turntable from 78 rpm to 33 1/3 rpm. Or imagine how angry you would become if the picture contrast of your television declined as you lowered the volume control. Fortunately for the operator, rate is independent of volume and volume of intensity. Unfortunately, not all actors can control all of their independent vocal variables. Work on vocal volume should isolate volume as one variable of your playing instrument.

EXERCISES

1. Using *AH,* extend the tone of your voice while accomplishing these independent tasks.

    a. Pitch increases, volume steady
    b. Pitch decreases, volume steady
    c. Pitch steady, volume increases
    d. Pitch steady, volume decreases
    e. Pitch increases, volume decreases
    f. Pitch increases, volume increases
    g. Pitch decreases, volume increases
    h. Pitch decreases, volume decreases

2. Use a poem to accomplish the independent tasks of the previous exercise.

3. Use the repetition of *TOO-TAH-TAY* to accomplish these simultaneous tasks:

a. Pitch steady, volume steady, rate increases
b. Pitch steady, volume steady, rate decreases
c. Pitch steady, volume increases, rate steady
d. Pitch steady, volume decreases, rate steady
e. Pitch increases, volume steady, rate steady
f. Pitch decreases, volume steady, rate steady
g. Pitch steady, volume increases, rate increases
h. Pitch steady, volume increases, rate decreases
i. Pitch increases, volume increases, rate increases
j. Pitch decreases, volume increases, rate steady
k. Pitch steady, volume decreases, rate increases
l. Pitch increases, volume steady, rate increases
m. Pitch decreases, volume steady, rate increases
n. Pitch decreases, volume increases, rate increases
o. Pitch increases, volume steady, rate decreases
p. Pitch increases, volume decreases, rate steady
q. Pitch increases, volume increases, rate decreases
r. Pitch increases, volume increases, rate steady
s. Pitch increases, volume decreases, rate increases
t. Pitch decreases, volume steady, rate decreases
u. Pitch decreases, volume decreases, rate steady
v. Pitch decreases, volume increases, rate decreases
w. Pitch decreases, volume decreases, rate increases
x. Pitch steady, volume decreases, rate decreases
y. Pitch increases, volume decreases, rate decreases.
z. Pitch decreases, volume decreases, rate decreases.

4. Use a practice poem to accomplish the simultaneous tasks of the previous exercise.

5. The great actor William Charles Macready could, after great trial and error, speak the single word *murder* with such effect that his audience would shudder at the mere sound of those two syllables! Work on that word seeking the same effect.

Intelligibility

Poor voice projection is not always due to insufficient volume. Many voices have been ruined or strained as actors increased volume in response to a director's scream, "I can't hear you!" The following factors contribute to effective projection:

a. *Articulation* and *pronunciation*. (See Appendix D.)
b. *Relaxation*. Tension interferes with breathing, resonance, articulation, and thus with comprehension.
c. *Pitch*. Sharp, sudden variations in pitch are difficult for an audience to follow.

d. *Breath control.* Actors occasionally swallow syllables and final words of sentences and phrases. Since thinking occurs at a faster rate than speaking, thought processes will conclude before your utterance concludes unless you concentrate on full utterance throughout expression. When your mind stops thinking about what is being said, your mouth stops saying it effectively!

e. *Understanding.* If you don't understand what you are saying or why, your audience will have difficulty understanding you.

f. *Movement.* If you have an overly animated head and neck you spray and diffuse the sound of your voice. Controlled movement enables control of voice projection.

g. *Visibility.* Gesture, movement and facial expression key the audience's perception of what you are saying.

EXERCISES

1. Repeat your practice poem with these factors of intelligibility in mind.

2. Go into a theatre with a fellow player. Stand on the stage with your friend seated in the farthest row. Begin to speak your practice poem in a whisper, observing the factors of intelligibility, gradually increasing your volume until your friend can hear you easily. You should be surprised how little volume is actually needed!

Rate

In the sixteenth century Leone di Somi also noted the nature of vocal rate on the stage:

> While an actor may think he is talking slowly, the spectator does not get that impression, provided that the words are not separated but given continuous delivery without being so mannered as to raise annoyance.[7]

The basic rate of utterance for the stage is slower than the basic rate in everyday discourse. A rate of approximately 140–170 words per minute is generally regarded as a satisfactory base rate. This rate is considerably slower than the rate at which we sight read. Reading can be by the eye or by the ear; speed reading is by the eye. Hearing each word in your mind's ear is reading by ear. Generally speaking, you would do best to always read aloud; failing that, you should *at least* read by ear. (A speed-reading actor can often become a speed-talking actor!)

EXERCISES

1. Count off 140 words and 170 words in a piece of prose. Mark where each number falls in the text. With a clock, practice reading the selection aloud until you can reach the 140 word mark at the end of exactly one minute; then practice until

you can reach the 170 word mark at the end of exactly one minute. The rate of delivery should be even throughout.

2. Listen to recordings of two performers reading or acting the same selection. Time their words-per-minute. Discuss the effect of rate on the impressions created.

3. Set a metronome and read a poem to it. Players with a greater sense of rhythm will have more frequent coincidences of accent and key word than actors with a poorer sense of rhythm. Adjust the tempo and repeat the reading, uttering one word for each beat, then two words for each beat, then a short phrase for each beat.

4. Walk around the room uttering one syllable of your poem selection for each step. Then utter one word for each step, two words for each step, and finally three words for each step.

5. Examine multisyllabic words for the rate of syllabic utterance. Some syllables are long and some short thus giving the word a definite rhythm. Note how accented syllables, vowel and consonant choices and placement give words definite rhythms and tempos.

6. Speak to a metronome uttering each syllable of an improvised speech to each accent. Vary the rate of the metronome and continue speaking. Pause in rhythm as well. Read something to the metronome, giving each syllable an accent, and each pause a regular interval.

Pausing

Closely related to rate is pause. Pauses should evolve from phrasing which, in turn, arises from the dramatic circumstances of action. In all cases, pauses to breathe must occur by plan not necessity. Usually such pauses come in logical places of phrasing. Breathing on stage should not be left to spur-of-the-moment reflex action as in everyday life. As Tyrone Guthrie warned us: "NEVER MAKE MEANINGLESS PAUSES. They usually occur when you have a breath which you have neglected to plan."[8]

To avoid monotonous patterns of logical pauses, each of an equal length, consider Stanislavski's idea of the *psychological pause:*

> Whereas the logical pause mechanically shapes the measures, whole phrases of a text and thereby contributes to their intelligibility, the psychological pause adds life to the thoughts, phrases, measures. It helps convey the subtextual content of the words.[9]

EXERCISES

1. Choose a poem and phrase it with logical pauses. Justify each logical pause psychologically and repeat the performance.

2. The incomparable British actor Lawrence Olivier has another view of the pause:

If they see your limits they lose interest. Yvonne Printemps, that lovely lady, gave me some advice from the great basso, Chaliapin. "Darling, always take a breath when the audience doesn't expect it—never at the end of a phrase or note." Best advice I ever got. It adds colossal power. The audience feels you have undying strength and can go on forever. If they sense you're tired, or fear for your physical self, you lose them.[10]

Review the poem chosen for the previous exercise, planning breaths when the audience doesn't expect them. Repeat the exercise justifying each unexpected pause.

3. Play your poem from the previous exercises in a small space, then in a large auditorium, then sitting, then standing, and then walking. Notice how the size of the playing space and the degree of physical activity affect your need for air and breath. Plan your pausing in light of the size of the theatre and the amount of physical activity you're engaged in while speaking.

4. Repeat the poem thinking of silence punctured by the sound of your voice rather than of continuous sound interrupted by pause. Hear silence throughout the reading. How does this change in attitude affect your reading?

THE STRUCTURE OF SPEECH

The sounds of language are grouped to form words and the words are grouped to form sentences. Words are your means of arousing feelings, desires, and mental pictures in your fellow players. The choice and arrangement of vowels and consonants into words, phrases, and sentences occasionally produce *onomatopoesis*—words sounding like that which they represent. You should consider all stage language as onomatopoetic. Assume a playwright has chosen particular vowels and consonants because of the effect they will produce in you as you mouth them and in your fellow players as they hear them. The Arabic of the *Koran,* for example, creates a particular religious feeling within those who recite from it by the sensations the formation of the words creates in the mouth. For this reason the *Koran* cannot ever be satisfactorily translated. Likewise, you thus can deprive yourself and your audience of important stimulation with poor articulation and enunciation.

Words can be classified according to communicative function. Nouns are words which name, verbs are words which assert, adjectives and adverbs are words which modify, prepositions and conjunctions are words which correct, and interjections are words which exclaim. All things being equal, words can be arranged in importance to the actor:

1. Verbs
2. Nouns and pronouns
3. Adjectives and adverbs

Verbs dominate your work by carrying action. Nouns and pronouns are the agents and objects of the action so they are second in importance.

Adjectives and adverbs describe the manner of the verbs and nouns; their sense depends upon the other two word types.

When verbs, nouns, adjectives, adverbs, prepositions, conjunctions, and interjections are combined into something meaningful, a sentence is formed. Sentences can be divided into three parts; they have a *subject*, a *verb*, and an *object*. The subject performs the action, the verb acts, and the object receives the action. For example, in the sentence "*John threw the ball,*" *John* is the subject, *threw* the verb, and *the ball* the object. A more complex sentence—*I came to you as a respectable man to drink wine, to enjoy women, to laugh, and to make others laugh*—has *I* as the subject, *came to drink; to enjoy; to laugh; to make laugh* as the compound verb, and *you as a respectable man; wine, women, and others* as the compound object.

The hierarchy of words and the structure of sentences can aid you in phrasing a speech specifically within the determining influences of a dramatic situation. Certainly the circumstances of an action provide the ultimate motivation and justification for phrasing, intonation, inflection and accent. Yet even within a given situation a variety of choices avail themselves to you. Familiarity with the mechanics of word importance can help you make the final choice.

Beginning actors often stress or accent too many words in a sentence, thinking it makes their voices more expressive, when, in fact, fewer stressed words in a sentence or phrase would clarify the meaning. Work to eliminate unnecessary accents, especially accented adjectives. Stanislavski believed that no adjective should be accented unless it directly contrasts with another adjective nearby. This is a good piece of advice.

EXERCISES

1. Take individual nouns, verbs, and adjectives from a practice poem and repeat them over and over until you make the words sound like the things they represent.

2. Choose a word which conjures up a particular mental image in your mind's eye. A word like *fire* can stimulate particular circumstantial images—campfire, hotel fire, match, birthday cake candles, lovers before a blazing fireplace. When you have a detailed sensory image in your mind's eye, speak the word to the eyes of a listening player. Let the listener describe the particular image your expressive utterance conjured in his mind's eye. Repeat your word, coloring its tone with the particular image in your mind's eye until your specific image is conveyed through your listener's eyes to his mind's eye.

3. Choose a practice poem and speak it stressing only the verbs, then only the nouns, then only the adjectives and adverbs. Do any new insights emerge? Eliminate unneeded stresses.

4. With the poem from the previous exercise, locate subject, verb, and object for each sentence. Speak the speech clarifying the subject, verb, and object.

Integration of Vocal Play

The following exercises begin to integrate the discussions of tension and relaxation, diaphragmatic breathing, breath control, resonance, rate, pause, pitch, volume and projection, intelligibility, and phraseology into a unified vocal experience. Stanislavski would have you speak to your fellow player's eye, not to his ear. Make your partner see in his mind's eye what you have in your heart.

As you conclude work on voice and speech, remember the great actor Louis Calvert's secret: An actor should train his voice so thoroughly in range, pitch, technique, and control that he will *seem* to speak naturally.

EXERCISES

1. Choose a poem and take the key vowels and consonants of the piece and create your own surrealistic interpretation of the mood and emotions of the piece using just sound and expressive movement. Let the sounds infect your whole body.

2. Assume the previous poem is a monologue from a realistic play. Invent circumstances for the monologue. Invent a character to speak the lines. Divide the speech into beats or units of action and give each beat a verb intention. Detail the circumstances in writing and play the piece.

3. Add a silent character to the circumstances invented for the previous exercise. Rethink the poem with this new element added. Explain the circumstances to another player who will play the silent character in the scene with you. Do not tell him what to do. React to whatever he does with the lines of the text. In playing, heed Stanislavski's advice to a student actor:

> . . . if you were really intent on getting your words over to her you would not have recited them like a soliloquy, without looking at her, without adapting yourself to her, as you have just done, and there would have been moments of waiting to see the effect of your words . . . the process is piece-meal: you convey, you pause, your partner absorbs what you conveyed, you continue, you pause again, and so on.[11]

Caress your partner's emotions with your words; infect him with your sounds and silences. Adapt your manner to your listener's reactions.

4. Invent a strenuous physical activity to accompany the previous exercise. Justify the activity within the circumstances. Note how physical action affects your psycho-vocal actions.

5. One effective technique for developing voice for the stage is oral reading. There is a vogue for speed-reading; nothing could be more detrimental to your vocal sensitivity. Speed-reading provides only facts; reading aloud integrates body, voice, mind, and motion into a single act. Reading aloud develops your rate; by reading slow enough to understand yourself, you will have discovered the appropriate rate for an audience's understanding of a first hearing. Oral reading builds breath control, resonance, and other vocal qualities so necessary for effective vocal play. Reading

aloud gives you all the vocal practice time needed. Read aloud everything you see—road signs, newspapers, novels, bills, menus, scripts. You will be developing your voice.

NOTES

[1]Taken from *Actors on Acting* by Toby Cole and Helen Krich Chinoy. Copyright 1949, 1954, © 1970, 1977, and 1980 by Toby Cole and Helen Krich Chinoy. Used by permission of Crown Publishers, Inc.

[2]Kristin Linklater, *Freeing the Natural Voice* (New York: Drama Book Specialists (Publishers), 1976), p. 1.

[3]Clive Barker, *Theatre Games* (New York: Drama Book Specialists (Publishers), 1977), p. 176.

[4]Guthrie, *On Acting*, p. 13.

[5]Ibid., p. 14.

[6]J. Clifford Turner, *Voice and Speech in the Theatre*, rev. by Malcolm Morrison (London: Pitman Publishing House, 1977), p. 133.

[7]Di Somi "Dialogues," p. 267.

[8]Guthrie, *On Acting*, p. 8.

[9]Stanislavski, *Building a Character*, p. 133.

[10]Curtis Bill Pepper, "Talking with Olivier," *New York Times Magazine*, March 25, 1979, p. 60. © 1979 by The New York Times Company. Reprinted by permission.

[11]Stanislavski, *Building a Character*, p. 116.

PART TWO

UNDERSTANDING THE PLAY

The more detailed, varied, and profound an actor makes this analysis by the mind, the greater his chance of finding stimulants for his enthusiasm and spiritual material for unconscious creativeness.

—Constantin Stanislavski[1]

5

Subjective Analysis

*Do not ask the poem to be more rational than you are. The way
to read a poem is with pleasure: with the child's pleasure in
tasting the syllables on his tongue, with the marvel of the
child's eyes . . . with the child's hand-clapping, rhythmic joy. In
short, to read a poem, come prepared for delight.*

—John Ciardi[2]

My first encounter with play analysis occurred in elementary school when
my friend and fellow dwarf in *Snow White and The Seven Dwarfs* proudly
announced that he had twenty-three lines. Quickly I took my mimeo-
graphed script and counted; so much for play analysis—let's have fun!
Unfortunately some adult actors do little more in preparing their performances. Michael Chekhov notes that "it is mostly in the initial stage of
our work that we often suffer from uncertainty and floundering."[3] Perhaps
the usurpation of drama by literature classes has put plays in the same
lively category with *Silas Marner* and "Trees"—works to be endured for
their pithy morals and ethical wisdom. The time has come to throw aside
such preconceptions and scamper to plays as children, delighting in and
demanding fun, play, and a helluva good time!

Plays are *play*, not objects to study, revere, and test. And actors are
players, not scholars or worshipful congregants. Unless a play engages your
fancy, you cannot play. Plays can only engage your fancy if they are understood as play. So let's begin a re-education in theatre and drama.

Before going on, important terms need definition to assure clarity in
our education. Drama theorist Bernard Beckerman offers astute expla-
nations of the relationship between theatre and drama by observing that
"theatre occurs when one or more human beings, isolated in time and/or

space, present themselves to another or others," while "drama occurs when one or more human beings, isolated in time and space present themselves in imagined acts to another or others."[4] Thus, *all* of your class exercises in Part I constituted theatre, while only the *imaginary* actions you performed were drama. Drama is a subform of theatre distinguished by its make-believe basis.

Drama, as you now should know from experience, can exist without a text. Plays are not prescriptive, but suggestive, written outlines of what may happen in a drama. Plays use language to suggest the three spheres of play—mental play, physical play, and verbal play. Scripts are blueprints or game plans for actors' play. An actor creatively fills in the outline, realizes the ideas of the blueprint, and carries out the game plan.

Acting becomes more specific as it moves from the general area of theatre to the category of drama. Using Beckerman's line of reasoning, *acting* may be considered to occur when a human being, isolated in time and space presents himself to another or others. *Acting a drama,* on the other hand, occurs when a human being, isolated in time and space, presents himself in imagined circumstances, (which includes the question "who"—in drama, the character is the answer) to another or others.

See a playtext as a chance to imagine circumstances for the presentation of self. The playwright helps by restricting your imagination; some playwrights restrict more than others, but none forbids creative invention. Reading the text starts the creative process of acting by stimulating your imagination.

An effective reading of the play maximizes the power of a play to stimulate your power of invention. Effective reading analyzes the play and your role in it. To analyze is to interpret; a process of questioning and answering results in a unique understanding of the character in action. Two actors answering the same questions will give two sets of answers, thus two different analyses, and two different interpretations. A play and its characters exist *only* within the actor's imaginative understanding of the play; theatre is, as Meyerhold reminds us, the art of the actor.

HOW TO READ A PLAY

To begin, you would do well to see a play as a story. Every play tells a story and, at first reading, you should take childlike delight in the story. Stories involve people doing and saying things to one another. The people are humans or non-humans—gods, demigods, plants, animals, ideas, memories, human qualities, emotions or symbols. The characters of the story do actions which have been arranged to form a unified and meaningful whole. With an appreciation of story in mind you can prepare to read the play.

First Reading

The actor reads not just any play but a particular play for performance or audition. Reading for either of these purposes affects the way you first become acquainted with the play and your character. Come to the play with an open mind, looking for an interesting story. The great French director Michel St. Denis cautioned:

> You must not enslave the text by premature conception or feeling of the character. You should not hurry to get on the stage and try to act, physically and emotionally, too soon. Psychological and emotional understanding of a character should come through familiarity with the text, not from outside it. You must know how to wait, how to refuse, so as to remain free. You must be like a glove, open and flexible, but flat, and remaining flat at the beginning. Then by degrees the text, the imagination, the associations roused by the text penetrate you and bring you to life. Ways are prepared for the character to creep in slowly and animate the glove, the glove which is you, with your blood, with your nerves, with your breathing system, your voice, with the light of your own lucid control switching on and off.[5]

You should realize that the play and the character cannot be grasped at once; the first reading plants seeds which will grow through subsequent readings and rehearsing. So, like a good gardener, maximize the conditions for successful growth.

Read the play at one sitting, in a quiet space, away from distraction. The play presents the playwright's comments as well as the actions of the characters. Read these comments, notes, and stage directions, visualizing yourself on stage in the setting described. (Watch out, though! Some stage directions are the creation of editors or stage managers. Disregard those.) Stand in your room, placing the audience before you and the setting around you. Some actors err by ignoring the playwright's comments; they assume dialogue—verbal actions—superior in communicating. This notion should seem clearly unacceptable after the exercises of Part I in mental, physical, and vocal play. The playwright communicates, like the actor, in all three modes; to ignore two-thirds of a play's evocative power is to cut yourself off from potentially helpful information.

But on the other hand, many plays contain no stage directions. The playwright's intentions exist in the lines themselves. If you are sufficiently analytical in reading, you will find tremendous insights into the physical and psychological play of the character. This process is much more difficult and valuable than learning to justify given stage directions. You will even find playwrights, like Shaw, whose comments are eminently interesting, but not particularly helpful in playing the action!

Plays have fewer descriptions than novels. You are not told of physical and mental play to the extent you are of verbal play. You must infer the former two from the latter. As you stand or sit amid the imaginary setting, begin to read the dialogue aloud, seeing in your mind's eye the characters in physical proximity to where you stand. When you read your own character's lines, move about the space as the playwright suggests. Often actors are encouraged to read from only sitting positions like directors or critics or designers. This tends to put the actor outside the play looking in at himself. Unlike the other contributors to the theatrical event, the actor is *inside looking out* and the initial perspective should enhance this uniqueness. Without this inside perspective a large part of your early work involves ridding yourself of the external view as you struggle to get into the play. As you read the text, see the entrances and exits of the characters and their physical movements all around you.

First Impressions

Your first impressions of the play and your character are very important. Your first impressions are similar to those of an audience's impression after seeing the play one time. Consequently, note your likes and dislikes, interests and disinterests, and difficulties, so that as you become more familiar with the play, you do not forget things which are difficult for an audience to catch at one time. One of America's most distinguished actors, Rip Torn, notes that "sometimes you have a complete picture of the character right away. I've done characters where from the first reading, I had a sense of the entire personality."[6] And Lynn Redgrave says that "there have been roles for which my initial picture was the one I stayed with."[7]

First impressions can also be dangerous. Later you should watch out for simply indicating the emotions felt during the first reading of the play. St. Denis' caution to resist jumping at the first idea is a good one. The first impression should be recorded to serve as a point of reference throughout the rehearsal process. Return to this record periodically for refreshment or revision. The first impression can keep you aware of your progress.

For too long actors have worked under the myth that writing or talking about a character drains an actor of his supply of creativity. The image of the inarticulate actor who can only express himself in stage action is, I think, a holdover from the nineteenth century. There is no reason why an actor needs to be inarticulate, nor is there a finite quantity of creativity which an actor must carefully spoon out in safe doses. The articulation of the actor, however, is not the articulation of the scholar or critic. Incomplete notes, phrases, misspellings, and ramblings give you something tangible to reread, amend, or challenge during the rehearsal and run of a play. Your analysis stimulates *you;* the scholar's analysis stimulates *others.* Take the character and yourself apart on paper to reassemble creatively on stage.

THE PLAY

1. What did I like about the play? What did I dislike?
2. What did I find interesting about the play? What did I find dull?
3. Did I find any of the characters in interesting situations?
4. Did the characters express any interesting thoughts?
5. Did the characters have any interesting reactions?
6. For whom was I most sympathetic? Least sympathetic? Why?
7. Did I laugh at anything? Did I find anything ridiculous?
8. What memories from my own life does this play bring to mind?

THE CHARACTER

1. How am I similar to this character?
2. How am I different from this character?
3. Whom do I know like this character?
4. Where would I be likely to meet this kind of character?
5. When have I been in circumstances like those this character is in?
6. When have I done similar things in similar circumstances?
7. When have I had similar desires?
8. When have I faced similar obstacles?
9. When have I used similar leverage?
10. When have I been in places like those the character inhabits?
11. How have I undergone changes like those of the character?
12. How are decisions I have made similar to those the character makes?
13. How are my beliefs and attitudes similar to those of the character?
14. When did time affect my actions like it does the character's actions?
15. What relationships have I had that are similar to those of the character?
16. When have I had hopes similar to those of the character at the beginning of the play?
17. How have I used similar means to bring about what I want?
18. When have I encountered similar unforeseen obstacles?
19. When have I reacted like the character when I couldn't get what I wanted?
20. When have I confronted someone like the character confronts?
21. Under what circumstances would I do what I consider the character's strangest or most shocking actions?
22. When would I use the means the character uses to pursue his goal?
23. What do I possess that is as important to me as that which the character values most?
24. What have I ever wanted as much as what the character desires most? When have I ever been willing to do what he does? Under what circumstances would I do what he does?
25. When has my attitude changed like the character's attitude changes? Were the circumstances similar?

To answer these questions imagine specific places, objects, times, and people, using memory as your resource. The first reading and initial analysis begins the process of moving you into the character by identifying similarities between personalities and circumstances. The great English actress, Sybil Thorndike, speaks of her reactions to Lilian Baylis' idea that Dame Sybil play Lady Macbeth:

> "I don't think I can play it, I don't know the beginnings of this foulness." She said, "Don't be nonsensical. You love your husband, don't you?" I said, "Yes." "Well," she said, "she loved her husband. She was only doing it for him, so there you are." And that started me off right.[8]

Ralph Richardson, another star of the English stage, likewise speaks of using memory to identify similarities:

> You think of all the people like that character you've ever met; it's surprising then how vividly you remember people in your past, that you think you've completely forgotten—some old schoolmaster, or somebody who ran a shop—memories come crowding back. You change their costume, make them up differently, in your mind, till you get nearer and nearer.[9]

The mental play of analysis forces you to discover yourself in the character. This process of self-discovery should prompt you to put down paper and pencil and *do* something. When this happens, stop your writing and begin to rehearse. When problems arise or you lose your urge to play, return to the text with paper and pencil to reread.

Rereading

French director Jean Vilar notes that "one can never read the play often enough. Actors never read it often enough. They think they understand the play when they follow the plot more or less clearly—a fundamental error."[10] An actor must read and reread as a detective looking for clues. Every play contains clues which, when found, can illuminate your performance. In rereading, stick to the facts of the character and the situation. From these facts, creative inferences are drawn. We must, as Stanislavski tells us, "dig down under the external events and in the depths find that other, more important, inner event which perhaps gave rise to the external facts."[11]

Read the play often. Stop to review what is occurring in the action and make notes in the text. In answering the second set of questions, refer to yourself as the character by writing in the first person voice—"I." This simple practice strengthens your ability to think, act, and speak as the character. Answer questions for the beginning and end of each act.

1. What do the other characters say about you? Are they right?
2. What do you say about yourself? Are you right?
3. What does the playwright say about you? Is he right?
4. What do your actions reveal about you?
5. Do your actions contradict what you say about yourself?
6. Does your behavior mask or hide something?
7. What do you seem to want?
8. Why do you want what you want?
9. Is there a conflict within you?
10. Is there a conflict between you and another character?
11. Are you in conflict with your situation or circumstances?
12. What created these conflicts?
13. When do these conflicts climax?
14. What discoveries do you make?
15. What decisions do you make?
16. When do you remember the past?
17. When do you describe the present?
18. When do you dream of the future?
19. When do you change your method of pursuing your goals? When do you stop pursuing a goal? When do you change goals?
20. Where were you prior to each entrance? What were you doing there? Why did you leave there to come here? Why do you exit? Where will you go? What will you do there?

View all of your answers as tentative, subject to modification in rehearsal process. Most answers will change during the sensitive interplay with the director. The ultimate function of your written analysis is for it to be thrown away, so that your discoveries emerge spontaneously onstage in action. The creative imagination uses analytical material as fuel for your playing instrument.

Research and Meaning

Actors hear a lot about researching a role and often waste many valuable hours researching useless information. The simple fact is that most of what you need to know is in the play. But do not be misled by this statement. Simply because much is in the play does not mean that everything is obvious! You need to broaden your background so that you can see what is in the script. For example, unless you are familiar with kingship and the Elizabethan conception of the world order, you will not "see" Shakespeare's history plays very well at all. If a play seems unclear you may need to read to broaden your basis for appreciation. To say that most of what you need to know about a play is in the play, is to assume you to be a well-read and intelligent actor. If you are less than that, use the library to make yourself one!

As an intelligent actor, your relevant research should center on references in the text which you do not understand as the character should understand them. All an intelligent actor playing Othello needs to know about Venetian society lies within Shakespeare's text. All the intelligent actress playing Laura in *The Glass Menagerie* needs to know about glass collecting is in Williams' play. All the intelligent actors in Odets' *Awake and Sing* need to know about America in the Great Depression exists within the text itself.

Playwrights do not present the world of history; they draw particular worlds deliberately filtered from history through their poetic imaginations. Consequently, misguided research can destroy the selective world created by the playwright; bringing historically accurate, but artistically damaging research helps no one. The Electra of Aeschylus, the Electra of Sophocles, and the Electra of Euripides are each different women living in different worlds. Every playwright's Lincoln is a different man. There are no historical figures in drama: there are particular characters created by individual playwrights from the dust of the historical past. For the actor, the character is more important than the historical figure, the invented situation more relevant than the historical one. A playwright's historical "errors" are not errors in the theatre; they are poetic truths.

Closely related to an actor's misunderstanding of research is preoccupation with meaning. What does this play mean? What is this play's theme? These questions have little relevance to the work of the actor. They occupy the time of literary critics and philosophers. Stanislavski warns us that "literary experts are not always competent in questions related specifically to our problems as actors."[12] You would do well to concentrate on what happens in the play rather than on what those happenings mean. As Beckerman points out, "a play does not mean; it *provokes* meanings. . . . The performance, a stimulant to experiences, provokes a range of meanings."[13] Early in the rehearsal process you and the director will discuss a way of reconciling your various views of the play's events into a single interpretation to give your work a sense of unity. That is, or should be, as close as you get to discussions of meaning.

Wherever "meaning" hunters lurk, "intention" seekers are sure to be found. These actors want to know what the playwright intended—how did the playwright want it done, what did the playwright intend his play to be, to do, or to mean. Again, these are irrelevant concerns. Intention does not change what exists. A man may have intended to build a skyscraper but ended up with a bridge. So what? Should we continue to force the bridge to perform as a skyscraper while complaining of its poor construction? Should our use of the bridge be governed by this "knowledge"? Should we investigate the biography of the architect to see if his own life's intentions can help us make the bridge work as a skyscraper? The same preposterous approaches are made to drama. Whether a playwright intended to write a tragedy, a comedy, a burlesque, or a grocery list doesn't change the text one bit. Whether the playwright had one arm, three arms, two mothers, or no mother doesn't change the text. Countless hours have been lost by theatre people debating whether or not *Death of a Salesman* is a tragedy or *The Cherry Orchard* is a comedy. Actors often forget that the family in *Long Day's Journey into Night* is the Tyrones and not the O'Neills! A play is what it is regardless of who wrote it or for what purpose. As Tyrone Guthrie discovered, "no author who's any good, . . . has the faintest idea really of what he's written."[14]

Marking the Text

At rehearsal the actor has only his script, not his papers of analytical notes. Consequently mark your text with information which can directly help you in playing on stage. Often I see actors with their lines glowing in pink or yellow highlight ink. Their lines stand out above all else. This helps the actor locate lines but it can also create a false psychological orientation. The actor sees himself apart from the context from which his lines emerge. It might be preferable for you to hunt through the script for your verbal actions as you hunt through your environment for your physical actions. In any case, highlighted or not, the following items can help you if noted in the script. (Pencil should be used since ideas change as rehearsals progress.)

1. Entrances and exits, including where you've been and where you're going.
2. Places where you express a desire.
3. Places where you confront an obstacle.
4. Places where you make a discovery.
5. Places where you make a decision.
6. Places where characters comment on you.
7. Places where the playwright comments on you.
8. Places where you comment on yourself.
9. Places where you contradict yourself.
10. Places where your conflicts climax.
11. Places where you remember the past.
12. Places where you describe the present.
13. Places where you dream of the future.

You can develop your own key or code for marking your script. Try all of the items listed to see which help you most in rehearsal.

EXERCISES

1. Read *The Glass Menagerie* by Tennessee Williams or one of the following study plays, and record your first impressions along the lines of the suggested questions.

Albee. *Who's Afraid of Virginia Woolf?*
Allen. *The Prime of Miss Jean Brodie.*
Anderson. *Tea and Sympathy.*
  I Never Sang for My Father.
Bullins. *The Electronic Nigger.*
Christopher. *The Shadow Box.*
Cowen. *Summertree.*
Crowley. *The Boys in the Band.*
Davis. *Ethan Frome.*
Elder. *Ceremonies in Dark Old Men.*
Frings. *Look Homeward Angel.*
Gardner. *A Thousand Clowns.*
Gibson. *Two for the Seesaw.*
Gilroy. *The Subject was Roses.*
Goodrich and Hackett. *The Diary of Anne Frank.*
Gordone. *No Place to be Somebody.*
Green. *The House of Connelly.*
Green and Wright. *Native Son.*
Guare. *The House of Blue Leaves.*
Hailey. *Father's Day.*
Hansberry. *A Raisin in the Sun.*
Heifner. *Vanities.*
Hellman. *The Autumn Garden.*
  The Children's Hour.
  The Little Foxes.
  Toys in the Attic.
Ibsen. *A Doll's House.*
  Hedda Gabler.
Inge. *A Loss of Roses.*
  Bus Stop.
  Come Back, Little Sheba.
  The Dark at the Top of the Stairs.
  Picnic.
Innaurato. *Gemeni.*
Kanin. *Born Yesterday.*
Leonard. *Da.*
Mamet. *American Buffalo.*
  Sexual Perversity in Chicago.
McNally. *Bad Habits.*
Medoff. *When You Comin' Back, Red Ryder?*

Miller, A. *All My Sons.*
  Death of a Salesman.
  The Price.
  A View from the Bridge.
Miller, J. *That Championship Season.*
Moore. *The Sea Horse.*
Mosel. *All the Way Home.*
Nash. *The Rainmaker.*
Norman. *Getting Out.*
Odets. *Awake and Sing.*
  The Country Girl.
  Golden Boy.
O'Neill. *Ah, Wilderness.*
  Beyond the Horizon.
Osborn. *Mornings at Seven.*
Patrick. *Kennedy's Children.*
Pomerance. *The Elephant Man.*
Rabe. *In the Boom Boom Room.*
  Sticks and Bones.
  Streamers.
Ribman. *The Journey of the Fifth Horse.*
Rice. *Street Scene.*
Saroyan. *The Time of Your Life.*
Schisgal. *Luv.*
Schnitzler. *La Ronde.*
Shepard. *Buried Child.*
Steinbeck. *Of Mice and Men.*
Stitt. *The Runner Stumbles.*
Tesich. *The Carpenters.*
Walker. *The River Niger.*
Weller. *Moonchildren.*
Wilder. *The Matchmaker.*
Williams. *Cat on a Hot Tin Roof.*
  A Streetcar Named Desire.
  The Night of the Iguana.
  The Rose Tattoo.
  Summer and Smoke.
Wilson. *The Fifth of July.*
  The Hot l Baltimore.
  The Rimers of Eldritch.
  Talley's Folly.
Zindel. *The Effect of Gamma Rays on Man-in-the-Moon Marigolds.*

2. Tell the story of the play you selected for the previous exercise from your character's point of view.

3. Continue the character analysis after rereading the play using the guideline questions presented in the chapter.

4. Write out, as the character, what you know has happened before the start of the play.

5. As your character, write about your hopes and dreams at the beginning of the play.

6. Find information about references in the text which are meaningful to the character. For example, in *The Glass Menagerie* research such items as the D.A.R., pleurosis, *The Pirates of Penzance,* and D. H. Lawrence.

NOTES

[1] Stanislavski, *Creating a Role,* p. 10.

[2] John Ciardi, *Dialogue with an Audience* (Philadelphia: Lippincott, 1963), p. 200.

[3] Chekhov, *To the Actor,* p. 146.

[4] Bernard Beckerman, *Dynamics of Drama: Theory and Method of Analysis* (New York: Drama Book Specialists (Publishers), 1979, pp. 10, 20.

[5] Michel St. Denis, *Theatre: The Rediscovery of Style* (New York: Theatre Arts Books, 1960), pp. 68–69. Used by permission of the publisher, Theatre Arts Books, 153 Waverly Place, New York, N.Y. 10014.

[6] Joanmarie Kalter, *Actors on Acting* (New York: Sterling Publishing Co., 1979), p. 52.

[7] Ibid., p. 75.

[8] Hal Burton, ed., *Great Acting* (New York: Bonanza Books, 1967), p. 57.

[9] Ibid., p. 71.

[10] Jean Vilar, "Murder of the Director," Christopher Kotsching, trans., *The Drama Review,* **3,** no. 2, (December 1958).

[11] Stanislavski, *Creating a Role,* p. 42.

[12] Ibid., p. 120.

[13] Beckerman, *Dynamics of Drama,* pp. 166–167.

[14] Tyrone Guthrie, "Directing a Play" (Folkways Record Co., 1962), Album No. FL 9840.

6

Structural Analysis

They found that even the Belly, in its dull quiet way, was doing necessary work for the Body, and that all must work together or the body will go to pieces.

—Aesop

Plays are certainly "play," but as works of art they have the distinguishing quality of beauty. One quality which lifts the play of everyday life into the realm of beauty is unity. Artistic play has a sense of wholeness, of design, of organization. To contribute to the unity and beauty of a play, you, the actor, should understand how you contribute to the structure of the whole, how your playful participation is shaped by the design of the play. This understanding requires another type of analysis; this analysis sees your play as part of a larger design. Often failure to see the structure of the whole results in a distorted performance which causes the play to lack unity and thus beauty.

Aristotle suggested that plays have six parts or qualities—plot, character, thought, diction, music, and spectacle—which, when combined by the playwright, are linked to one another in a unified manner. Usually these six parts are studied from the playwright's or audience's point of view. In this chapter, the structure of a play will be examined according to six qualitative parts defined for their relationship to the actor's work. These six reconsidered parts become plot, character, thought, diction, pattern, and movement. The second of these six qualities—character—will be further examined according to its structural components—script, relationships, units of action, transactions, and personality composition. These aspects were examined in Part I as constituting the basis of an actor's mental play. By using the same method for character analysis as for self-analysis, you will possess an easy technique for finding yourself in the character and the character in you.

The six qualities of a play are related to each other in a special way: plot, character, thought, diction, pattern, and motion are arranged hierarchically, that is, according to their importance in determining the structure of the action.[1]

Plot

↓

Character

↓

Thought

↓

Diction

↓

Pattern

↓

Movement

The quality above determines the shape of the quality below. In addition, each quality provides the material out of which the one above is composed.

Plot

↑

Character

↑

Thought

↑

Diction

↑

Pattern

↑

Movement

An examination of this form-to-material relationship can help you clarify the structure of individual plays and your action in them.

PLOT

The plot of a play is what happens onstage before an audience. Plot differs from story; story includes action which happens before the play begins and offstage during the performance. The story of a play is referred to by the characters; the plot of a play happens right before our eyes. Amanda

Wingfield's girlhood in Memphis and Laura's traumatic high school days are parts of the story of *The Glass Menagerie* but not part of the plot. The story can affect the plot, the story includes the plot, but the story does not equal the plot.

The playwright determines the plot by arranging the action sequence, the order of events. In a certain sense, the plot determines the form of the characters: a playwright creates particular characters to do the action he envisions. Tennessee Williams needed to create Amanda to dominate her children, Laura to cower from her mother, and Tom to escape from his mother. The playwright uses his plot to shape his characters just as an engineer uses his plan for a bridge to shape his steel.

While the playwright's plot can tell you *what* happens, you determine *how* the happenings occur and to what purpose. Playwrights tell you what happens by recording what is *said*, rarely *why* those words are said (mental play), *how* those words are said (vocal play), or what occurs while those words are said (physical play). These concerns are left largely to the purview of your creativity.

By inventing appropriate mental, vocal, and physical play, you create a score of actions known as the *subtext*. The subtext is your imaginative contribution to the playwright's plot. From this point of view, you-as-character shape the action of the plot. The subtext is the reason an audience leaves its reading chairs to attend the theatre; they want to experience the subtextually illuminated plot, usually unavailable to them in reading. Such illumination is the art of the actor and the art of the theatre.

CHARACTER

Your imagination is limited to the creation of a character capable of carrying out the actions the playwright has plotted. As you carry out the actions, the character is revealed; character comes into existence through action. You are what you do. As you do more, the summary character impression you create changes. Thus, while a character may be *talked* about in general, you can only play him in particular, at specific moments in the play.

A character is always changing. Each action *reveals* a certain aspect of the character, while, at the same time, *creating* that aspect. You can see one character at the beginning of the play and a second at the end; playing character involves transforming the first character into the second. Tom Wingfield is not temperamental until he explodes in anger. Laura is not shy until she hides. Each new action changes and transforms the equation known as character. Consequently, you need to take care to avoid playing qualities before the action of the plot requires their revelation. Plot, thereby, dictates character; until circumstances require a certain action, you should not play the quality which makes that action possible.

While plot determines the order in which you will reveal a character, character is the basic material of the plot. Characters are needed to carry out the actions; a plot cannot exist, does not occur, outside the characters. A son could not escape the tyranny of a mother and sister without Tom escaping Amanda and Laura. Characters are the particular agents of the action.

Characters in drama are particularized just as you are particularized. Characters have a script goal, relationships, units of action, transactions, and personality aspects like you. And, like the six qualities of a play, these five qualities of character are ordered hierarchically:

Script Goal
↕
Relationships
↕
Units of Action
↕
Transactions
↕
Personality

The quality above determines the shape of the quality below; the lower aspect is the material out of which the higher aspect is made. Thus, a character's script goal or superobjective is most important in determining the shape of every other quality, while a character's personality is basic to every other quality. A review of Laura in *The Glass Menagerie* reveals this relationship.

Laura's script determines the structure and direction of her actions by mobilizing them toward a script *objective* and *counterobjective*. Her actions seem to reveal two goals—love and escape. These objectives are composed of relationships—Laura's relationships further her script goals. Laura avoids relating with her mother since it does not further either goal. Tom provides Laura a protective relationship which allows her to pursue an intimate relationship with her glass menagerie. Laura's glass animals give her escape and the fanciful love of their fantasy world. In withdrawal, Laura can imagine herself and her life as one of romance, security, and love. Her mother and others threaten her make-believe world; Laura tries to escape them, to protect her freedom by withdrawing to a wonder world of intimacy and joyful love. Her animals and Tom's protection give her the possibility of reconciling two almost contradictory goals. In this way, relationships are determined by a character's script while providing the basic material of the script itself.

Relationships determine the nature of a character's *units of action*.

Withdrawal allows Laura to avoid the time of the real world which reminds her of her loveless life. With her animals time does not exist; Laura relates to her mythical friends in an eternal world created from the scraps of past brief happiness. With strangers, even the superficial rituals of greeting strain Laura's resolve. The game of "Why Don't You—Yes But" allows Laura to justify her inability to form relationships, while "Wooden Leg" gives her an excuse for withdrawal. Units for structuring action are material for the construction of relationships.

Units of action shape the individual transactions a character makes. Laura's withdrawal involves silent internal dialogue among her personality aspects. When forced to deal with others, she tries to complement whatever is said to avoid conflict and to hurry the smooth end of communication. Only when her solitude and fantasy world are threatened, does Laura cross another character. The ulterior level of her games reveals her childlike need for love and protection. Intimacy with her glass animals involves Laura in free Child-to-Child exchanges. In this way, transactions constitute the essential material of beats.

Transactions construct and reveal a character's personality. By observing Laura in action, you could conclude the existence of a large Child aspect, a small and contaminated Adult aspect, and a small and primarily nurturing Parent. Her personality is principally that of a distorted and deluded child. Transactions are made of emanations from a character's personality. Thus, ultimately, character is composed of various personality tendencies. By watching a character transact, you can conclude the personality or thought of your character.

THOUGHT

The conscious mind is composed of a personality's various feelings, desires, impulses, beliefs, attitudes, and tendencies. A character determines his thought and, essentially, the thought of a character—his personality—is what distinguishes one character from another. Thought, then, is the primary material out of which character is made. A character's thought is ultimately determined by the character's script goal as he formulates the best means of reconciling contradictory objectives. Tom, Amanda, and Laura are distinguished primarily in their thoughts as they seek their objectives. Thought is revealed by what characters say and do. Consequently, thought is revealed in the pursuit of script goals, formation of relationships, structure of action, and individual transactions. The playwright communicates his knowledge of the character's thought through the words of the text. Thus, the thought of your character is first perceived by you through the diction of the text.

DICTION

The diction of a text contains the words of the characters and the play-wright. Diction expresses what your character says and does through words. In this way the thought of your character determines the words the play-wright chooses for him. The diction of the text is the chief means you have to begin your imagining of the character in action. Using the text's words you begin to imagine the character's thoughts in vocal and physical play. Consequently, the basis of both vocal and physical play is mental play in the form of words. As your character speaks and moves a continuous stream of mental action underlies the activity. This stream is known as your *inner monologue*. The inner monologue expresses your character's thought at every moment of the play. In some plays a character alone vocalizes the inner monologue, as Tom does at the beginning and end of *The Glass Menagerie*. Diction is the practical formulation of all of your character's onstage thought.

PATTERN

Diction is the pattern of the thought within you while onstage as the char-acter. This pattern covers your mental, physical, and vocal playing. All three aspects of your play are patterned by the mental thoughts of your character. Vocal and physical play create patterns in sound and sight. These patterns create sensations and perception in those around you. Perception itself requires pattern; every human sense perceives through pattern. Act-ing requires the patterning of sensory stimuli to communicate character.

The playwright's choice of diction communicates a character's thought to you who then patterns the thought through your total sensory apparatus in performance. One's eye must move in a certain pattern to perceive you moving from stage left to stage right; one's eardrums must vibrate in a certain pattern to perceive you saying *to*, or *two*, or *too*. In this way pattern shapes motion.

MOVEMENT

Patterns set up movement. To communicate, you set up patterns of motion; to perceive, fellow actors and audience recognize those patterns of motion. Patterns are comprised of shaped motion. As a place of total sensory per-ception, the theatre communicates character through *all* of your sensory equipment. The art of acting consists of translating the visual diction of the playscript into the total sensory expression of a character. Such a trans-lation constructs patterns which shape sensory movement.

Motion is the basic material of your work and consequently of theatre and drama. Everything of the theatre requires motion for perception; if it doesn't move itself, it should generate movement. When motion is patterned, it is perceived; color, shape, pitch, and volume all need particular patterns of motion for accurate perception. For the playwright, motion and movement are determined by the plot; for you, character shapes the mental, physical, and verbal motions. Your character determines your movement.

Motion or movement is not used in this discussion in the narrow sense of walking, gesturing, or facial expression. By motion, I mean all motion stimulated by the presence of the actor. You-as-character stimulate total movement in your audience by carefully selecting patterns. By selecting patterns you generate movement in your onstage and offstage audiences. Movement allows our perception of you-as-character.

All perception depends upon patterned movement. Depth is perceived by the patterned distribution of two-dimensional light on the eye's retina. Vision itself occurs when the retina responds to light energy by generating a pattern of neural impulses. Light and color are perceived by patterns of wave lengths. Sound is created and perceived by the regular pattern of air particles moving to the ear as sound waves. Hair cells in the nose respond to odors by transmitting patterns of nerve impulses to the brain. Receptor cells in the taste buds trigger a pattern of neural activity which identifies taste qualities. Similar receptor cells in the skin transmit neural impulse patterns to the brain, communicating pressure, temperature, and pain. Kinesthesis, our very sense of movement and balance, depends upon the patterned movements created by the other senses, in conjunction with nerve endings in the body's joints.

All sensory perception requires movement of stimulus to the body and the motion of neural impulses from receptor cells to the brain. Plot, character, thought, and diction are then finally communicated sensorily through patterned motion. Plot, as structured action, is the determiner of the other five qualities; movement is the basic material for the construction of all other qualities. To act is thus to *initiate* motion, *through* motion.

The implications of this hierarchical order are important. You should understand (1) your character's place in the plot—how the action defines your character, how your character shapes the action, (2) your character's thought—how your character's personality shows itself through transactions in the pursuit of script objectives in the action of the plot, (3) your character's diction—how your character's thoughts are expressed through mental, physical, and verbal play, (4) your character's pattern of movement—how your character's presence transmits sensory data which reveals your thought, character, and place in the plot. This last point suggests that you should have considerable input, not only in stage movement and voice production, but also in costume, makeup, personal accessories, and all other sensory considerations which reveal your character. Part III details this method of characterization.

Marking the Text

The information from structural analysis may be added to the score you are creating in your play text. Add these notations to the ones made in the previous chapter:

1. Indications of character script goals.
2. Indications of character relationships.
3. Indications of character units of action.
4. Types of transactions.
5. Personality aspect revealed in each line.
6. Ideas for patterns:
   a. mental patterns—internal monologue
   b. vocal patterns—stress, inflection, rate, volume, intensity, etc.
   c. physical patterns—movements, gestures, properties, makeup, costume, cologne, color, etc.

EXERCISES

1. Tell the story of *The Glass Menagerie* or study a play from the previous chapter. Which parts of the story constitute the plot? In what order are the events of the plot presented?

2. Choose Amanda, Laura, or Jim O'Conner and discuss the relationship between script goals/relationships/units of action/transactions/personality.

3. Discuss how the entrance of Jim O'Conner changes the script goals, relationships, units of action, transactions, and personality of Tom, Laura, or Amanda.

4. Choose a character from a study play and briefly discuss how

   a. the plot determines the character's script goals.
   b. the character's script goals determine his relationships.
   c. the character's relationships determine his transactions.
   d. the character's transactions determine his personality.
   e. how (a.) through (d.) change the course of the action.

NOTE

[1]This analysis evolved from the perceptions of Hubert Heffner, as contained in Hubert C. Heffner, Samuel Selden, and Hunton D. Sellman, *Modern Theatre Practice,* 5th ed. (Englewood Cliffs, N.J.: Prentice-Hall, 1973).

7

Stanislavski and Analysis

A simpler technique, a more human result would be difficult to find.

—Edward Gordon Craig

The man who has influenced actor training more than any other is Constantin Stanislavski (1863–1938). Almost every book written on acting this century comes under his influence; almost every performance given by an actor utilizes his theories. Part I of this book introduced some of his ideas. Stanislavski's ideas should be more fully examined now in the analysis of drama and character.

Stanislavski was a cofounder of the Moscow Art Theatre who began to perfect a method of acting in 1909. He noticed that great actors had a "truth" to their performances which, in his own acting, only occurred by accident or chance. Stanislavski set out to consider great actors—Shchepkin, Talma, Duse, Salvini—and make conclusions about what they did. He was not interested in actors who followed a system; he was interested in learning how certain actors thrilled an audience consistently. The results of his observations became a way of training actors for practical work in the theatre. Stanislavski's goal was not a universally used and identically interpreted methodology, but rather actors who could consciously thrill their audiences. Until the time of his death, Stanislavski rethought, amended, and discarded parts of his conclusions, trying to perfect the circumstances for great acting.

Americans know the theories of Stanislavski through three books, *An Actor Prepares, Building a Character,* and *Creating a Role.* Stanislavski intended the first two books to be one volume but, due to his illness, they were published in America at two separate times. *Creating a Role* consists of three

FIGURE 7-1: Constantin Stanislavski in 1936. Photo courtesy of the Gorki Museum of the Moscow Art Theatre.

essays. The first essay was written between 1916 and 1920, the second was written just before the publication of *An Actor Prepares,* and the third was written after the writing of the *An Actor Prepares* and *Building a Character* treatises. Since the ideas of Stanislavski evolve, the works should be examined in the chronology of composition, rather than in order of American publication.

Creating a Role, Part 1

In this essay Stanislavski discusses three phases of an actor's work on Griboyedov's comedy, *Woe from Wit*—study, emotional experience, and physical embodiment. In study, the actor analyzes the play, putting life in the factual circumstances through his imagination—"like a child, he must know how to play with any toy and find pleasure in his game."[1] Imagination creates internal circumstances within you-as-character. Analysis, imagination, and the development of inner circumstances—desires, impulses, urges—lead you to feel certain emotions as the character. By asking what you would do in that situation you begin to move close to the character. The answers lead you to formulate objectives which could satisfy the desires aroused by the situation in your imagination. Physical and psychological objectives within the situation begin to form a logical line of action, the basis of your score. Playing the objectives of the score excites you as you sense that the objectives lead ultimately to one larger objective, the super-objective. The movement from one objective to another toward the su-perobjective is your through-line of action.

Action in pursuit of objectives leads you to physicalize the character while always remaining yourself:

> An actor can alter the circumstances of life portrayed on the stage, he can find it in himself to believe in a new super-objective. He can give himself up to the main line of action which goes, through a play, he can combine his recalled emotions in one way or another, he can put them in this or that sequence, he can develop habits in his role which are not native to him, and methods of physical portrayal as well, and he can change his mannerisms, his exterior. All this will make the actor seem different in every role to the audience. But he will always remain himself too.[2]

Creating a Role, Part 2

In this essay Stanislavski reverses the order of work suggested in the previous essay. After first acquaintance with the play *Othello*, Stanislavski leads his actors to create the physical life of their roles before embarking on analysis. He explains that you need a technique flexible enough to let you work with a variety of directors. First acquaintance with a play focuses on sections which create the greatest impression on you. The second reading fires your feelings, desires, and mind. Inspired, you improvise the memorable scenes, using simple physical actions leading to an objective. This use of physical action helps you 1) discover the subtext of the action from which the text emerges, and 2) trigger internal feelings about what is occurring. The period of analysis seeks creative stimulation for your work by detailing the circumstances of the action. You continue to ask not how you would *feel,* but what you would *do.* "When you reach the moment of creation do not seek the path of inner stimulation . . . but stick instead to the physical being of your role."[3]

An Actor Prepares

In the first volume of Stanislavski's two-part discussion of acting, an internal approach to acting is offered to acting students. You need a conscious technique for aiding your instinct and subconscious release of emotion. Bodies and voices need training sufficient to allow the subconscious, instinctual feelings easy expression. Without such a technique and rigorous training, you can rely only on inspiration and accident.

Action is the basis of your work. Consequently, Stanislavski says, you need to *justify*—invent reasons or purposes—for everything you do on the stage. Purposeful action can stimulate emotions; feelings are thus the result of action. The *magic if*—what would I do if I were this character in these circumstances—leads you into the character and situation. Belief in the possibilities of the circumstances given by the playwright and invented by you and the director can stimulate your emotions. Actual and imagined circumstances create a film of images playing before your mind. These images hold your attention.

By pursuing an objective, you can arouse emotion. Consequently, you can break your role into *units of action* or *beats,* each of which works toward the realization of a particular goal or *objective*. In every physical objective resides a psychological objective, and vice versa. An objective should be named as a verb which incites action. You can break your actions into smaller and smaller units until you can believe in the reality of the action; building from these small units toward larger ones eventually leads you to a believable execution of all the actions in the role.

Stanislavski creates a psycho-technique involving units of action, objectives, physical action, and imagined circumstances which should lead to the evocation of emotion in the actor. *Feelings* about the circumstances are the most important contributors to your work on the stage. If feeling does not manifest itself spontaneously, you can turn to your mind, the second contributor, to imagine more evocative circumstances. The *will* is the third member of your internal "triumvirate." The will directs the actions. The three components of your psycho-technique interact: your mind is stimulated by thought, feeling by tempo-rhythm, and will by your mind and tempo-rhythm. Together they lead you to create an unbroken line of action leading to a superobjective. Thus the groundwork for inspired acting is laid.

Building a Character

In the second volume of Stanislavski's discussion of acting, he explores the physicalization of character. Physical characterization may develop spontaneously from analysis, but, if it doesn't, you need a technique for creating a physical embodiment of your inner understanding of character. To this end, you need a healthy and responsive body and voice capable of creating unbroken physical and vocal lines of action. A sensitivity to tempo and rhythm are essential to physical characterization. Stanislavski concludes by summarizing his system as one based upon a principle of physical action, a search for evocative circumstances, and a conscious technique to uncover subconscious "truth." What he has done, he says, is simply make natural processes conscious, so that you can believe "naturally" in unnatural situations.

Creating a Role, Part 3

In this essay Stanislavski advocates a method based heavily on physical actions. When working on *The Inspector General,* scenes are often improvised before the play is read. You begin your work with the simplest physical actions and objectives, such as entering a room. A list of physical actions leading to an objective begins your work of formulating larger, more inclusive objectives after mastering smaller ones. The method of physical actions activates a process of natural analysis—doing physical actions automatically prompts you to justify your actions by imagining circumstances.

Many of Stanislavski's ideas should be familiar to you after your work on understanding yourself in Part 1. By using the same technique to explore self and character, you can easily see yourself validating Stanislavski's belief that actors always remain themselves. Your analysis of character can, therefore, begin to employ an analysis of circumstances, a division of action into units, an identification of objectives, and an exploration of subtext. In *The Glass Menagerie's* second scene, Laura presents an opportunity for a demonstration of these techniques.

CIRCUMSTANCES

The circumstances of any particular moment differ for each character. The following description could constitute the circumstances within which Laura begins Scene 2:

Who am I?
I am Laura Wingfield. I live here in St. Louis with my mother and brother, Tom. My father was a telephone repairman who, as mother says, "fell in love with long distance." Mother doesn't say so, but she is disappointed in me— I'm not the kind of daughter she wanted—pretty, vivacious, witty. I've got this brace on my leg that clomps and makes everyone stare. I can't stand being looked at like the freak I am! At least my animals don't stare—they're sensitive and can't walk either. But we have fun dreaming and playing together and listening to music. They need me to care for them.
What do I want?
1. I want to care for and love my animals. In our own little world Mother isn't nagging at me about typing school or gentlemen callers, and my brother isn't threatening to leave. With my animals we dream of a time and a place where all of us are happy, beautiful, and loved.

2. When I hear Mother's footsteps I want to convince her that I've been practicing my typing lesson. I want to avoid another scene with Mother yelling about my foolish animals and sentimental music.

Why do I want it?

1. I want to escape to my animals to hide from all the people who stare at my leg and from my Mother's disappointment in me. I can't take all her plans to change me!

2. When I hear Mother's footsteps I want to convince her I've been practicing because I want her to smile at me, to love me, to think I am a good daughter. I couldn't stand to have her disappointed with me again!

How will I get it?

1. a. Give my animals a bath.
   b. Dress my animals for the dance.
   c. Introduce my animals to gentlemen callers who come to take them to the dance.
2. a. Hide my animals.
   b. Put paper in the typewriter.
   c. Sit at the desk and open my book.

What stands in my way?

1. My animals hate baths and don't know any gentlemen callers. They don't even know how to dance! Mother is coming!

2. It will not take Mother long to get into the room. I don't want to hurt or scare my animals when I put them away. My brace slows my speed of walking to the desk. I can't find a piece of paper!

What leverage do I have?

1. I know from Mother how to convince little ones to take baths. I remember a boy from high school who would make a wonderful gentleman caller for anyone. I have seen people dancing in the ballroom nearby.

2. I remember enough to pretend to type.

Where am I?

1. I am far away from St. Louis in a world without braces, pleurosis, typing schools, disappointed mothers, or unhappy brothers.

2. I am in my livingroom at the table with my animals, all the way across the room from the desk!

When is it?

1. I don't know or care! Evening, I guess, since the animals will go to the dance soon.

2. It can't be four o'clock already! Mother's D.A.R. meeting usually ends at four. She's home early from the meeting!

Analysis of circumstance uses the factual data of the text in a subjective, personal manner. You invent details, rounding out the information provided, to stimulate action and, thereby, your emotions.

UNITS OF ACTION AND OBJECTIVES

The analysis of circumstance revealed one unit of action and the beginning of another before the first line of dialogue was uttered. Laura's first intention is "to get the animals ready for the dance." Her second is "to convince

FIGURE 7-2: From THE GLASS MENAGERIE by Tenessee Williams at the Tyrone Guthrie Theater. Directed by Alan Schneider. Ellen Geer as Laura and Ruth Nelson as Amanda. Photo courtesy of The Guthrie Theater, Minneapolis, Minnesota. 1964.

Mother I have been practicing my typing lesson." Further units can be detected by investigating the rest of the scene's action. A very useful technique for seeing the *line of action* is to isolate the character's words and actions. The following are Laura's words and actions in Scene 2 after she has seated herself at the typewriter:[4]

(1) [*Seeing her Mother's expression Laura touches her lips with a nervous gesture.*]
Hello, Mother, I was—[*She makes a nervous gesture toward the chart on the wall.*]
[*Shakily.*] How was the D.A.R. meeting?
Didn't you go to the D.A.R. meeting, Mother?
Why did you do that, Mother?
Why are you—
Mother, you know my age.
Please don't stare at me, Mother.
Has something happened, Mother?
Mother, has—something happened?
Mother, I wish that you would tell me what's happened?
(2) Oh . . .
[*Laura draws a long breath and gets awkwardly to her feet. She crosses to the victrola and winds it up.*]
(3) Oh! [*She releases the handle and returns to her seat.*]
I've just been out walking.
It is. I just went walking.
All sorts of places—mostly in the park.
It was the lesser of two evils, Mother. I couldn't go back there. I—threw up—on the floor!
It wasn't as bad as it sounds. I went inside places to get warmed up.
(4) I went in the art museum and the bird houses at the zoo. I visited the penguins every day! Sometimes I did without lunch and went to the movies. Lately I've been spending most of my afternoons in the Jewel Box, that big glass house where they raise the tropical flowers.
(5) [*Laura looks down.*]
Mother when you're disappointed you get that awful suffering look on your face, like the picture of Jesus Mother in the museum!
I couldn't face it.
(6) [*Laura twists her hands nervously.*]
Yes. I liked one once. [*She rises.*] I came across his picture a while ago.
No, it's in the yearbook.
Yes. His name was Jim. [*She lifts the heavy annual from the claw-foot table.*] Here he is in *The Pirates of Penzance.*
The operetta the senior class put on. He had a wonderful voice and we sat across the aisle from each other Mondays Wednesdays and Fridays in the Aud. Here he is with the silver cup for debating! See his grin?
He used to call me—Blue Roses.
When I had that attack of pleurosis—he asked me what was the matter when I came back. I said pleurosis—he thought that I said Blue Roses! So that's what he always called me after that. Whenever he saw me, he'd holler, "Hello, Blue Roses!" I didn't care for that girl he went out with. Emily Meisenbach. Emily was the best dressed girl at Soldan. She never struck me, though, as being sincere . . . It says in the Personal Section—they're engaged! That's—six years ago! They must be married by now.
(7) [*Laura utters a startled, doubtful laugh. She reaches quickly for a piece of glass.*]
But, Mother—
[*In a tone of frightened apology.*] I'm crippled!

Obstacles

The scene reveals Laura pursuing several objectives. Each is numbered at the moment it seems to begin. Each objective faces an obstacle and, in Laura's case, the obstacle prevails in each unit, forcing her to the next intention.

Objective	Obstacle
1. To convince Mother	1. Mother's silent stare
2. To escape to fantasy world of music	2. Mother's voice
3. To defend my actions	3. Mother's disbelief
4. To impress Mother with my actions	4. That sort of thing doesn't impress Mother
5. To escape Mother's disappointment	5. Mother carries on about how I have ruined our lives
6. To withdraw into the past to reminisce about a happy time	6. None, until I realize the time wasn't all that pleasant due to Emily
7. To excuse myself from Mother's idea of marriage	7. Mother insists

These seven intentions could eventually dissolve into the larger objective of *to escape*. The scene contains expository material but, as analysis shows, no words are ever expository to an actor. Lines and actions are never done simply *to tell, to ask, to show,* or *to find out*. These are vague and general verbs which are more effective as part of active objectives expressed in compelling verbs.

Subtext

When you seek the subtext of a particular line, your discovery will be consistent with the objective of the contextual unit of action. The following are possible subtexts for sample lines from the scene:

Line	*Subtext*
It was the lesser of two evils, Mother.	defends
I couldn't go back there.	refuses
I—threw up—on the floor!	confesses
It wasn't as bad as it sounds.	assuages
I went inside places to warm up.	
I went in the art museum and the bird houses at the zoo. I visited the penguins every day!	boasts

Subtext reveals the action behind the line, showing the character's mental play at each moment.

When detailing the circumstances, dividing the text into units, determining objectives and obstacles, or finding a subtext, remember that there are no right answers. Your work is *your* interpretation, an act of creation

FIGURE 7-3: From a City Center production of THE GLASS MENAGERIE. Angus McBean Photograph, Harvard Theatre Collecton.

which works for *you* as the character. Different actors will have different circumstantial emphases and details, different units and objectives, and different subtexts. All are equally acceptable *if* they are effective in justifying the actions of that character in that particular situation in a compelling manner.

126

Marking the Text

Mark your study script for circumstances, units of action, intentions, and subtext. Add the following to the score you are creating:

1. Indications of circumstance and circumstantial change.
2. Places where objectives change.
3. Obstacles encountered.
4. Subtexts.

EXERCISES

1. Choose another scene in *The Glass Menagerie* or a scene from a study play and detail the circumstances for a character at the beginning and, again, at the end of the scene.

2. Divide the previous scene into units of action, label each objective and obstacle.

3. For each unit of action you identified in the previous exercise, list the specific actions you plan to take to accomplish that goal.

4. Choose a long speech from the previous scene and identify the subtexts in the speech. The verb list in Appendix 3 should help you locate precise verbs.

NOTES

[1]Stanislavski, *Creating a Role,* p. 20.
[2]Ibid., pp. 85–86.
[3]Ibid., p. 210.
[4]Tennessee Williams, *The Glass Menagerie* (New York: Random House, 1971). Reprinted by permission of Mitch Douglas, International Creative Management. Copyright © 1945, 1971.

8

Theatrical Analysis

Every creature of fantasy and art, in order to exist, must have his drama, that is, a drama in which he is a character. This drama is the character's raison d'etre, his vital function, necessary for his existence.

—Luigi Pirandello[1]

There is always a play-within-the-play . . . . The characters of drama are actors.

—Michael Goldman[2]

"All the world's a stage and all the men and women merely players." Shakespeare's lines from *As You Like It* have been repeated so frequently that they have become almost meaningless. Recently, however, scientists have investigated the implications of the sentence. Sociologists like Erving Goffman and psychiatrists like Eric Berne have transformed the metaphor into a technique for understanding human behavior. The vocabulary of the theatre is now common in sociological and psychological discussions.

Throughout history, actors have looked to life for inspiration in creating stage characters. Earlier in this book the importance of observing everyday behavior was explored as a means of understanding the actions of dramatic characters. Today the observing actor sees everyday life described in theatrical terms! People play "roles" and act out "scripts." Consequently, if human actions are the material upon which character actions are constructed, then an actor can view dramatic characters as fellow actors.

CHARACTER AS ACTOR

You can look at the character you are to play as a fellow actor. Each character also has a performance to give for a particular audience. A script is rehearsed, scenery, costumes, and properties assembled, and performance presented. In this chapter you explore a method of analyzing *characters-as-actors.*

You already know the importance of circumstance to the Stanislavski method of analysis. In addition to that significance, it gives you and the audience important information which clarifies the situation. The circumstances tell the audience what it is expected to believe or to pretend to believe and tells you what you may do. Circumstances clarify the action. By clarifying the circumstances, you exercise control over your audience's beliefs and expectations. When you communicate who you are, you limit the possible identities an audience may give you. When you define the place, you deny an audience's inclination to assume other places. So the conscious clarification of the circumstances becomes an important goal for you.

If every character is an actor, then one of every character's goals is to control *his* audience's perception of the situation. But who is the character's audience? The other characters in the play! Consequently, a character seeks to define the circumstances for his fellow characters just as ardently as you seek to define them for your audience. The character wants his fellow characters to accept his definition of who *he* and they are, of *where* they are, of *when* it is, of *what* they are doing, have done, or will do, of *why* they are doing, or have done, or will do certain things, and *how* these deeds will be done. Laura's audience in Scene 2 of *The Glass Menagerie* is Amanda; Amanda's audience is Laura. Laura tries, at first, to define Amanda as the proud mother of a duteous daughter. Meanwhile Amanda tries to cast Laura as the deceitful, ungrateful daughter of a martyred mother. Laura attempts to convince Amanda that they are in Laura's study; Amanda tries to convince Laura that they are in a courtroom. At the end of the scene, Laura tries to define herself to Amanda as a cripple; Amanda defines Laura instead as a lazy, yet very eligible young lady. By controlling the definition of the circumstances, a character can control his companions to achieve his objective more easily.

Dramas abound with examples. Moliere based the action of *George Dandin* on the title character's attempts to prove to his wife's parents (his audience) that his wife, Angelique, is unfaithful to him. Angelique, on the other hand, tries to define the situation differently to her parents (her audience); she wants them to see George as a deluded and cruel husband. She is aided by a shill in her audience, her maidservant, Claudine. In Scene 2 of Brecht's *Galileo,* the physicist tries to convince one audience—the Venetian Senate—that he is a humble and devoted scholar with only the best interests of the state in mind, while simultaneously trying to convince another audience—Sagredo and Virginia—that he is a wily and clever manipulator, far superior to the crass merchants of the Senate. Amanda Wingfield's performance for the Gentleman Caller highlights the final scenes of *The Glass Menagerie*.

PERFORMANCES

Characters in plays give performances of roles just as surely as you do upon a stage or people do in everyday life. They perform whether they are or aren't taken in by their roles. Martha of *Who's Afraid of Virginia Woolf?* sincerely believes she wears the pants in her house. Blanche DuBois believes she *is* a delicate, innocent belle. Laura Wingfield *believes* her physical disability makes her repulsive. Orsino of *Twelfth Night* would kill anyone who told him he didn't love Olivia. Tom Lee of *Tea and Sympathy* begins to believe he *is* a homosexual. Sincere and believing characters give unconscious performances.

Characters can, on the other hand, consciously try to deceive their audience. Amanda tries to deceive the gentleman caller into thinking of Laura as a domestic wonder. Judge Brack in *Hedda Gabler* has successfully deceived Tesman and Aunt Juliana into accepting his performance of family friend. Nora of *A Doll's House* has successfully deceived Helmer into thinking that she is utterly dependent upon him, even though she has secretly saved his life. Viola succeeds in deceiving everyone in Illyria into believing that she is Caesario.

Honest or deceptive, the roles characters play are always conceptions of self. This conception could be of a past self, of a present self, or of a future self. For example, Amanda conceives of herself as still a Moon Lake belle beset by courting beaus (past); Laura sees herself as a freak (imaginary). Tom considers himself a potential Shakespeare but for the demands put on him by Amanda and Laura (future). Jim O'Conner imagines himself as just a few courses away from being a television whiz-kid (future). *Death of a Salesman* reveals Willy Loman playing all varieties. In flashbacks, we see him play the role of admired father to his sons. To Linda, we see him play his present role—weary, confused husband. To his brother Ben, Willy plays his future role—successful, cocky businessman. In *A Doll's House*, Nora plays her old role—carefree, innocent chirping pet—with less and less enthusiasm until she abandons it to a stunned audience—Helmer. Hedda Gabler can be seen as a frustrated actress: the role she was trained to play is reserved for men. She casts Eilert Loevborg in the role under her direction. When he fails in the role, she plays it herself, defiantly, to a horrified and disbelieving audience composed of Tesman, Judge Brack, and Thea.

Characters playing inappropriate parts can create comedy as well as tragedy. Viola's successful portrayal of Caesario compels Olivia to cast her as would-be lover! Malvolio thinks he has been cast as lover. Sir Toby tries to cast Viola in a duel with Sir Andrew, a script the latter dreads as well! A theatregoer can get great comic pleasure both from the onstage audience's displeasure with how badly yet sincerely an inappropriate role is played, and from the character's discomfiture in the onstage audience's delight in his successful playing of a painful role!

Characters, like people in real life, either do not themselves believe, or do not want others to believe, that they are playing roles. Whether sincere or deceptive, the character must try to convince his audience that he is not playing a role, that he is behaving as he always does. Inexperienced actors often feel compelled to remind the actual audience that the character is not telling the truth. This is unfortunate since the character's onstage audience can see what the actual audience can see. To be effective with the actual audience the character must be convincing to the onstage audience. The attainment of a character's objective depends not on showing the actual audience that you are playing a role, but on convincing your onstage audience that you are *not* playing a role!

A successful performance tries to avoid the trappings of a performance. Characters try to make their playing as believable and as natural to the circumstances as do actors. Also, a successful performance is done seriously. Especially in comedy and farce, the seriousness with which a character performs is in direct proportion to the audience's enjoyment.

Sometimes characters perform in pairs. Often two characters decide to further both of their objectives by teaming up for a performance. Laura and Tom are Amanda's reluctant partners in the show she plans for the Gentleman Caller. Likewise at the beginning of *Who's Afraid of Virginia Woolf?* George is irritated that Martha has booked another performance for them without consulting him. At the end of *Twelfth Night* Sir Toby and Sir Andrew conspire to play the roles of battered victims to win the forgiveness of Olivia. Angelique, Clitandre, and Claudine stage brilliant joint performances for the benefit of George Dandin's parents-in-law.

Occasionally, two teams of characters entertain one another, alternating the functions of performer and audience. Nick and Honey entertain Martha and George. Galileo and his assistants Andrea and Federzoni perform before Prince Cosmo Di Medici on the same bill as the University Professors. In *Right You Are* by Pirandello teamwork may be turned in on itself. Signora Frola and Signor Ponza try to convince the onstage audience—the Agazzi family, Sirelli and his wife, and Signoras Nenni and Cinni—of their true relationship. Laudisi functions as stage manager for the two performers who may be working as a team trying to convince their audience that they are performing solos! The perfection with which their two stories fit together raises the possibility that this brilliant team performance was manufactured by Laudisi to keep their real relationship hidden from both the onstage and actual audiences!

SETTING AND COSTUME

Every performance needs a setting—an arrangement of space, furniture, light, properties and costumes—which aids the character define the situation, exercise control over his audience, and ultimately achieve his objective. A character's performance is designed for this environment; the environment is designed for this performance. The setting helps everyone— character and audience—believe in the performance. As critic John Lahr states, "Carefully selected props define a character, silently punctuating the performance, tantalizing the spectator and inviting the imagination to play. The stage performer wants to hint at the ideas he embodies; he wants the audience to discover his meaning. Everything he does or wears should reinforce the idea behind his characterization."[3]

Settings are extensions of performances, and thus, of character. Their purpose is to aid the character define the situation. The question arises— whose situation does the setting define? Whose set is it? Every setting has a character or team of characters who have designed it to create a particular effect upon an audience. Amanda's first thought is to rearrange her setting before the arrival of the gentleman caller/audience. Both she and Laura must also have new costumes for the imminent performance. Settings may change from scene to scene or range from particular to general in nature. *In every case, the situation-definition provided by the setting is purposeful.* For example, the setting described in Ibsen's *A Doll's House* is more particularized for the characters than is the setting for *King Lear*. The setting for *A Doll's House* is constant; the settings for *King Lear* change. Why? Ibsen seems to be particularly interested in the performances of the characters who designed the set, and in the effect of this set on the performances of visiting characters. Shakespeare seems interested in showing more—in showing the performance of Lear in his own set, the performances of others in Lear's set, Lear's last performances in others' sets, and other characters' performances in their own sets.

In all cases, performance depends upon the kind of setting. A particular setting should suggest a particular performance. Helmer and Nora have designed their setting for their performances:

A comfortable room, tastefully but not expensively furnished . . . Between the two doors, a grand piano . . . Near the window, a round table with arm chairs and a small sofa. Toward the back of the right-hand wall, a door, and further forward, a porcelain stove, two armchairs and a rocking chair, grouped around it. Between the stove and the side door, a small table. Engravings on the walls. Shelves with china and small objects d'art. A small bookcase filled with beautifully bound books. Carpet on the floor, fire in the stove. Winter day.[4]

From the setting alone an audience could guess quite accurately the kind of impression Helmer and Nora wish to create—a warm, cozy, picture-book home inhabited by an intelligent and loving family, safe from the cold, brutal world. A visitor to their home would make the same conclusion. The character is the scene designer of his setting.

Contrast Ibsen's setting with the one which opens *King Lear*—"King Lear's Palace." That's all. Why no more detail? What is in the palace? Is the palace warm or cold? Is the castle in good repair or deteriorating? Why no more information? Did Shakespeare forget? Did Shakespeare's editor consider scenery unimportant? No. All that is important to King Lear is communicated in his setting—he is the king. All else is secondary to the primary situation Lear wishes to define. In this setting we should expect a performance which communicates the situation of kingship to an assembled audience. The condition of the walls or the temperature of the palace are irrelevant to Lear's concept of kingship. To the Elizabethans, to Lear, to Shakespeare, to the onstage audience, and to the Globe Theater audience, it is sufficient to know that a king is in his own setting. All else is unimportant. Scene 2 shows Gloucester in *his* setting, Scene 3 Lear's daughter in her setting, and so on. Shakespeare mixes settings and performers more than Ibsen. *King Lear* is, in part, a play about an old actor who refuses to give up his lifelong role, even though he has given away all of his setting; his performance is unsuited to any other setting. Characters, like sports teams, seem to perform best in their own settings.

Waiting for Godot presents a country road and a tree at evening. Characters travel roads from one setting to another but this road is a setting for two characters without a setting in their future. Beckett's characters have no set to go to because they have no performance to give; one can't have a set without a performance. The characters are waiting—waiting to be given roles or parts. As they wait they rehearse roles or performances they have observed others give. Pozzo and Lucky stop off to give a performance for them. The setting in *Waiting for Godot* functions as a casting director's waiting room; performers wait for roles to play and settings to inhabit.

Characters who have settings try to keep the onstage and offstage areas distinct. They design their settings and performances so that their audience can't see their offstage behavior. In some plays the setting is all onstage space; only when the audience leaves can the characters assume an informal backstage posture. In other plays, the stage itself is divided into onstage and offstage areas. For example, when Jim O'Conner is dining with Tom and Amanda, Laura retreats to the living room, her offstage space. When, however, Jim joins her, the living room becomes his stage leaving Amanda peeking in from the wings. The restaurant in *The Matchmaker* is divided into dining compartments which can function as offstage areas for some characters and onstage areas for others. In *A Streetcar Named Desire* Blanche's bedroom serves as her offstage space even though it is visible to the actual theatre audience. Biff's bedroom in *Death of a Salesman* functions as an offstage space for the boys as they consider appropriate performances for the following day. The setting for *Right You Are* functions as theatre lobby and auditorium area. Most of the play's action features an audience discussing the performances of Ponza and Frola between their appearances (during the intermissions!).

With the stage divided into onstage, offstage and even auditorium or lobby, where is the actual theatre-going audience? The actual audience functions, I think, as an invisible ally to the performers. In some cases—in plays with soliloquies or asides—the audience is a *visible* ally to the performing character. The actual audience sits "in the wings." You could benefit by thinking of the real audience as sitting backstage during your character's performance for the onstage audience. Asides could then be considered as opportunities for the character to communicate with the offstage personnel who are collaborating with you on your performance. Soliloquies could be considered times when the character reviews his performance so far. For example, in *The Glass Menagerie* Tom opens the play by introducing the cast and setting to the actual audience; he gives the epilogue to that same audience in which he instructs Laura's actions like a stage director in rehearsal. Prince Hal in *Henry IV Part I* says in soliloquy:

> I know you all, and will a while uphold
> The unyoked humor of your idleness.
> Yet herein will I imitate the sun,
> Who doth permit base contagious clouds
> To smother up his beauty from the world,
> That, when he please again to be himself,
> Being wanted, he may be more wondered at
> By breaking through the foul and ugly mists
> Of vapors that did seem to strangle him.
> If all the year were playing holidays,
> To sport would be as tedious as to work.
> But when they seldom come, they wished-for come,
> And nothing pleaseth but rare accidents.
> So, when this lose behavior I through off
> And pay the debt I never promised,
> By how much better than my word I am,
> So much shall I falsify men's hopes.
> And like bright metal on a sullen ground,
> My reformation, glittering o'er my fault,
> Shall show more goodly and attract more eyes

Than that which hath no foil to set it off.
I'll so offend, to make offense a skill,
Redeeming time when men think least I will.

In this monologue the prince tells the backstage people (the actual audience)—who know from history that he should be playing the role of future king—not to worry; he will play the appropriate role at a time when it will have the greatest impact and make him look like the greatest actor to take the role of king. Perhaps Shakespeare's history plays examine the ways various actors have tried to play the role of king. Erving Goffman explains a character's need for soliloquies and asides. "The higher one's place in the status pyramid, the smaller the number of persons with whom one can be familiar, the less time one spends backstage, and the more likely it is that one will be required to be polite as well as decorous."[5] The more isolated the character is in situations the more he needs to use us, the actual audience, as confidants and backstage co-workers. In fact, as a character becomes more isolated, cut off from his fellow characters *for whatever reason,* the more likely an aside or soliloquy will appear.

AUDIENCES

Characters function not only as performers but also as audience. The clarity by which performer and onstage audience were differentiated in the Greek theater has been gradually replaced by a more fluid assumption of function. However, just as a Greek chorus tries to define the circumstances of the moment through its responses to the protagonist, the onstage audience still functions with the dynamics of a theatrical audience trying to learn the situation.

Uncertain situations create uncertain audiences. As author David Cole points out "we realize that we have all had similar sensations of uneasiness in the presence of actors, irrespective of the role they happen to be playing."[6] Onstage audiences are also uneasy. Jim O'Conner is an uneasy audience member who blossoms when allowed to take center stage and perform for Laura. Think of Nick and Honey's manner as George and Martha begin their "games." Helmer is uneasy as Nora begins a new role. Olivia is uneasy at the performances of Malvolio in crossed garters and of Viola as Caesario. Monsieur and Madame de Sotenville are wary of George Dandin's performance as he thinks he has trapped his wife and her lover in his house. Galileo is momentarily stunned by Cardinal Bellarmin's performance of declaring the physicist's theory a heresy. Stella Kowalski trembles as Blanche plays martyr to Belle Reve.

Why are audiences uneasy? The answer lies, I think, in the fact that each member of an audience has at one time or another been a performer.

Each audience member knows from experience the intentions of a performer. They know the performer seeks to make his conception of the circumstances dominate. They know the performer will try to exercise control over them. They know they are about to be used by the performer to further his own objectives. Jim, Nick, Honey, Helmer, Olivia, the de Sotenvilles, Galileo, and Stella are uneasy because they have been actors themselves and know the motives of performance.

The uneasiness of an audience is due to contradictory feelings within the audience. They want the performance because it will clarify an unclear situation. They do not wish the performance because the definition of the situation will be imposed on them. Laura wants Jim to perform so that she can learn if Emily succeeded in marrying him; at the same time, Laura fears the consequences of Jim's performance. This attraction/repulsion polarity can be seen overtly in Tesman and Aunt Juliana's anticipation of their relationship with Hedda Gabler, and in Gertrude and Ophelia's attitude toward Hamlet in his "antic disposition."

The size of an audience affects a performance; an audience must be present for the performance to take place. Performances may even be given to imaginary audiences. An audience could even be within the character's mind. Characters often perform from their Child aspect to their Parent. Such performances may seem inappropriate to the onstage and actual audiences, yet completely understandable and fitting to the unseen one. Hedda Gabler, Hamlet, Willy Loman, and Martha in *Who's Afraid of Virginia Woolf?* may be performing for their absent fathers. Performances for absent audiences are difficult for actors; the lack of feedback and final applause makes the actors push harder and harder. Their performances resemble final dress rehearsals before an empty auditorium.

Audiences tend to willingly suspend their disbelief at performances only if their own well-being is not threatened. An audience at performance seems to follow one of R. D. Laing's "knots": "They are playing a game. They are playing at not playing a game. If I show them I see they are, I shall break the rules and they will punish me. I must play their game, of not seeing the game."[7]

EXERCISES

In reading a text you can try to see your character as a fellow actor and the other characters as either audience or cohorts. Use the following list of questions to guide your analysis of a character in *The Glass Menagerie* or a previously used study play.

1. When does your character seem to be giving performances? What is the nature of those performances? What does the character want his audience to believe about him?

2. Are the performances sincere or deceptive?

3. Are the roles old roles, current roles, or roles the character wishes he had?

4. Are the roles appropriate to the actual situation? Does the character know this?

5. Does the character believe he is playing a role? Does he want others to see that he is playing a role? How does he try to hide the "acting" aspect of his performance?

6. Does the character perform with anyone? Does pairing further both of their objectives?

7. What setting is used for the performance?

8. How do the settings affect the portrayal of the role?

9. Does the character play in his own or another character's setting? How does this affect the performance?

10. What constitutes the onstage area of the set? What constitutes the offstage area?

11. Who is in your character's audience? Did your character choose the audience?

12. Does the audience affect your character's choice of role? How do they affect the performance?

13. Does the audience accept your character's performance as believable?

14. When does your character become an audience member?

15. Does your character help another performer choose a role to play? How does your character affect other characters' performances?

16. Does your character accept the other characters' performances as believable?

NOTES

[1]Luigi Pirandello, *Naked Masks: Five Plays of Luigi Pirandello*, Eric Bentley, ed. and trans. (New York: Dutton, 1952).

[2]Michael Goldman, *The Actor's Freedom: Toward a Theory of Drama* (New York: Viking Press, 1975), pp. 16–17.

[3]John Lahr and Jonathan Price, *Life Show: How to See Theater in Life and Life in Theater* (New York: Viking Press, 1973), p. 43. Quoted by permission of the author.

[4]Henrik Ibsen, *A Doll's House*, Christopher Hampton, trans. (New York: Samuel French,), p. 5.

[5]Excerpt from *The Presentation of Self in Everyday Life* by Erving Goffman. Copyright © 1959 by Erving Goffman. Reprinted by permission of Doubleday and Co., Inc.

[6]Copyright © 1975 by David Cole. Reprinted from *The Theatrical Event*, by David Cole, by permission of Wesleyan University Press.

[7]R. D. Laing, *Knots*. Copyright © 1970 by The R. D. Laing Trust, Random House, Pantheon Books.

PART THREE

UNDERSTANDING THE CHARACTER

The leap from literature into enactment takes its force from the actors. Whether the playwright wants his characters portrayed as plausible psychological studies or as puppets or stock figures or archetypes, they will be incarnated by human beings. The actors constitute the life of the performance, its vitality. Even when a character does not understand his own thoughts and feelings, the sources of his speech and behavior, the actor must try to understand them or he cannot embody them.

—Albert Bermel[1]

INTERNAL TECHNIQUE

9

Psychological Character

Dreams are the touchstones of our characters.

—Henry David Thoreau

A character is distinguished chiefly by his thoughts. Memories are thoughts of a character's past, observations of his present, and dreams of his future. A character acts to make his dreams the reality of his present circumstances. Thus, to characterize a role, you can begin by identifying the way a character's thoughts affect his actions—how the pursuit of the dream affects the character's use of memory and moment-by-moment observation.

Characterization means understanding a character backwards to play it forwards. You see your character moving to the end of the play; your character merely sees himself moving toward or away from his dreams. Consequently, you should see your character as one personality at the beginning of the play and as another at the end.

CHARACTER PERSONALITY

After reading the play, you have certain impressions of the character. You may see the character change in the action of the play. From reading what the character says and what the character does you can deduce strengths and weaknesses in the character's personality. Certain of the character's lines seem directed from particular aspects—Parent, Child or Adult. A character who frequently acts or speaks from one aspect can be said to have a large aspect of that type; infrequent expressions, on the other hand, suggest a weakness in that personality quality. A valuable tool is diagraming the character's makeup at the beginning and again at the end of the play, thereby establishing a character's *polarity*. Figure 9-1 could represent, for example, actors' interpretations of the Wingfield family in *The Glass Menagerie:*

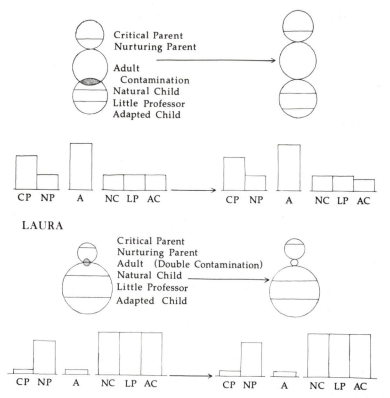

FIGURE 9-1: Impressionistic diagrams can help actors visualize their characters' change in the action of the play.

Tom's contamination in his Adult clears as he leaves home and purges his guilt by "remembering" the play; escape shows Tom less adaptive to his mother's wishes. Laura's double contamination begins to clear following the bittersweet encounter with the Gentleman Caller.

It could appear that in working on a characterization that you have really three characters to develop. Tom could have distinct vocal and physical manners to match the particular mental patterns of his Parent, Adult and Child. Characteristic rate, pitch, volume, intensity, gesture, or tempo-rhythm can identify each personality aspect in action. Consequently, a character change can be conveyed by changing the frequency or scope of the physical or vocal traits associated with the developing personality quality. Contamination could be represented by combining the vocal qualities of one aspect with the physical traits of another, or vice versa. For example, when Laura expresses her distorted view of her handicap, Adult gestures could accompany a childlike voice to reveal the fact that she has accepted her childlike fears as objective fact. As Laura changes, Adult vocal qualities could emerge to replace childlike ones. Congruence of vocal and physical manner is a characteristic of an unprejudiced and undeluded character.

EXERCISES

1. Choose a character in a study play and draw your impression of the character's personality at the beginning and at the end of the play. Discuss how and why the change occurs.

2. Identify lines in the study play which you think emanate from your character's three main personality aspects.

3. With your study character, begin to invent physical and vocal qualities for each of the three main personality qualities.

4. Pretend your study character is in some simple everyday situation doing a simple activity. Improvise your character doing the actions using appropriate personality aspects.

5. Improvise a scene from the study play's beginning utilizing your physical and vocal characterization. Improvise and play a scene from the end of the play showing the changed personality.

CHARACTER IN ACTION

Once you have established the general outline of a character's personality change, turn your attention to how the change manifests itself in action. Each line and action can be seen as part of a *transaction.*

Transactions occur as your character tries to fulfill certain needs and goals within particular circumstances. Thus, the identification and analysis of transactions requires (1) the description of circumstance, and (2) the determination of goals. Since both of these requirements have been fulfilled for Scene 2 of *The Glass Menagerie,* let us use that scene to illustrate the identification and analysis of transactions.

Laura's first transaction is in response to her mother's presence and the nonverbal stimulation Amanda provides. Amanda's Parent successfully scares Laura's fearful Child. But since her goal is to convince her mother of her good behavior, Laura changes the nature of the relationship. On the overt level, Laura's Adult tries to demonstrate a phoney studious nature. But the demonstration is false, as her nervous Child reveals itself by seeking

Amanda:
She purses her lips,
opens her eyes very wide,
rolls them upward and
shakes her head.

Laura:
Seeing her mother's ex-
pression Laura touches
her lips with a
nervous gesture.

parental approval. Amanda's words rebuke her daughter overtly, while her "martyrdom" seeks protection from a nurturing Parent.

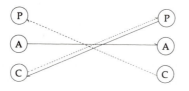

Laura:
"Hello, Mother, I
was—" She makes a
nervous gesture
toward the chart
on the wall.

Amanda:
Amanda leans against
the shut door and
stares at Laura with
a martyred look. "De-
ception? Deception?"

You can, in this way, continue to diagram moments you consider significant to your work. As transactions are clarified, psychological motivations are discovered as the subtext is brought to the surface. For example, these early exchanges show Laura trying to act as an Adult and Amanda trying to act as a hurt Child, while the ulterior, psychological level of their exchange shows Laura as a frightened Child and Amanda as an angry Parent.

With ulterior transactions, you confront the character's tensions of playing two verbs, one overt and one hidden. For example, Laura tries to convince and to please Amanda; Amanda tries to shame Laura and to arouse her pity. You can achieve richness in your performance by playing the tension created in the dual level of the double verbal action. Sometimes dramatic and unexpected revelations occur when you deliver lines from unlikely personality aspects. For example, suppose Laura begins her dialogue in a Parent demeanor, almost criticizing her mother for coming home early and disrupting her work. The eventual movement to her pained Child is thereby all the more significant since the progression is from Parent to Adult to Child rather than simply from Adult to Child. Try all of your lines from each personality side to discover unique insights into a scene's dynamics.

EXERCISES

1. Choose another scene from *The Glass Menagerie* or from a study play and detail in writing the circumstances of your character at the beginning of the scene. Break the scene into units of action and identify each objective and obstacle. Diagram key transactions, assigning subtextual verbs to each of your character's lines.

2. Improvise the previous scene in your own words, clearly attacking the beginning of each new unit of action. Attend to the pursuit of your goals and the obstacles standing in your way.

Character Units of Action

Characters pass their time on the stage by doing actions. The actions are grouped by you into units or beats, each fulfilling a purpose or need of your character. Characters in drama engage in withdrawal, rituals, activities, pastimes, games, or intimacy. Intimacy is a goal for every character, however disguised his pursuit may be.

Characters can engage in withdrawal, moments of isolation. *The Glass Menagerie* itself is a moment of withdrawal in the memory of Tom Wingfield. The play enables him to review his past so that he can purge the guilt he feels about leaving his mother and sister. Purged, Tom can more satisfactorily pursue his dream of becoming a writer. Guilt is his writing block and the play is his way of overcoming that block. On the other hand, Laura, *in* the play, withdraws to her glass collection to avoid the painful need for intimacy she feels; the creation of a fantasy world in withdrawal gives Laura make-believe intimacy. You can find moments in a play when your character remembers the past or dreams of the future in moments of withdrawal.

Characters often engage in rituals, a second kind of unit of action. *The Glass Menagerie* begins and ends with rituals—eating and blowing out candles. Amanda is most concerned with maintaining rituals within the Wingfield family; establishing grace before meals and manners of politeness help her hold onto her family. The tales Amanda tells of her youth in Mississippi and her plans for a gentleman caller have a ritualistic quality for Tom and Laura, but for Amanda they are moments of withdrawal to happier times.

Activities either further characters' goals or stand in their way. Tom's job at the factory stands in the way of his dream of adventure. Typing school lessons block Laura's desire to withdraw to her glass collection.

D.A.R. meetings further Amanda's need for security and stability in her economically feeble world. Preparations for the gentleman caller engage the family in a major concerted activity.

Pastimes can also constitute units of action. Reading D. H. Lawrence is one of Tom's pastimes, as is smoking. Listening to her mother's reminiscences of days in Mississippi gives Laura a pastime. In *The Glass Menagerie,* pastimes frequently become another type of beat—games.

Games help a character reinforce beliefs. With Eric Berne's *Games People Play* in hand, you can identify games in drama and use the analysis to clarify your character's actions and relationships. For example, Laura's game of "Wooden Leg" is basic to her character. The game lets her limp serve as an excuse for declining anything she doesn't want, anything which contradicts her dreams and beliefs. "Wooden Leg" lets Amanda play one of her favorite games, "I'm Only Trying to Help." (Relationships are often formed among characters with complementary games!) While Laura's game aims at removing her from a position of responsibility, Amanda's game seeks to alleviate her guilt. Both games reinforce Amanda's belief that (1) Laura cannot take responsibility for herself, and (2) Amanda is not responsible for Laura's behavior; the games also support Laura's conviction that (1) no one can help and (2) she is therefore free to withdraw into her fantasy world.

Games give characters ways to justify their lack of intimacy and love. Intimacy is spontaneous—it catches characters off guard. Intimacy comes to Amanda when Tom surprises her with the news that he has found a gentleman caller. At that moment Amanda and Tom share tenderness and happiness. Laura finds an intimate relationship briefly when Jim O'Conner surprises her with a kiss; she likewise initiates a moment of intimacy with Jim when she gives him her broken unicorn.

An examination of Scene 2 in *The Glass Menagerie* shows how units of action structure time. Scene 2 reveals Laura trying to win her mother's approval through games. When games fail, Laura withdraws until forced to play the game which always stumps her mother—"Wooden Leg."

Beat	Intention	Structure
1	To convince mother	Fake *activity* interrupted for *ritual* greeting as part of good version of *game* "Cops and Robbers" (intentionally setting self up to be caught for doing something good)
2	To escape to fantasy world of music	*Withdrawal*
3	To defend my actions	*Pastime*
4	To impress mother with my actions	Good version of *game* "Ain't It Awful" ("Ain't I Wonderful")

Beat	Intention	Structure
5	To escape mother's disappointment	*Withdrawal*
6	To withdraw into the past to reminisce about happy times	*Withdrawal*
7	To excuse myself from mother's idea of marriage	*Game* "Wooden Leg"

EXERCISES

1. Choose a long speech of a character in *The Glass Menagerie* or a study play and break the speech into units of action, labeling each objective. Identify the subtext. Detail in writing all of the sensory images described in the speech. Memorize the speech and speak it, clarifying the beginning of each beat while seeing, hearing, tasting, and touching in your mind's eye or ear the sensory images you described in writing.

2. Choose an emotionally charged expression your character has and repeat it over and over with growing conviction. Think of the circumstances surrounding that expression as you repeat the words.

3. Choose a scene from *The Glass Menagerie* or a study play and identify the units of action your character uses in the scene.

CHARACTER RELATIONSHIPS

Friends and enemies affect a character's pursuit of his dreams. You should identify the relationships which help or hinder your character. The cause for establishing alliances and the reason for animosity are important to you. For example, in *The Glass Menagerie* Tom is Laura's ally until he agrees to bring a gentleman caller home. Amanda is Laura's enemy because she won't let Laura withdraw. Tom is Amanda's enemy until he agrees to her request for a gentleman caller for Laura. Laura is Tom's ally since she shares his desire to escape. Amanda has no allies in her struggle to help her children find love and security; she believes that only by helping them will they have reason to love her. The opposite is true—the more Amanda tries to love her children through unsolicited assistance the more they resent her intrusion. Help makes Amanda her children's enemy and thus the obstacle to their objectives.

Jim O'Conner is seen by everyone in the Wingfield family as a potential enemy or ally. Jim's entrance makes possible Tom's, and maybe Laura's, exit. Amanda sees him as answering her prayers. Laura at first sees Jim as an enemy to her withdrawal and then as an ally in her desire for love. When he announces his engagement, the actress playing Laura can choose whether to see him as ally or enemy, thereby clearly interpreting the end of the play.

Relationships affect a character's *power*. By allying themselves to bring a gentleman caller home, Tom and Amanda increase their power while lessening Laura's. Relationships also affect dependency—Amanda depends upon Tom's ability to earn money to support the family and to find gentlemen callers; Laura depends upon Tom's ability occasionally to protect her from Amanda's plans. When Tom throws his power to Amanda, Laura feels alone, powerless, and utterly dependent. She is thus extremely susceptible to the charming power of Jim O'Conner.

Characters in drama use *power plays* to make their dreams come true. Amanda uses her high intensity power plays with Tom and Laura when guilt-through-playing-the-martyr fails. Laura uses defensive power plays, such as illness and physical handicap. When Tom's alliance with Amanda fails, he breaks off all relationships rather than return to the old, pre-gentleman caller distribution of power. Leaving home puts Tom in his father's footsteps.

Individual scenes in plays may be seen as *drama triangle* role exchanges. The dynamics of a scene's subtext may reside in the playing of Persecutor, Rescuer or Victim. Scene 2 of *The Glass Menagerie* can again serve to illustrate:

1. Amanda enters as Victim trying to force Laura into the Persecutor role.
2. Laura assumes a fake Rescuer role—being a secretary will rescue the family from its worries about her future.
3. When Amanda fails to get Laura to play Persecutor, she takes the role and forces Laura into the Victim position.
4. Amanda joins Laura as co-Victim to bewail their station in life.
5. When Amanda gets the idea of marriage she moves into the Rescuer role as the scene concludes.

EXERCISES

1. Choose a scene from *The Glass Menagerie* or study play and outline the dynamics of your character's relationships, discussing alliances, power plays, and drama triangle exchanges. Improvise the scene to clarify these features.

2. Perform the scene used in the previous exercise trying to establish a secret relationship with another character.

3. Perform a study scene with music which you think reflects your character's inner life.

4. Play the study scene with a rope tied around your waist and the other character's. Use the rope to physicalize the dynamics of the relationship.

5. Play a study scene using properties to reveal the dynamics of the relationship.

6. Play a study scene making direct physical contact with another character at each new phrase, thought, or intention.

7. Perform a study scene using pauses to heighten, strengthen, change, or reveal the dynamics of the relationship.

8. Perform a study scene with direct eye contact with another character throughout; avoiding direct eye contact; and with no eye contact.

Substitution and Relationships

Sometimes an actor cannot believably play certain moments from a play simply by relating to the actual circumstance's of his character. In these instances, you will need to *substitute* images from your own life which mean to you what the circumstances mean to the character. For example, if you cannot relate to the shyness Laura feels toward Jim, imagine to whom you did, could, or would feel similar shyness. Then, when playing a scene with Jim, see in your mind's eye and hear in your mind's ear the person who could cause you to behave like Laura.

Substitution often becomes necessary in moments when a character's remembering describes something. You can substitute images which can stimulate you in ways analogous to the images actually described by your character. Substitutions are very personal and are often best left undiscussed. What is moving to one actor can be laughable to another. If the substitution works for you, then use it. If it doesn't work, find another, no matter how similar the one you tried is to the one actually involving the character. Time and memory can change your images' ability to stimulate. Sometimes something which was actually frightening when it happened, can become an image capable of arousing laughter when recalled. Be pragmatic in your use of substitutions.

The substitution of a personal image for a character's image should produce actions. As you relate to a personal image, notice what your body and voice are doing. Sometimes a mechanical repetition of those physical and vocal actions can help generate the image in your mind's eye when you seek to recall it. Sometimes the physical action becomes all that is necessary for you to relate believably to the character's image; at those times the substitution of a personal image is unnecessary. Substitution led you to find actions which made the character's images more stimulating.

CHARACTER GOALS

All of a character's relationships exist in units of action which lead the character toward his dreams in his superobjective and counterobjective. Using a script checklist can help an actor clarify the overall shape of his character's pursuit of his twin and, often, contradictory objectives.

Superobjective

First, an actor should seek to locate his character's superobjective. This unites your character's actions into a coherent, directed whole. The requisite *through line of action* or *spine* as it is sometimes called, aims at the attainment of a primary "want" objective.

> A want is a linking function, integrating present experience with the future where its gratification lies and also with the past which it culminates and summarizes. Wants grow from where one has been; making sense out of the sensations and feelings which lead to this moment of wanting. Only by touching into where one is and what one wants right now can one forge the central link in the chain of events and experiences which make up one's life.[2]

You can determine your character's objective by listing all of your character's wants as they appear. List not only those wants which your character expresses, but also those wants which the other characters and the playwright attribute to your character. Don't always assume that the character or the playwright knows what the character wants; use the character's actions as your guide. Often a character (or playwright) will say a character wants one thing while actions suggest another. For example, in O'Neill's *Beyond the Horizon* Robert Mayo dreams of going to sea yet his actions show him trying to find any excuse he can to stay home. His goal seems to be to blame his failure to pursue his dreams on others or on "life." An actor who decided that the character's goal is to go to sea would have great difficulty reconciling his actions to this desire. A character's actions prove the old saw—"actions speak louder than words." The wants of the characters in *The Glass Menagerie* may include the following:

Amanda

to cling to the past
to keep Laura pretty and fresh for marriage
to escape the embarrassment my children cause me
to shape a clear and secure future for my children
to get into the mainstream of life
to protect my children from unpleasantness
to convince my children to listen to me
to force Tom to keep his job
to instill in my children an appreciation of spiritual things
to plan for my children's future
to convince Tom to go to night school
to secure success and happiness for my children

Laura

to help mother around the house
to avoid mother's stare

FIGURE 9-4: Helen Hayes and Lois Smith in THE GLASS MENAGERIE, 1956.

to stay away from school
to resist mother's arrangements for me
to decline meeting Jim O'Conner
to excuse myself from meeting Jim O'Conner
to hide in my music
to hide
to get Jim to autograph my program
to let myself go

Tom

to escape from this house
to refuse to listen to Mother
to leave the house
to die rather than go to work in the factory
to give up my hopes for Mother and Laura's well-being
to stay out of Mother's grasp
to get out of this situation without hurting Mother or Laura
to move out into a new future
to rid myself of the image of Laura suffering because I deserted her

Note the repetition of certain wants. A character often repeats those wants which *are* most important or *seem* most important. When choosing your character's superobjective and counterobjective, choose desires and word them in such a way as to include, encompass, and justify every other want. This act of choosing primary objectives and subjugating others in hierarchy is your first act of creative interpretation.

In locating and playing a character's objectives you should avoid falling prey to what critic Albert Bermel calls the *Spokesman Fallacy*. This fallacy can affect adversely the way in which you pursue your objectives and, in turn, everything you do on the stage. The fallacy is based on two assumptions. First, the playwright "creates one or more characters whom he likes better than he likes his other characters." Second, "all plays bring us, courtesy of the favored characters, a message." These assumptions damage a performance. An actor analyzing under these fallacies tries to label his character as either good or bad and, consequently, his wants as desirable or undesirable. Don't misperceive the function of a play as discouraging harmful desires and encouraging nice ones.

> The Spokesman Fallacy presupposes that a play tries to resolve issues when, as a work of art, it does nothing of the sort. A play *airs* issues. It illustrates their complexity by looking at them from several viewpoints, none of which is necessarily the author's or—to turn things around—all of which are necessarily the author's. The playwright's only spokesman is the play, the whole play and nothing but the play.[3]

Every objective is desirable to the character who has it. No one in life (nor in the drama) assumes a goal for the sake of demonstrating to all around the undesirability of having such a goal. Characters may regret that they are compelled to certain ends and wish that they could change, but in actual pursuit they relish the game. Understand the reasons for your character's objectives but do not editorialize in the manner of your playing. After all, the audience has come to the theatre to see the character pursue the objectives and not to see your opinion of those objectives.

Script Decisions

Since every script objective involves a decision to pursue, you can often gain a firmer understanding of your character by improvising a monologue in which the decision to seek a particular goal is made. Sometimes playwrights include references to such moments in the play itself. Willy Loman in *Death of A Salesman* gives such a monologue as he describes the funeral of Dave Singleman:

> And I was almost decided to go, when I met a salesman in the Parker House. His name was Dave Singleman. And he was eighty-four years old, and he'd drummed merchandise in thirty-one states. And old Dave, he'd go up to his room, y'understand, put on his green velvet slippers—I'll never forget—and pick up his phone and call buyers, and without ever leaving his room, at the age of eighty-four, he made his living. And when I saw that, I realized that selling was the greatest career a man could want.[4]

Robert Mayo in *Beyond the Horizon* describes the childhood circumstances which motivate his superobjective:

> Well, in those days, when Ma was fixing meals, she used to get me out of the way by pushing my chair to the west window and telling me to look out and be quiet. . . . So I used to stare out over the fields to the hills, out there—[*He points to the horizon.*]—and somehow after a time I'd forget any pain I was in, and start dreaming. I knew the sea was over beyond those hills,—the folks had told me—and I used to wonder what the sea was like, and try to form a picture of it in my mind [*with a smile*]. There was all the mystery in the world to me then about that—far-off sea—and there still is! It called to me then just as it does now. [*After a slight pause*] And other times my eyes would follow this road, winding off into the distance, toward the hills, as it, too, was searching for the sea. And I'd promise myself that when I grew up and was strong, I'd follow that road, and it and I would find the sea together. [*With a smile*] You see, my making this trip is only keeping that promise of long ago.[5]

Sometimes such moments occur within the play itself as with Tom (and perhaps with Laura) in *The Glass Menagerie*.

Disposition

You come to a determination of your character's self-image and view of the world by considering his disposition. This attitude toward the self and others reinforces your character's desires and suggests his basic technique for pursuing his dream.

Often a character's desired disposition and his *actual* disposition conflict and spur him on toward victory. Characters try to attain their dreams, to "win," even if the goals are self-destruction. Death is often a victory or a confirmation for a character. Willy Loman believes his suicide will give him victory. Robert Mayo believes dying in a ditch beside the road in the rising sun will give him, his brother, and wife new lives. Tom's disposition moves between a positive and negative self-image and a positive and negative image of others. At the beginning of the play he seems to have primarily negative feelings about himself while at the end he tries to remove the last negative feeling by purging the guilt he feels about Laura. Tom wants to feel "okay" and he can do that only by deserting his mother and sister.

Heroes

Characters often have heroes who influence them significantly. In *The Glass Menagerie* Tom's hero may be D. H. Lawrence or it may be his father, who, until Tom leaves, is the villain of his fantasy. The "plot" in Tom's fantasy scenario enables him to become his hero through the deal he makes with Amanda. Laura may have a heroine in *The Pirates of Penzance,* the high school operetta which starred Jim. Mabel "whose homely face and bad complexion/Have caused all hopes to disappear/Of ever winning man's affection" is beloved of Frederick, the role played by Jim O'Conner. Mabel is thrilled by her newfound joy, as Laura will be with Jim:

> Did ever a maiden wake
>   From dream of homely duty,
> To find her daylight break
>   With such exceeding beauty?
> Did ever a maiden close
>   Her eyes on waking sadness,
> To dream of such exceeding gladness?

But Frederick is taken from Mabel in a fluke of fate leaving Mabel alone; the plot of Laura's scenario mirrors this Gilbert and Sullivan development. (Perhaps the music Laura plays throughout the play is from *The Pirates of Penzance!*)

Heroes often have the same wants as characters. Blanche DuBois in Williams' *A Streetcar Named Desire,* and Marguerite of *Les Dames aux Camelias* share many traits and goals. As Virgo, Blanche may use the astrological descriptions of her character as a self-fulfilling prophecy. Dave Singleman, Ben, and his own father could all contribute to Willy Loman's hero. Robert Mayo may have found a hero in the romantic poetry of Arthur Symons that he reads at the play's opening.

Occasionally, a character derives his strategy from fairy tales. In *Who's Afraid of Virginia Woolf?* the "Who's Afraid of Virginia Woolf?" refrain reveals Martha's Child fears and Parental aggression in the melody and her heroine in the substitution of "Virginia" for "Big Bad." You can view Martha as one who sees men as wolves, a slang term for sexually aggressive males. Martha has constructed a strong masculine personality to protect her from aggressive, sexually hungry "wolves." She goads her husband George into wolflike attempts to penetrate her defenses. Each time she outsmarts him, thus reinforcing her fear of male aggression and her negative view of others. When George refuses to attack Martha, he draws her out of her "brick" personality so that he can destroy it by killing their imaginary child, the symbol of Martha's home. Martha then admits fearing the "wolf." To play Martha, you can view yourself as a vulnerable little pig who must protect yourself with a strong defense and by outsmarting the males around you.

A character's physical center can give you a clue toward physicalization. Willy Loman's feet and his need for arch supports present a focus for an actor's initial attempts at physicalization. Robert Mayo, through the poetry he reads and the dreams he recites, is, like the smoking Tom Wingfield, an oral person. Laura's physical center focuses on her legs. Jim O'Conner's gum chewing mouth marks him as another oral character.

Psychological Circumstances

An understanding of the injunctions and attributions under which the character lives can aid you in determining the psychological circumstances. The advice and warnings a character gives another character are often the ones ruling that character's own behavior. A character's psychological motivation achieves its direction, in part, from the psychological circumstances created in a character by parents' or parental figures' *injunctions* and *attributions*. Laura's objectives are partly shaped by the following restrictions Amanda places on her:

> Do nothing; stay fresh and pretty for gentlemen callers
> You are not an adult
> You deliberately court illness
> You deliberately deceive me
> You have a little defect which is hardly noticeable
> Wish on the moon for happiness and success
> Don't be satisfied sitting at home
> You are prettiest when physically deceiving
> Your disobedience will not be excused
> Be normal
> Things have a way of turning out badly

The restrictions Laura tries to put on others are, as they are for all characters, ones she herself follows:

> Don't wake up Mother or make her nervous
> Apologize to Mother

Do what is asked of you
Be careful of fragile things

When these messages contradict each other, a character is forced to invent actions which reconcile them. These parameters for action lead Laura to pursue a characteristic superobjective and a characteristic counterobjective in distinct ways.

Counterobjective

Whenever a character's actions seem to contradict the achievement of his superobjective, the character may be pursuing a counterobjective. Some of the injunctions and attributions lead toward the superobjective, some toward the counterobjective, and some toward both. *Counterscript actions* provide you with opportunities to display an aspect of your character which seems to conflict with the superobjective. For example, Laura's delight in Jim's conversation and Tom's residence at home seem to contradict their desires to escape; in actuality, these activities point to other goals in a counterobjective—love and approval. Willy Loman learned to appreciate nature and to take pride in manual labor from his father. Flute music haunts him as a symbolic reminder of his father's injunctions about outdoor life. Willy tries to foster meagre bits of this past life by observing the beauty of trees, warm sunshine, and the soothing breeze coming through his car's window. He recalls by name the many trees and flowers which once grew in his backyard. During the crisis, Willy's preoccupation with seeds and planting shows his desperate attempt to follow this counterobjective suggested by his father. He seeks in counterscript actions the dream denied him by following script actions.

Love Often characters do not attain their dreams. As discussed earlier, relationships can help or hinder desires. The one universal desire which every character pursues, the one universal relationship desired, and the one universal dream sought, is love. Every character believes that if the goal set is achieved, love will follow. If a character cannot hope for love, hate will substitute. Either of these two most powerful emotions will be sought since they are necessary components in the confirmation of existence. Plays show how characters pursue love, compensate for a lack of love, pass their time waiting for love, and even avoid love. Willy Loman wants love and substitutes the sex of a prostitute when other sources are unavailable. Laura avoids a loveless world in the world of glass animals. Martha seeks love through aggression. Tom Lee in *Tea and Sympathy* needs love but doesn't know how to pursue it. As author Ira Tanner writes, "fear of love is the root cause of every attitude and form of behavior that separates us from each other."[6] Love, then, is one of the superobjectives, not only in our own lives, but also, in the lives of dramatic characters.

SUMMARY

When investigating the mental play of a character you can perform the following steps to gain a fuller appreciation of the psychological aspect of the character's inner life:

1. Diagram the character's personality impressionistically for the beginning of the play and for the end of the play.
2. Begin to consider physical and vocal qualities to distinguish three basic personality aspects.
3. Review the character's individual actions as they represent parts of transactions seeking the fulfillment of particular needs or goals.
4. Detail the circumstances for action in each of your character's scenes.
5. Divide each scene into units of action, labeling each objective and obstacle.
6. Use the psychological level of ulterior transactions to aid your identification of the subtext in each scene.
7. Discover the progression of units of action in each scene.
8. Identify the nature of your character's relationships as they aid or hinder your character's pursuit of goals. Note how the relationships change in the progression of the action.
9. Determine the superobjective and counterobjective for your character.
10. Establish your character's disposition at the beginning and the end of the play. Identify the cause of any change.
11. Research passing references in the text which could lead to the identification of heroes.
12. Review the injunctions and attributions which govern your character's actions.
13. Evaluate your character's actual ending with his desired outcome.

EXERCISES

1. Make a list of your study character's desires and note repetitive desires. These are often the character's most important desires. Number the character's wants in order of importance. Compare your ranking with others in your group. Express each character's primary want as an active verb infinitive. It should encompass and justify other wants.

2. Discuss how the superobjective (number 1 on the list in the previous exercise) and counterobjective (number two on the list in the previous exercise) satisfy all of the other desires the character has. Invent and perform an improvisation as the character in which these two objectives clash.

3. Determine the disposition of your study character. Improvise their actions revealing those dispositions at the beginning and end of the play.

4. Perform Michael Chekhov's exercise in Chapter 2 for the Psychological Gesture for your study character.

5. Using your fingertips, mold your face into a mask for your study character. Let the mask communicate what you want, your disposition, traits of any hero, and

the influence of your physical center. Use stage makeup to supplement your natural mask-making.

6. While wearing the mask, clothe yourself in the character's garments. With a full-length mirror communicate physically *as* the character *with* the character. Walk to the image. Run to the image. Declare love. Attempt to seduce. React to a crisis. React to heat. React to cold. Talk to your hero. Hate. React to hate. Say your want list with growing conviction.

7. Wearing the mask and clothing, fantasize your character's dream, the attainment of his objective. Improvise the scene with those who would be there, doing and saying what you would do and say. Next, fantasize your defeat as a nightmare. Improvise the event.

8. To determine the psychological circumstances under which your character may pursue an objective, list all of the injunctions and attributions given to others, or which parent figures (if in the play) give.

9. Choose a character in a study play. Analyze the character's name. How does the name affect the character's behavior, expectations, and transactions? Do other characters have expectations based on the name? Does the character use the name or a nickname? Use a dictionary of names to aid you in this research.

10. Locate the counterscript actions of Tom Wingfield, Martha, Tom Lee, or Blanche DuBois. Relate these activities to a counterobjective learned from parent figures. Is there a conflict between superobjective and counterobjective? Is one an obstacle to the other? Does the character ever fantasize or daydream on the outcome of the might-have-been objective?

11. Determine obstacles to your character's victory. Which parental injunctions? Which characters? Which fears? Which fantasies? Which physical influences? Play against these barriers in performance.

12. Appear before the group or cast in your character's clothing and mask, prepared to answer the following and other questions *as your character.* (Some characters wouldn't answer some questions; others might not understand.) In answering the questions, each answer should be based on either textual evidence or logical creative imagination. View each answer as either helping you toward or standing in the way of your victory. All of these questions may not be applicable to characters in all types of plays. Nevertheless, consideration of each is necessary before applicability can be decided.

Physical Qualities:

1. Who am I?
2. Who am I named after? Do I like my name?
3. What is my sex? What do I think of sex?
4. How old am I? What do I think of my age?
5. How does my posture express my age, health, and inner feeling?
6. How is my complexion? What do I think of it?
7. What is my height? What do I think of it?
8. What is my weight? What do I think of it?
9. What is the pitch, volume, tempo, resonance, or quality of my voice? What do I think of it?

10. Is my articulation careless or precise? Is my articulation standard or colloquial? Do I have a dialect?
11. What is my hair color and style? Do I like it?
12. Do I have any deformities? What do I think of them?
13. Do I have any mannerisms? What do I think of them?
14. Do I have any handicaps? What do I think of them?
15. How energetic or vital am I? Do I like it?
16. Do I suffer from any diseases past or present?
17. Are my gestures complete or incomplete, vigorous or weak, compulsive or controlled?
18. Do I like my walk?
19. How do I sit?
20. How do I stand?
21. Do I have any objects with me? How do I handle them?
22. Is my basic rhythm jerky or smooth, volatile or even-tempered, impulsive or deliberate, ponderous or light, broken or continuous?
23. What do I like to wear? What do I have to wear? How do I wear my clothes? How do I handle them?
24. Do I carry any accessories or hand props? Why?
25. How do each of these physical traits affect my manner of movement and manner of speaking?

Social Qualities:

1. What do I do when I wake up each morning?
2. What is my relationship to my environment? Do I like it?
3. What is my educational background? How much discipline was I subjected to? How intelligent am I?
4. What was my childhood like? What are my strongest memories?
5. How much money do I have? How much do I want?
6. What is my nationality? What do I think of it?
7. What is my occupation? Do I like it? What other jobs have I had? When and why did I choose this one?
8. What are my political attitudes?
9. Am I religious?
10. Whom would I choose to be if I could be anyone else?
11. Did I have any childhood heroes? What did I like about them?
12. Do I like members of the opposite sex? What do I like about them?
13. Who were my parents? What do I like about them? What do I dislike about them? What can I still hear them saying to me?
14. Do I like my family? What do I like? What do I dislike about them?
15. How has my mother influenced me? How has my father influenced me?
16. What do I think of my brothers and sisters?
17. What was my favorite fairy tale? Why?
18. Who are my friends? Who are my enemies? How can I tell if someone is a friend or an enemy?
19. What ideas do I dislike? What ideas do I like?

20. What hobbies or interests do I have?
21. Do I have children? If not, why not? Do I like my children? Why? Do they like me? Why?
22. What advice do I have for my children?
23. What do I like about my spouse? What do I dislike?
24. Why did I marry the person I did?
25. How do my physical traits affect each of these social traits?
26. How do each of these social traits affect my script objective?
27. How do each of these social traits affect my wants?
28. How does the locale of the play make me feel?
29. How does the time of the play make me feel?
30. How does the period of the play affect my actions?
31. What will be carved on my tombstone?
32. Where have I been prior to each of my stage entrances? How does this affect my actions verbally and physically? What would I like to see or do when I enter?

Psychological Qualities:

1. What choices do I face?
2. What choices do I make?
3. How do my social traits affect my psychological make-up?
4. How do my physical traits affect my psychological make-up?
5. What makes me angry? What relaxes me?
6. What are my driving ambitions?
7. Do I have any instincts?
8. Do I do things impulsively?
9. What do I worry about?
10. What do I want? What do others think I want?
11. What do I like about myself? What do I dislike about myself?
12. What do I need?
13. What do I fear?
14. Why can't I get what I want?
15. Do other people like me? Why?
16. How are each of my psychological traits manifested physically?
17. How are each of my psychological traits manifested vocally?
18. Why do I make each of my stage entrances? What do I want each time? How do these wants affect me vocally and physically? What am I thinking about at each stage entrance?

Moral Qualities:

1. Are the choices I will make based upon expediency or upon some ethical standard?
2. Whom do I admire?
3. Will the pursuit of my needs lead to a moral choice?
4. What is my attitude toward the choice I make?
5. How do I express this attitude vocally and physically?

Playing Qualities:

1. What metaphors, similes, or personifications are used to describe me?
2. How are these figures of speech related to my physical, social, psychological and moral traits?
3. How are the traits inherent in the figures of speech expressed physically and vocally?

You must consider the answer to every question, even though the character in performance may be, and probably is, ignorant of many.

13. Write an autobiography for a study character up to the beginning of the play. Use the following sample student biography as an example.

Autobiography of Karen Wright
in Lillian Hellman's *The Children's Hour*
by Connie Bonner

I am Karen Wright, age thirty. I am 5′7″ and weigh 119 pounds. I was born on April 12, 1904. My hair and eyes are both brown. I come from a well-educated, old, Protestant family. My father, Harry S. Wright, Jr., a very gentle, correct man, was principal of a local high school outside Boston. My mother, formerly Jean Courtly, taught French and German at my father's school. I had a younger sister, Denise, but she died of pneumonia when I was fourteen, two years before my father's death.

After my father died, my mother continued to teach and started taking courses to obtain a higher degree. Occasionally I went to her classes when she couldn't attend. Because of this I learned many languages and developed a great interest in learning and teaching. I graduated valedictorian from my father's high school and attended Wellesley College in Mass. on the Ella White Scholarship for language majors.

During my Wellesley years I made many friends, got homesick, joined the tennis team, studied, and sang in the choir. In the evenings I would sit in the lounge and study or sew or occasionally play the piano. That was how I met Martha Dobie. She came from a small town in Maine and used to enjoy going to the lounges to study at night. We became close almost immediately. Our temperaments and habits seemed to match perfectly. Junior and senior year we roomed together. We used to talk about all our plans for the future, joking about all our plans for the future, joking about becoming teachers or principals. Senior year we became serious and realized our dreams of teaching could be reality. We started planning for a school. The school would be a girls' boarding school in the country. It would be a place of instruction in every area pertinent to society and a woman's life: English, sciences, histories, speech, sewing, music, and manners.

In 1934 we opened the Wright-Dobie School for Girls. We had found an old farm near Lancet, Mass. and turned it into the school. It took us two years of hard work, borrowing, and struggle. We had to borrow money from several of the influential members of the town, but through the years we've almost paid everyone back.

I met Joe during those first two years of struggle. He was just starting out in his practice at the hospital and Martha and I asked him if he could be on call for the school in case of any emergency. I think I loved him from the first. He was so warm and secure. We are going to marry as soon as Martha and I are out of debt.

NOTES

[1]Albert Bermel, *Contradictory Characters* (New York: Dutton, 1973), p. 4. Reprinted by permission of Albert Bermel. Copyright © 1973 by Albert Bermel.

[2]Erving and Miriam Polster, *Gestalt Therapy Integrated* (New York: Vintage Books, 1973), p. 228.

[3]Albert Bermel, "The Playwright as Moralizer," *Columbia Forum*, Winter 1970, p. 45.

[4]Arthur Miller, *Death of a Salesman* (New York: Viking, 1958), p. 81.

[5]Eugene O'Neill, *Beyond the Horizon*. Copyright 1919, 1925, 1926, 1927, 1928, 1940, 1946 by Eugene O'Neill. Random House.

[6]Ira Tanner, *Loneliness: The Fear of Love*. (New York: Perennial Library, 1973), p. 12.

EXTERNAL TECHNIQUE

10

Physical Character

The face is the mirror of the mind, and eyes without speaking confess secrets of the heart.

—St. Jerome

In the preceding chapter you examined ways of understanding and interpreting the internal dynamics of a character. Regardless of how ingenious, detailed, or revealing the inner characterization, you will fail without considering the means of presenting that characterization to an audience through your body and voice. To create the outer form of your inner creation, you should consider the character's physical appearance and movement based upon your understanding of human behavior. In the process of externalizing character, you may discover new and sometimes better inner justifications for action.

An audience deduces internal characterization from what it sees and hears you do; an audience concludes your motivation *after* seeing your action. Through the creative use of costume, makeup and properties, you can disclose the inner life of your character. The process of making a characterization manifest helps you to believe the reality of your character's psychological life. One of the greatest faults of young actors (and American actors in general) is a lack of attention to the physical details of characterization. Conscious and early effort must be given to the physical life of a character. You would do well to follow Rip Torn's advice:

> I select my elements by the way I choose to walk, the way I move, the way my voice operates, the actual pitch of it, the sound of it. I select those in the same way a painter takes colors from his palette to create an impression. So while my identification is instinctive, my selectivity is conscious; that's where the artistry comes in.[1]

In this chapter various techniques will be examined which can help you invent the physical side of your character.

METAPHOR ABSORPTION

"Sly as a fox." "Slow as molasses in January." "Like a bull in a china shop." Metaphors and other figures of speech colorfully describe our actions. Often characters in plays are compared to animals or inanimate objects either by other characters or by the playwright. These comparisons provide you with an opportunity to absorb some of the physical characteristics of

FIGURE 10-1:   Daumier, Head, 1935–2687. Courtesy of The Museum of Fine Arts, Budapest, Hungary.

FIGURE 10-2: *Que de Soins M'ont Coute Cette Tete Charmante.* Honore Daumier. Bequest of William Babcock B 4215. Courtesy, Museum of Fine Arts, Boston. This and FIGURE 10-1 could help an actress through the technique of *metaphor absorption.*

the object or animal into your own body. *To absorb* means literally to assimilate, to incorporate. You can incorporate some of the physical qualities of the fox, the molasses, or the bull as a means of transforming your own physical self into that of the character.

The absorption of a character's metaphoric qualities requires close observation of the relevant object or animal. In *The Glass Menagerie* characters are frequently compared to animals or objects, leaving the actor free to choose the one which he believes captures his character's essence.

Amanda: hawk, Jesus' mother, bird, a Daumier print
Tom: oyster
Laura: piece of translucent glass, a deer
Jim: cow

If there are no metaphors, or if the existing references do not excite your creative imagination, ask yourself what animal the character would be if the character were an animal. Or discover an object closely associated with your character.

In *The Glass Menagerie* objects can be used in place of metaphors.

Amanda: handkerchief, purse, jonquils, macaroons, old-fashioned cut-glass pitcher
Laura: glass unicorn, blue roses, penguins, candle
Tom: cigarettes, movie ticket stubs, rainbow colored magician's scarf, coffee cup, newspaper
Jim: gum, mints, white chinaware

These objects or others invented by the actor can be used to discover the key to the physical life of the character. The following steps can help you in absorbing physical qualities—movement, rhythm, tempo, gesture, mannerism—from animals or objects:

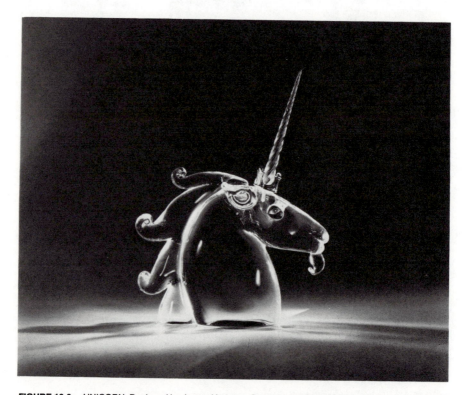

FIGURE 10-3:   UNICORN. Designed by James Houston. Courtesy of STEUBEN GLASS. An actress playing Laura might examine a glass unicorn using the technique of *metaphor absorption.*

1. Study the actual animal or object closely, attending to your sensory reactions. What colors does it have? What do you associate with those colors? How does it feel? How does it smell? What do you associate with those sensations? How does it taste? What do you associate with that taste?

2. How does the animal or object move? How could it move? Move like the object could move. How would you run if you were the object? How would you dance? If you were a human being with these movement qualities, how would you walk, run, dance, sit, or rise?

3. How would you move as the character, if the character had these movement qualities?

4. Move about the stage setting as the character would move, if the character had those movement qualities.

EXERCISE

Using a character from *The Glass Menagerie* or a study play, absorb metaphorical qualities from an animal or object associated with that character. Use the suggested four-step process as your guide.

CHARACTER AND THE MASK

Frequently actors discover that the physical life of their character starts at the top of the head but ends at the neck. Mobilization of the entire body into the creation eliminates *face acting*. Masks can help you energize and utilize your entire body in the creation of character. As playwright Eugene O'Neill found,

> It was interesting to watch, in the final rehearsals of *The Great God Brown,* how after using their masks for a time the actors and actresses reacted to the demand made by the masks that their bodies become alive and expressive and participate in the drama. Usually it is only the actors' faces that participate. Their bodies remain bored spectators that have been dragged off to the theatre when they would have much preferred a quiet evening in the upholstered chair at home.[2]

Masks are as old as the theatre itself and function as extensions of the actor. With a mask you cannot rely upon eyes or face. When working with a mirror, you should discover your focus in your body. Small psychological gestures demand magnification without the loss of truthfulness and honest motivation. Actors discover great freedom when concealed behind the mask of character. Yet that very freedom reveals every fault and inadequacy in movement and posture. The mask is a demanding teacher and the first lesson is to give it room to teach. As master mask artist Bari Rolfe advises,

A first lesson the actor learns is to get out of the way, as it were, to let him or herself be influenced by the mask; not to impose anything upon it but instead to be receptive to it. Getting out of the way means simply doing nothing at first, nothing of one's own habits of walking, standing, sitting, gesturing.[3]

Masks simplify and clarify the essential physicality of character. The masks suggest all necessary movement; the actor follows those suggestions:

The mystique of the mask is powerful. One immediately feels different behind it. When an actor is responding to the commands of the mask, he experiences a sense of wholeness, relaxation, and well-being. There is a calm sensation of being taken over by it. If he is improvising he feels himself doing unexpected things, feeling impelled to obey the choices suggested by the mask.[4]

EXERCISES

1. Choose a monologue from a Greek drama. Find a mask which suggests the essential quality of the character. Wearing the mask, stand before a mirror. Begin to slowly move your head, then your torso, then one hand, then the other. Slowly approach the mirror; slowly retreat from the mirror. Recite the monologue slowly to yourself while observing the mask leading your body. Recite the monologue aloud, letting the mask guide your every action.

2. Repeat the previous exercise with an animal mask appropriate for a character in your study play.

3. Repeat Exercise 1 with a mask you made or found for a character in your study play.

Masking Through Makeup

Stage makeup is the masking device most frequently used by the contemporary actor. Makeup thus serves an important function for the actor. Skill in its application and use should be an early goal for the aspiring actor. Amateurish or incorrect makeup application can ruin an otherwise wonderful performance. Good makeup can, on the other hand, add tremendously to a performance.

The purpose of this discussion is not to teach the fundamentals of stage makeup, but rather to examine makeup as a function of your physicalization of character. The great Constant Coquelin speaks of another great actor, Lessuer, and his use of makeup:

No one has ever done more with his second self, or created out of his own personality characters more different in themselves, or with more intense expression. It was really astonishing. But then he studied with the fury of enthusiasm. In his house there was a sort of dark-room, with closed windows and all paraphernalia. There, alone before his mirror, he would sit trying experiments with his face by the light of lamps. He would make up a hundred times, before he would succeed in producing the ideal which he felt to be the true one, and of which he could say, "Yes, that is he." And when he had put the finishing touch to the likeness, he would work for hours at one wrinkle. The result was so extraordinary that judges of acting will never forget. . . .[5]

Would that today's actors paid as much attention to this important extension of character! Take a course in stage makeup or begin to learn from a good text as soon as possible!

Makeup must always be used to extend the psychological reality of you-as-character. Besides extending the psychological character, makeup has many other functions. Makeup makes you look natural in the unnatural stage light. Without makeup, every character's face would wash into flat pie plates of sound. With makeup you can accentuate positive facial features and tone down negative ones. And through prosthesis—the use of artificial facial pieces—you can completely change your appearance.

EXERCISES

1. Observe people analytically with regard to their skin color and texture, bone structure, hair, wrinkles, sagging flesh, etc. Pay particular attention to how these features show psychological character. List the textual references to your study character's face. Describe the face of your character using some of the features you observed.

2. Collect photographs of faces from magazines, catalogues, or circulars. Faces of unique or interesting people can provide a reference file for future use in capturing the outer look of a character. Collect faces with features you envision for your study character. From these photographs begin to imagine the psychology of the person—social position, temperament, health, etc.

3. Choose a strong line your study character has which expresses an intense attitude or emotion. To a count of five, let your face assume an expression which projects that attitude. Freeze your face and say the line, then dissolve the expression to another five count. Use stage makeup to accentuate the frozen, mask-like expression.

4. Mold your face into the face of your character as if your face were made of clay.

5. Alone with a mirror and some rudimentary stage makeup, try to capture some of the features of your study character on the face you have molded in the previous exercise. Imagine you are painting the mask you have formed.

COSTUME: EXTENDING THE CHARACTER'S BODY

The first impression an audience makes of your character comes from the clothes you wear. As the action progresses, apart from face and hands, your moving costume creates the greatest reaction in the audience. From a distance an audience can perceive familiarity or strangeness, sex, emotion, nationality, social position and even elements of psychology from the moving costume. Needless to say, you should attend to such an important extension of your character as costume.

Costume affects not only the audience's impression of character, but also the actor's ability to stand and move as that character. Costume projects the messages a character wishes to send about himself. Russian director Alexander Tairov discounts common misconceptions about costume:

> Genuine theatrical costume is not finery for the purpose of adorning the actor, it is not a model of stylish costume of this or that period, it is not a fashion picture from an old journal, and the actor is not a doll or a mannequin, whose chief goal is to show the costume off to advantage. No, the costume is the actor's second skin, it is something inseparable from his essence, it is the visible mask of his scenic figure. It must become so integral a part of him that, just as with the words of a song, not one line may be discarded or changed without at the same time distorting the whole image.[6]

Great actors accomplish this goal! The great American actor Alfred Lunt once said "I wouldn't change that shirt for anything in world. It doesn't show, but somehow or another I suppose it helps me feel the character."[7] To make costume part of the physical life of the character you must begin early in the rehearsal to consider your "second skin."

The actor who understands what a costume can convey is better able to begin working with a costume. To one degree or another, a costume can reveal, intentionally or unintentionally, a character's sex, social class, age, historical period, nationality, locality, mood, occupation, and even sexual attitudes. When costume serves a decorative function it may enhance sexual attractiveness, display awards, frighten or intimidate, provide a place to carry accessories, extend or enhance various bodily parts. Author James Penrod elaborates this idea:

> Mankind has in various periods decorated his body with objects on the head, the neck, the arms, the waist, the legs, the fingers and even the toes. Women have variously exposed or hidden their breasts, cinched their waists, enclosed themselves in corsets, hidden under voluminous skirts and padding, often abused their bodies in various ways to conform to the prevailing idea of beauty. Men, in keeping with their aggressive role, have often worn clothing that allowed for greater mobility. Social status or rank has usually been indicated in clothing by style, fashion, fabric, and sometimes color.[8]

All of this is mentioned not to propose that you must know the history of fashion and decoration, but to impress upon you the great importance of costume in communicating psychological character to an audience.

You should, early in the rehearsal process, talk with the costume designer and director about your clothing. You know your character and the designer knows the possibilities of costume. Together you can evolve the best expression of the physical character. Don't tell the designer and director what you want—they are creative artists in their own right. Together you discuss your understandings of the character and the circumstances as they exist and evolve in the play. These discussions could cover the following topics.[9]

1. Kind of costume
2. Justification for costume
3. Distortions of the body by costume
4. Tightness or looseness of costume fit
5. Effect of costume fabric on movement
6. Effect of sleeves and collar on movement
7. Effect of hair style on movement
8. Undergarments
9. Costume accessories

Following this discussion you can begin to put together a rehearsal facsimile of the costume you will wear. Don't wait for the designer or stage manager to get you one; it is up to *you* to perfect your movement through costume! The actress Lynn Redgrave describes how the process can work:

> I always try to approximate in rehearsal the sort of costume I'm going to be wearing. I find it's less panicky when I finally get the real thing, and bits of business—problems or difficulties—come out of it. In other words, if you're going to be in a long dress and you rehearse in jeans, you will just automatically sit different, no matter how much you try to be aware of the difference and take it into account. Everything about the two costumes is different—the way you walk, the way you stand. The same is true if you're going to be in a high heel and you're rehearsing in a low heel. Not only does it throw you when you finally get into the right costume, but you miss out on all the possibilities you could have worked with. Maybe the character doesn't walk very well in high heels, but you're never going to find that out if you leave it until the moment when everything else is hitting you. If it's a modern play and no one is sure what they're going to be wearing, I try to persuade the designer to hold off deciding until I have time to experiment. If it's a classical play and the designer has decided all these things, then either I try to get the real costume—which is almost impossible—or I duplicate it out of junk I have at home.[10]

High-heeled or heelless shoes, long or short skirts, coats, hats, and underwear (or the lack thereof) should become part of your early work in externalizing the physical character. These character adjuncts can stimulate wonderful ideas as you work to master and exploit your ability to reveal the psychological nuances of character.

1. Observe people's clothing as extensions of their personalities. Discuss how clothing expresses or hides your fellow actor's or another person's:

   a. sex
   b. nationality
   c. social standing or class
   d. age
   e. locality
   f. degree of formality
   g. degree of conformity
   h. taste
   i. wealth
   j. mood
   k. occupation
   l. sexual attitude

Analyze the circumstances in which the clothing is worn. How do the circumstances seem to affect the person's choice and use of clothing?

2. Choose a character from *The Glass Menagerie* or a study play and list the references to costume in the text. Elaborate on that list to discover how the items listed in the previous exercise may be utilized. How do the moment-by-moment circumstances affect the character's attitude toward his clothing? Which items on the list become important for the character to emphasize or suppress through costume as the play develops?

3. Choose a particular scene from *The Glass Menagerie* or a study play and improvise your character's actions focusing on exploiting the possibilities of costume to reveal the character's subtextual life.

PROPERTIES: EXTENDING THE CHARACTER'S ACTION

Critic John Lahr wisely observes that "properties help to say part of who we are."[11] The art of selecting and profiting from stage properties is an essential component of the creative player.

Hand properties are extensions of the character and should be explored as early as possible in rehearsal. Effective actors rarely use properties for their literal function. The magnificent British actress Edith Evans exemplifies this ability:

> The only thing you don't do with a fan is fan yourself. You poke the fire with it, you hit someone, you do every sort of thing, but you never fan yourself. If you've got a fan and you know how to use the thing, you can quite easily talk behind it, or above it, or round about it; or slowly wave it if you don't

FIGURE 10-4: Paul Rudd and Pamela White use properties to reveal their relationship in the Circle in the Square production of THE GLASS MENAGERIE by Tennessee Williams. Photo courtesy of Inge Morath.

FIGURE 10-5: Ruth Nelson cradles properties in a scene from THE GLASS MENAGERIE directed by Alan Schneider. Photo courtesy of The Guthrie Theater, c/o The Guthrie Theater, Minneapolis, Minnesota, 1964.

want to think about something else while you're pretending to talk to someone over there, you see.[12]

Properties can reveal the subtext of a scene as they serve as manifestations of ulterior transactions. You should explore every possible use of properties, especially the sounds they can make; properties can punctuate a performance. Director Jose Quintero speaks of Geraldine Page and properties:

> I have never worked with anyone else who knows how to use properties the way that Geraldine can. She can change a handkerchief, a broom, or a tablecloth into her inner landscape. She can let you know through these ordinary things her joy, unhappiness, longing, and also those undefinable and by no means ordinary mysteries hidden in all of our lives![13]

Choose properties carefully and plan their use imaginatively. Playwrights often help. In *The Glass Menagerie* the characters are given many properties to use:

> *Tom:* cigarettes, newspaper, manuscripts, noisemaker, door key, ticket stubs, empty bottle, matches, magician's scarf, cup of coffee
> *Amanda:* bowl of dessert, handkerchief, telephone, newspaper, hairbrush, powder puffs, jonquils, candles, candelabrum, glass of wine, glass pitcher, plate of macaroons

Creative actors pick properties which are not specified in the script but which logically extend the character in the particular situation. The simple handling of properties can release tension, involve you in the physical reality of the present moment, and result in the generation of sincere emotion. The great American actor Edwin Booth played *Hamlet* with the skull willed to him by his friend, Lovett, who was hanged for horse thievery. Imagine the great actor's experience as he gazed at his friend's skull in his hand and spoke of Hamlet's friend Yorrick! Compelling actors select their properties not only for their relevance to the dramatic character and situation but also for their personal association value.

EXERCISES

1. Observe people using properties. Discuss how the objects are used in non-literal ways. How does the manipulation disclose the psychology of the user?

2. Select a property of a character in *The Glass Menagerie* or a study play and exploit its possible uses. Use the object logically, not like using a cigarette as a lawn mower! The more uses the better.

3. Choose a scene from *The Glass Menagerie* or a study play and invent a property for use by your character in the scene. The object should be one not specified by the text.

4. Improvise an invented scene in which properties reveal your study play character's objectives.

5. Choose a scene from a study play and use properties as obstacles to your character's objectives.

6. Repeat the scene from the previous exercise using properties as leverage to achieve your objectives.

7. Improvise a scene of eating for your study character or perform an eating scene from *The Matchmaker, Ah Wilderness, Life With Father, JB,* or *The Glass Menagerie.*

8. Improvise a drinking scene for your study character or play a scene from *Kennedy's Children* or *The Time Of Your Life.*

9. Improvise a scene of changing clothes as your study character or play a scene from Noel Coward's *Red Peppers.*

10. Choose and perform a silent scene from your study play or one of the following scenes from *The Glass Menagerie:*

   a. the silent beginning of Scene 2
   b. Tom's exit from Scene 3
   c. the silent opening of Scene 4
   d. the slient scene in Scene 4 prior to Tom's apology

11. Select a long speech by your study character and deliver it while

   a. doing a jigsaw puzzle
   b. dressing or undressing
   c. setting a table
   d. threading a needle and mending some cloth

Let the actions affect the phrasing and psychophysical life of your character.

SUMMARY

Physical character emerges from the psychological character as you use stored observations, freewheeling imagination, and diligent experimentation to externalize the character. To these discoveries you apply a sense of timing and rhythm to move your character into the realm of art. But as Jose Quintero reminds us, the art of physical characterization begins in life:

> If you are going into the theatre you must understand that your identity is made up of everything that you have seen or heard. You are a composite. The ability to be a beggar, a lottery ticket salesman, an usher in a theatre, a

waiter in a restaurant, the King of Persia, a Japanese, an African, a Caucasian, is not known to your head, but to your whole body. You must know how it feels to wear white gloves and Edwardian pumps. How it feels to have no gloves at all and to walk down Eighth Street with boots that you bought at the Salvation Army, already ragged with holes, so that in the morning you head to the nearest garbage can, and search for a copy of a newspaper to stuff ever so gently into the shoes to cover the holes. No acting teacher, no speech teacher, no right-walking and sitting-down teacher can teach you that.[14]

EXERCISES

1. Choose a scene from *The Glass Menagerie* or a study play and consider the rhythm of your character by playing the scene first with a metronome for each character and then without the metronomes. Experiment to find an appropriate rhythm for your character in the circumstances of the scene.

2. Repeat your study scene with attention on the three types of movement—preliminary, arrested, and suspended—discussed in Part I of this book.

3. Play your study scene silently, saying the lines to yourself. Observe your physical actions. Simplify and clarify your movement. Time your actions to those of the other characters. If you find yourself "face acting," repeat the scene silently while wearing a mask.

NOTES

[1]Kalter, *Actors on Acting*, pp. 50–51.

[2]Eugene O'Neill, "A Dramatist's Notebook (1933)." Used with permission of Yale University Library as legatee under the will of Carlotta Monterey O'Neill.

[3]Bari Rolfe, *Behind the Mask* (Oakland, Calif.: Persona Books, 1977), p. 11.

[4]Ibid., p. 14.

[5]Benoit Constant Coquelin, "Acting and Actors," *Harper's*, May 1877.

[6]Alexander Tairov, *Notes of a Director* (Coral Gables, Fl.: University of Miami Press, 1969), p. 125.

[7]Lewis Funke and John E. Booth, eds., *Actors Talk About Acting* (New York: Random House, 1961) Copyright © 1961 by Lewis Funke and John E. Booth.

[8]James Penrod, *Movement for the Performing Artist*. Used with permission of Mayfield Publishing Company. Copyright © 1974 by James Penrod.

[9]Suggested by a list in Penrod's *Movement for the Performing Artist*.

[10]Kalter, *Actors on Acting*, p. 78.

[11]John Lahr and Jonathan Price, *Life Show* (New York: Viking Press, 1973), p. 88. Quoted by permission of the author.

[12]Burton, *Great Acting*, p. 130.

[13]Jose Quintero, *If You Don't Dance They Beat You* (Boston: Little, Brown, 1974), p. 63.

[14]Ibid.

11

Vocal Character

Speech is the mirror of the soul; as a man speaks, so is he.

—Publilius Syrus

A character is made up of his sayings and doings. Not only from *what* a character says, but also from *how* he speaks does an audience learn the psychological composition of a character. Conversely, a character's vocal identity is the outgrowth of his pyschological constitution or personality, his physical qualities, and his present circumstances. In consequence, the study of a character's psychological and physical life could have already created ideas in you about your voice.

Examination of the words and rhythms of a text helps you capture the appropriate vocal play of your character. Remember that natural speech is not the actor's goal; on the contrary, the actor uses his vocal technique and understanding of the character's words and situation to create the *illusion* of natural speech. To further this goal, you would do well to begin by following the advice of the noted acting teacher, Robert Lewis.

> We don't want to admire acting at the expense of the dialogue. You have to be very careful that you build the dialogue up with all your work on the subtext, the characterization, the emotion. And each time you work on one of these elements, use it to make the words that much clearer, not that much vaguer. . . .[1]

PRELIMINARY STEPS

If the investigation of your character's psychological and physical aspects hasn't prompted you to construct a characteristic voice, then such work must involve conscious effort. Every character, like every person, has distinct vocal traits. One way to begin to characterize your voice is to repeat the *metaphor absorption* technique, this time focusing on the sound qualities and associations of the object or animal:

1. Study the animal or object closely, attending to your sensory reactions.
2. What sounds does the animal or object make? What sounds could it make? Make sounds like the object does or could make. How would you sing if you were the object? How would you laugh or cry? If you were a human being with these vocal qualities, how would you talk, sing, yell, whisper, laugh, or cry?
3. How would you sound as the character, if the character had these vocal qualities?
4. Read some of your character's lines with these vocal qualities.

Another technique for exploring the vocal side of a character is to experiment with various optimum pitches, volumes, and rates, to find a combination which seems to capture the essence of your character's personality. Remember to establish and rehearse a volume level appropriate to your character *on stage* rather than in the rehearsal room.

EXERCISES

1. Using a character from *The Glass Menagerie* or a study play, absorb metaphorical qualities from an animal or object closely associated with your character. Use the suggested four-step process as your guide.

2. With a sentence from one of your study character's speeches, experiment with a variety of optimum pitch/volume/rate combinations. Tape record each variation for playback and evaluation.

Working on the Vocal Score

Working on a text can seem dull and inartistic, but the labor is necessary before subsequent creativity can begin. You must know what you are saying and how to say it correctly. Thus, a dictionary should accompany your check of unfamiliar words for definition and pronunciation. The structure of the speeches should be understood, and significant figures of speech noted. With this preliminary work behind, you can move to phrasing and pausing.

Paraphrasing can often help you phrase your speeches. Sometimes paraphrasing helps you empathize with the subtextual level of various long speeches, common expressions, and complicated sentences.

Original:
RODERIGO: Tush! Never tell me? I take it much unkindly That thou, Iago, who hast had my purse As if the strings were thine, should'st know of this.

IAGO: 'Sblood, but you'll not hear me! If ever I did dream of such a matter, Abhor me.

Paraphrase:

RODERIGO: Damn it! I can't believe you kept this from me! You, Iago, whom I let take whatever money you needed! You knew!

IAGO: Jesus Christ, there's no use in talking to you! If I so much as thought of such a thing . . . hate my guts.

Paraphrasing changes the words of a character to clarify meaning and intention.

EXERCISES

1. Choose a scene or a long speech from *The Glass Menagerie* or a study play and check the definition and pronunciation of each unfamiliar word. Write out the lines using the International Phonetic Alphabet (see Appendix D).

2. Paraphrase your lines from the preceding exercise. Practice the scene using the paraphrase, gradually introducing the actual words of the text until you are using the exact wording.

THE POETIC CHARACTER

Nothing can panic the young actor so much as the prospect of playing a character whose lines are written in poetry. Poetry and the theatre were inseparable for most of the theatre's history, yet today poetry puts off many potentially fine actors. Perhaps poetic drama is associated with the hollow, bombastic histrionics of the worst nineteenth century acting. Perhaps *poetic* and *real* are seen as opposite rather than as complementary modes. Perhaps actors are confused by the many notions of not only how to act in the poetic drama but also of what poetry is!

Definitions of poetry abound. Coleridge said that "prose is words in their best order," while "poetry is the best words in their best order." Tennyson considered poetry "the Rhythmical Creation of Beauty." Emily Dickinson said that she knew she was reading poetry "if I feel physically as if the top of my head were taken off." Poetry seems to be, like beauty, in the eye of the beholder.

You should begin by considering poetic language to be the logical expression of a poetic character. Just as everyday prose is "natural" for an everyday character, poetry is "natural" for a character who has a different' view of what it means to exist as a human being on earth. The poetic conception of self and circumstance is the subject for the psychological analysis of character, so you should take language into account when constructing a psychological basis for a poetic character. Create a psychological and physical character for whom poetic diction would be the only natural and logical method of expression. With such a beginning, the technique for speaking the verse should seem relatively easy.

Actors usually consider poetic drama to be poetry with a regular rhythm, sometimes known as *verse*. All language has rhythm, based on a system of stressed (′) and unstressed (-) syllables. Take the last sentence, for instance, and notice the pattern of accent:

All language has a rhythm, based on a system of stressed and unstressed syllables.

To read that sentence aloud with meaning, the voice naturally emphasizes certain sound units and de-emphasizes others.

When the emphases of language are regularized, verse emerges.

Humpty Dumpty sat on a wall

Humpty Dumpty had a great fall

All the King's Horses and all the King's Men

Couldn't put Humpty together again

The regularity of stress gives the language a musical and rhythmic quality. When language does not provide a continuous tonal stress pattern, rests of silence fill in the meter.

Old King Cole was a merry old soul

And a merry old soul, was he; ____

He called for his pipe and he called for his bowl,

And he called for his fiddlers three. ____

The words between the accents are compressed or extended so that the accent rhythm remains steady.

With a sense of poetry's musicality, you are ready, as the poet and playwright W. B. Yeats tells us, to develop an ability to speak verse:

> The sing-song in which a child says a verse is a right beginning, though the child grows out of it. An actor should understand how so to discriminate

cadence from cadence, and so to cherish the musical lineaments of verse or prose that he delights the ear with a continually varied music.[2]

The great English actor, Sir John Gielgud echoes this poet's concern:

Actors are so often unmusical, and often, too, the rhythm of the verse turns to a singsong and the meaning is obscured. Or they break up every speech with realistic pauses and breaks to give the illusion of spontaneous thought. This is equally fatal. The phrasing and rhythm and pace should support one, as water does a swimmer, and should be handled with the same skill and pace.[3]

According to Dame Edith Evans, the accentuation provided by the verse can help you speak the lines:

You learn to go from emphatic word to emphatic word like springboards, and when you want to slow up you lean on them a bit. Once you know about that, it's ordinary talk really, it's life, it's the way we talk. After all, we don't emphasize every word when we talk do we?[4]

Speaking Verse

In speaking verse, avoid extremes. Your goal is neither to make the audience forget you are speaking poetry, nor is it to remind them of the fact. Rather your goal is to make the poetry seem natural for the character and the situation. A character for whom poetic utterance seems necessary must exist in circumstances which seem to require poetic utterance. Delivery should have a rapid and nimble articulation, a subtle and supple rhythm, and a sustained resonance, *all the while avoiding the impression that the words are memorized or that they are the result of spur of the moment musing.* Lord Laurence Olivier describes how he found the key:

It was Michel St. Denis who put it into words for me when I was working with him on *Macbeth*. He said, "It must be absolutely true, and you must find the truth *through* the verse, and you must not discard the verse and pretend it's prose, and you mustn't be carried away by the verse into utter unreality; therefore, you must find the truth *through* the verse.[5]

To avoid pausing at the end of each line to maintain a sense of form and to keep clear of slurring the verse structure to make it sound "real," author Robert Hillyer suggests a rule to follow when a thought continues into the next line: "Draw out the last syllable of the first line; then *without pause or change of pitch,* launch into the second line."[6]

EXERCISES

1. Choose a long speech from a verse play. Say the lines naturally for meaning and natural stress. Underline the key words. Place the modifiers in parentheses.

2. Speak your practice speech emphasizing the rhythm as much as possible. Sing the speech as opera. Paraphrase the speech and speak your paraphrase as a realistic speech.

3. Deliver the speech following Dame Edith Evans's suggestion, Lord Olivier's advise, and Mr. Hillyer's rule. Speak for the sense of what you are saying with an awareness of the rhythm.

4. Identify the sense images—sights, sounds, smells, tactile sensations, temperatures, tastes, and movements—in your practice speech. Recite the speech experiencing each sensation as you speak of it. Create in your listeners the same sensations described by the language.

DIALECTS

Dialects are regional usages and pronunciations of language. Playwrights or actors sometimes decide that a particular character should have a distinct manner of speaking. Often Americans feel compelled to use a British accent when playing English plays, although they feel no such need when playing Norwegian, Spanish, or Italian dramas. Common dialects include Southern, Yankee, Bronx, Cockney, and Irish.

When considering a dialect, take care; they can be large problems for beginning actors. Usually the less an actor knows about dialect, the thicker he makes it. However, if you must use a dialect, the best method of perfecting one is to visit the actual region where it is used and watch and listen to the natives. Often short wave radio broadcasts can provide examples of native dialects. Phonograph records, dialect dictionaries using the International Phonetic Alphabet, and phonetics records and texts offer less desirable alternatives. Practice your dialect in restaurants, stores, and other public places. Remember that characters, like people, try *not* to have an accent rather than try to *have* one.

SUMMARY

A review of your work on vocal score shows the following phases of work:

1. Assume characteristic pitch, volume and rate.
2. Check pronunciations and definitions.
3. Paraphrase to clarify subtextual dynamics.

4. Locate key words and parenthetical modifiers.
5. Enjoy the sensations of utterance.

EXERCISES

1. Choose a scene from *The Glass Menagerie* or a nonverse study play and examine a character's vocal life using the suggested steps.

2. Choose a scene from a verse drama and examine a character's vocal life using the suggested steps.

3. Choose a scene from a dialect play[7] and examine a character's vocal life using the suggested steps.

4. Sometimes a character's vocal life becomes stale if you anticipate the justifications for your lines. To combat this tendency and to discover new insights and adaptations, play your lines against those of another actor from a scene in another play. You will both need to listen carefully. Your goal is to justify each of your lines in light of each preceding line. React to what you hear as the character and then adapt your own line as logically as possible. This exercise is similar to actors' experience with *sides*—pages of text with only your part and a few cue words. With sides, reactions and adaptations are usually fresher for at least the first few rehearsals.

NOTES

[1]Robert Lewis, *Advice to the Players* (New York: Harper & Row Pubs., 1980), p. 142.

[2]W. B. Yeats, "The Reform of the Theatre," in *Plays and Controversies* (New York: Macmillan, 1924), pp. 45–49.

[3]Funke and Booth, *Actors Talk About Acting*, p. 17.

[4]Burton, *Great Acting*, p. 130.

[5]Ibid., p. 18.

[6]Robert Hillyer, "On Reading Verse Aloud," Copyright © 1939 by *The Atlantic Monthly Company*, Boston, Mass. Reprinted with permission.

[7]Dialect scenes can be found in the plays of Tennessee Williams, Sean O'Casey, Paul Green, G. B. Shaw, and Eugene O'Neill.

PART FOUR

PLAYING IN THE THEATRE

There I was, the promising young actor, and, being filled with rapture and bliss, and a youthful sense of the dramatic, I got down on my knees and begged her to marry me. And she? . . . She said: "Give up the theatre!"

—Vassily Vassilyitch Svetlovidov speaking of his beloved
(in a scene from *Swan Song*)[1]

Man plays only when he is man in the full sense of the word and he is totally man only when he plays.

—Schiller

Style

Style is not something superficial or merely external.

—Michel St. Denis[2]

Actors can waste many hours pointlessly arguing about style in acting. Everyone either argues about what style *is* or insists that there is no such thing as style.

Style is what you end up with, not something for which you strive. Every actor has style; every play has style; every production has style. It may be pleasing or offensive, appropriate or incorrect, but like it or not, everything which moves has its own style. A well-trained actor can use his internal and external technique, and his ability to analyze a play, to work with a variety of directors' ideas of style in a wide array of plays. When confronted by questions of style you would do well to ignore them. A consideration of the inner nature of your vocal, physical, and mental techniques of playing, a thorough analysis of the play text, and an imaginative characterization through psychology, voice, and movement will give you an appropriate style.

WHAT IS STYLE?

Style is not posing, affectation, or elegance. Style is a function of the whole structure of a performance. Long ago I heard Professor Hubert Heffner predict that one day I would encounter people who said that they "just didn't know what style meant, anyway," and that "there is no such thing as style." He told me and the other students to tell such people that *we* knew: "*Style is the way in which means are related to manner.* In acting the manner is the imaginative embodiment and rendering of a personality. The means are the visual and vocal traits and devices which serve to individualize that personality."[3]

Every individual has a distinct style. And every actor's personal style should be clear enough to distinguish his individuality yet pliable enough to respond to a variety of influencing performance conditions. Historian Garff Wilson describes this unique mixture of personality and malleability:

> Nature supplies an actor with certain basic endowments of body and voice, mind and spirit. These are the raw materials out of which he shapes his art. His training and experience, molding his natural endowments, occurring in a particular social and aesthetic milieu, and applied to a particular role in a particular play presented in a particular playhouse, will determine his style.[4]

Wilson's concise description suggests a number of external factors which contribute to an actor's performance style.

THE CIRCUMSTANCES OF PERFORMANCE

When discussing human action in Part I and character action in Parts II and III, the circumstances of the moment were found to be paramount in determining the action. The moment-by-moment *circumstances of dramatic action* constitute the first and dominant part of the *circumstances of performance.* You need not consciously analyze these circumstances as meticulously as you did the circumstances of action. You must, however, be aware of and sensitive to the effect they will have on your performance. Three factors constitute the basic *circumstances of performance:*

1. Circumstances of character action
2. Director
3. Playing space

The first of these has been discussed earlier; let us turn our attention to the remaining two aspects.

The Director Determines the Style

For better or for worse, in the contemporary theatre the stage director determines the *mise en scène* or style of the whole production. All designers and actors work within his understanding and interpretation not only of the play but also of the historical period in which it was written. Each director has his own notion of Greek style, Elizabethan style, and Restoration style. Consequently you must catch on to each individual director's vision of period style. Each director decides which *conventions*—theatrical assumptions, givens, or rules—from an historical period to use in his production. Some directors use masks in Greek tragedy, others don't. Some directors cast all men to play Shakespeare, others use women. Some directors ignore the historical setting of both play and playwright and opt for an historical period of their own choosing! Some directors mix the conventions of a variety of historical periods in one production!

If this weren't enough, the contemporary director has even more options with which to "stylize" (whatever that means) his production. *Expressionism, impressionism, constructivism, surrealism, futurism, cubism, dadaism, naturalism, realism, romanticism, symbolism, and theatricalism* may be clear in an historical context, but they become semantic hobgoblins when applied to practical production concerns. Add to these "isms" various directors' conceptions of epic, Brechtian, Artaudian, environmental, and multimedia approaches to theatre and the actor's dilemma increases. What are you to do? First, analyze the moments of dramatic circumstance; second, listen carefully to the director; and third, examine the playing space.

The Playing Space Affects Style

If the choice of directorial approach to a play is beyond the actor's control, adaptability to performance space isn't. Plays have been and continue to be produced almost everywhere. From outdoor amphitheatres to garages, barges, streets, and living rooms, every space is ripe for some director's production. You need the ability to adapt your performance technique to the variables of the playing space.

Certainly a different technique is called for if the auditorium holds 15 or 15,000, if the audience is above or below, if the spectators are near or far, or if the performance is indoors or outdoors. A flexible actor can and must maximize the impact of his performance regardless of the performance circumstances.

What, then, can you do to prepare for the smorgasbord of theatrical styles on which you may be asked to dine? It seems to me that an actor should work to extend the techniques already explored in this book to a variety of performance circumstances. Exercise to broaden the use of your voice, movement, stage business, position on stage, and costume and makeup.

The following exercises can begin this growth. In each, determine:

1. The actor's use of voice—ordinary, artificial, declamatory, chanted, sung.
2. The actor's use of movement—ordinary, simplified, detailed, exaggerated, dancelike.
3. The actor's use of stage business—detailed, archetypal, nonexistent.

4. The actor's physical relationship with the audience—direct, indirect, close, far, above, below, before, among.
5. The actor's use of costume and make-up—ordinary, fantastic, contemporary, historical, symbolic, exaggerated, nonexistent.

EXERCISES

1. Research the performance circumstances of the fifth century B.C. Greek theatre. Arrange a physical approximation of those circumstances and perform a Greek monologue or scene within those conditions. In what ways are the performance circumstances perfect for the text? In what ways did the playwright exploit the performance circumstances in writing the text? Remember to begin your work with an analysis of the dramatic circumstances of the character. Extend your characterization to exploit the performance circumstances. Notice how the circumstances dictate many of your choices. The following books can aid your research:

Arnott, Peter. *Greek Scenic Conventions of the Fifth Century, B.C.*
Barton, Lucy. *Historic Costume for the Stage.*
Brockett, Oscar G. *History of the Theatre.*
Nicoll, Allardyce. *The Development of the Theatre.*
Webster, T. B. L. *Greek Theatre Production.*

2. Repeat the previous exercise for the performance circumstances of the Elizabethan theatre. The following books can help your research:

Barton, Lucy. *Historic Costume for the Stage.*
Beckerman, Bernard. *Shakespeare at the Globe.*
Brockett, Oscar G. *History of the Theatre.*
Nagler, A. M. *Shakespeare's Stage.*
Nicoll, Allardyce. *The Development of the Theatre.*
Styan, J. L. *Shakespeare's Stagecraft.*

3. Repeat the exercise for the performance circumstances of the Restoration theatre. The following books can help your research:

Barton, Lucy. *Historic Costume for the Stage.*
Brockett, Oscar G. *History of the Theatre.*
Hotson, Leslie. *The Commonwealth and Restoration Stage.*
Lynch, James J. *Box, Pit, and Gallery.*
Summers, Montague. *The Playhouse of Pepys.*
    The Restoration Theatre.

NOTES

[1] Anton Chekov, *Swan Song* in *The Brute and Other Farces,* Eric Bentley and Theodore Hoffman, ed. (New York: Samuel French, 1958), p. 15.

[2] St. Denis, *Theatre: The Rediscovery of Style,* p. 61.

[3] Hubert C. Heffner, Samuel Selden, and Hunton D. Sellman, *Modern Theatre Practice,* 5th ed. (Englewood Cliffs, N.J.: Prentice-Hall, 1973), p. 250.

[4] Garff B. Wilson, *A History of American Acting* (Bloomington, Ind.: Indiana University Press, 1966), p. 13.

13

Glossary of Stage Terms

I hate definitions.

—Benjamin Disraeli

Hate them or not, definitions are necessary for the actor to communicate efficiently in the theatre. The terms in this chapter are given their common explanation; certain regions or companies may have their own variations.

acting area   the part of the stage used for playing a scene.

apron   the part of a stage which projects beyond the proscenium arch and into the auditorium.

arena stage   a stage surrounded on all sides by the audience.

aside   a short line of dialogue delivered to the audience unbeknown to the other characters.

blocking   planned movement and stage composition developed during early rehearsals.

body positions   the degree to which the actor's torso is "open" to the audience in a proscenium stage theatre.

 full front: the actor's torso and head directly facing the audience.

 one-quarter: the actor 45 degrees away from the audience.

 profile: the actor's side toward the audience.

 full-back: the actor's back toward the audience.

 three-quarter: the actor halfway between full-back and profile positions.

build   increase rate, volume, and/or intensity of vocal or physical play to a climax.

business   invented physical actions usually involving properties, costumes, or other actors.

center line   an imaginary line at the center of the stage drawn between the footlights and the back wall.

cheat   open the body position more than necessary to perform an action so that the audience can see better.

close in   turn the body away from the audience.

FIGURE 13-1: Basic body positions.

company   the people involved in the production of a play.

countercross   a few steps taken in the opposite direction of the actor making the main cross. The countercrossing actor usually moves at a slower rate while keeping his focus on the crossing actor. *CX*

cover   (a) to block someone or something from view by being downstage of it, (b) to invent business or dialogue to disguise an error in performance.

cross   approach someone or something by moving toward it. *X*

cue   a signal for vocal or physical action.

curtain line   the last line of dialogue in a scene or act.

double   play more than one character in a play.

ensemble   a company whose playing is characterized by unity and balanced technique.

fake   pretend an action which would not be feasible, such as drinking poison or stabbing someone.

fourth wall   the imaginary fourth wall of a three sided set through which the audience views the play.

freeze   stop all movement.

gabbling   "the verbal transference of memorized lines between persons who, though they are facing each other and standing in good light, are not really seeing each other at all."[1]

give stage   allow another actor to attract the audience's focus of attention.

green room   the place where actors wait to be called to the stage.

indicating   demonstrating an attitude or emotion.

kill   to remove or eliminate, such as "kill a laugh."

mug   exaggerate facial actions to indicate an emotion.

open turn   a turn made toward the audience.

open up   turn more of the torso and face toward the audience.

overplay   give a line or action greater emphasis.

point   emphasize a particular word or action.

prompt   supply an actor with forgotten, missed, or corrected lines.

proscenium stage   a raised stage with the audience facing one side and watching the action as through a picture frame (the *proscenium arch*).

share   play on the same plane in equal body positions with a partner. Both actors are equally open to the audience.

soliloquy   a long speech delivered to the audience by an actor alone on stage.

stage areas   the geographical divisions of a stage floor.

stage positions   the geographical locations on the stage floor.

   right or left stage: the actor's right or left as he faces audience.

   downstage: toward the audience.

   upstage: away from the audience.

   above: upstage of.

   below: downstage of.

FIGURE 13-2: Stage areas.

steal   move inconspicuously from one point on the stage to another.

steal a scene   draw disproportionate attention to oneself to the detriment of the ensemble.

take stage   assume a strong body position or move to an emphatic stage area to attract the focus of the audience's attention.

telescope   pick up cues before they have been sent, to overlap action or dialogue, building a scene to a climax.

throw away   underplay the significance of a line or action.

top   build upon a preceding line or action by performing one's own action with greater volume, rate, or intensity.

underplay   give a line or action less emphasis.

upstage   take the audience's attention away from where it should be by assuming an upstage position, forcing the focal actor into a closed position. Avoid upstaging by playing on the same plane as your partner.

wings   offstage areas, left and right on a proscenium stage.

FIGURE 13-3:   A curtain call.

NOTE

[1]Charles Marowitz, *Stanislavski and the Method,* p. 64.

14

Working in the Theatre

*The theatre is play, in which inspiration and child-like wonder
are more important than sweat and tantrums.*

—Jean Vilar[1]

The actor is never alone. Even in a one-character play the actor works as
a part of a production team. Your work in developing your skills in acting
would be wasted if you could not function as part of this team. In this
chapter the work of the actor exists as part of a larger process—the process
of creating a theatrical work of art.

AUDITIONING

Auditions are distasteful to all concerned. Actors dislike the business of
revealing themselves for evaluation and probable rejection; directors endure endless numbered names of would-be actors eager for one particular
role. However, auditions must be endured and mastered before you can
practice your craft as an actor.

Directors look for specific qualities when casting a play or company.
If auditioning for a company, the qualities are more general than for a
specific role in a play. Physical appearance, voice and diction, a sense of
movement and rhythm, audience appeal, projection, and evidence of technique—intelligence, experience, responsiveness, sensibility, openness,
imagination—matter to directors and audiences alike. You should prepare
to present yourself displaying the qualities a director wants to see. You
should have several audition pieces ready to perform. They should be of

a variety of period and form—classical and modern, serious and comic, poetry and prose. Most important, they should be pieces which you enjoy doing and which show you off to best advantage. You get no credit for play selection! *Do only what you do best, no matter how simple or easy; your goal is to look better than everyone else auditioning by being not just very good, but by being terrific!*

Compose your audition carefully:

1. Time each piece to a maximum of two minutes.
2. Choose roles in your age range.
3. Avoid dialects or accents.
4. Cut or construct your material—cut problem lines, combine speeches.
5. Find unfamiliar material from novels, magazines, anything unique. Consider writing your own material.
6. Avoid climactic or intense speeches.
7. Determine your volume ahead of time. Louder than necessary is preferable.
8. Choose self-explanatory material. Say only your name and the title of your scene.
9. Rehearse your demeanor, walks onto and off of the stage, transitions, and final thank-you.
10. Take and dominate the stage with geniality rather than gregariousness. Assume a businesslike yet charming attitude.
11. Rehearse everywhere, for everyone, at anytime until you are absolutely confident.

A serious auditioner should have Michael Shurtleff's *Audition* on his bookshelf.

Occasionally a director asks you to read from the play being cast or to perform an improvisation. Try to read the play ahead of time so that when reading, you can talk the lines and listen to your partner. Use your partner's line readings as motivations for your own readings. If asked to improvise, you will probably be evaluated as to some evidence of imagination, the ability to invent objectives and pursue them, an uninhibited willingness to share your privacy in public, and a responsiveness to the director and other actors.

REHEARSALS

Rehearsal is the time for the actor to discover the character and to reveal the character through action. Psychological development occurs as the actor becomes the character through action. The actor learns the mental, physical, and vocal life of the character in particular situations. Director Richard Schechner identifies a basic rehearsal fact:

Rehearsal is a way of making unknown material (the play to be performed) so familiar to the actors that the audience can successfully believe that what they see is a way of living. The professional actor is a person who is skilled in this kind of magic deception; or invocation of belief.[2]

Experimentation and repetition constitute the hallmarks of the rehearsal process. Actors experiment at home and test the results of their experimentation with their co-workers. At least 60 percent of an actor's work occurs at home. Rehearsals clarify problems which the actor needs to solve at home. The actor comes to rehearse with particular goals. The four or five weeks of rehearsal time is precious and must be used efficiently. To maximize his effectiveness, the actor is punctual, healthy, rested, and cooperative.

The director sets the schedule, tone, and methodology of rehearsal. You should have a technique adaptable to the most and to the least helpful directors. A typical rehearsal schedule is composed of reading, blocking, experimentation, runthrough, technical, dress, and preview phases.

Reading Rehearsals

At the initial rehearsals the actors read the play or listen to the play read to them by the director or playwright. You should have read the script before the first rehearsal. When reading the text, *talk* your lines rather than act them; speak the lines as if you are having a conversation. Read to see how you affect the person to whom you are speaking. Listen purposefully.

After reading the play, the director and actors discuss the play. The director will speak of the play—the kind of play it is, its importance or relevance, his interpretation—and then try to initiate discussion. The director wants to excite you about the play. Often subsequent readings are interrupted for discussions of meaning, definition, ideas about character, comments on tone or style. Designers may present sketches of costumes or a model or groundplan of the setting. Whatever happens at these rehearsals, speak only when you need to speak; don't try to impress everyone, and especially don't debate!

Blocking Rehearsals

At some point discussion will end and you will find yourself standing on stage or in a rehearsal room with the setting's outlines painted or taped on the floor. A first concern in staging a play is the actors' positions or placement in relationship to the setting and other actors. This *blocking* is either provided by the director or is the result of actors' trial and error. Each director has his own method of achieving blocking.

You must motivate and justify each piece of blocking given by the director, even though the primary reason for the movement or position may be stage composition, balance, emphasis, or stability. If the director encourages experimentation in blocking, you can be guided by the actions inherent in your subtext. In any case, record the blocking in your script with a pencil.

Experimentation Rehearsals

Gradually attention turns from your position on stage to actualizing the ideas you have come upon while doing homework on the psychological, vocal, and physical aspects of your character. Homework doesn't produce products to display to your director and fellow actors; rather, homework leads to an experiment you wish to conduct at the next rehearsal. The results of your experiments are the materials for subsequent homework—adaptation, adjustment, modification, abandonment, reinvention—based upon the reactions of the other characters and the director.

Try everything! Beginning actors are often timid about trying things; they wait to be given things by the director. Experienced actors are occasionally reluctant to try anything new; they prefer to repeat past performance highlights in different costumes and with other lines. Both kinds of actors are on the road to obscurity. On the other hand, directors don't want actors whose sole goal is to be unprecedented; these actors often neglect to consider that certain things haven't been tried because they are either wrong or not worth trying! Directors tend to prefer actors whose invention abounds within an intelligent understanding of the play. Within a thorough understanding and appreciation of the text, a fearless actor can and will delight his director by trying things he has never done before and even things he fears he cannot do. Even try things you think may be wrong; soon you will know for sure. Actress Helen Hayes believes in this dauntless approach to acting:

> Do anything, do anything that comes to your mind, but don't ever allow yourself to be afraid to try things, because it just might be that something glorious will come out. Of course, nine times out of ten it's terrible. That's what I mean by the process of elimination: I do all the wrong things, and then I finally get down to maybe what's right—I hope.[3]

You must trust the director not to let you make a foolish choice your final choice. Without painful trial and error, you will probably make safe, clichéd, and tired choices about your character. With daring experimentation, you can make exciting final choices about your character.

Actors and directors have a variety of ideas about when and how to memorize lines. For some actors memorization comes easily; for others it is a tedious, frustrating, and embarrassing process. P. Kabanov, the director of the Gorki Museum of Moscow Art Theatre wrote to tell me of Stanislavski and memorization: "In rare instances he wrote in on the margins first letters of words of the text of a role for easier memorization."[4] Even the master resorted to a kind of rote learning process!

Some actors memorize their lines before rehearsals begin. The advantage of this approach is that it leaves you free from the temptation to hide behind your script. With lines memorized at the beginning, you are immediate master of the lines. Actors who prefer to delay memorization do so until shortly after the blocking is established. Lines are easier to remember when associated with movement or stage position. Delayed memorization also eliminates the possibility of memorizing superficial perceptions and interpretative readings with the words before experimentation has begun.

Your relationship with the director is critical in the experimentation phase of the rehearsal period. Rehearsal strategy should account for a wide array of directors. Every director represents the audience as he tells you of your experiments' effectiveness. Some tell and show you more than you'd like, others less than you'd want. Some allow great freedom, others dictate every movement and intonation. Whatever a director does or doesn't do should not affect your attitude toward your work. Don't argue with a director about his methods; if you cannot work with him, resign your role.

Directors will give you notes or comments on your work. Some may seem unfair—too few, too many, too harsh. At such times try to remember that directors want to suit the quality of their notes to the individuality of each actor. Whatever notes are given should be recorded in your script or notebook for part of your homework. Review the notes just prior to the next rehearsal; directors do not like to give the same note twice!

Your fellow actors should be treated as you would like them to treat you. This simple watchword is too easily dismissed. Personal etiquette among actors is imperative to successful rehearsing. A few suggestions can put you on the right track:

1. Never offer suggestions or criticisms to another actor. If you have any, give them privately to the director to do with what he will.
2. Leave your personal problems at the stage door. Rehearsals are not singles' bars or group therapy sessions!
3. Don't prompt. There is a prompter or stage manager to do that.
4. If you are part of a company, welcome newcomers. Longevity is not a sign of superiority.

Rehearsals can be either a rewarding experience or a tedious and traumatic nightmare. More advice can diminish the likelihood of the latter:

1. Arrive early to warm-up your body and voice and to prepare your psychological framework. Late actors upset everyone.

2. Welcome accidents. Use whatever happens. Often unexpected discoveries result from chance occurrences.

3. Don't assume you know what others will do at any moment. Believe that whatever your fellow actors do is a deliberate choice designed to test your character's reaction.

4. Forget about finding the right way. In acting there are just millions of wrong ways, some less objectionable than others.

5. Use your offstage time to work on your role. Jokes, school work, and gossip are not appropriate between-scenes activities.

6. Have patience; you can't be great all at once.

7. If you have something new to try, try it; don't tell the director about it first. Your actions will speak more clearly and efficiently than your words.

8. If you get bored on stage, do something exciting.

9. When you are not alone on stage, use those around you.

10. Expose unknown aspects of yourself. No one will believe it is you; they will think you are just "acting."

11. Great acting is over-acting without getting caught. Dare the outrageous rather than the safe. If you *believe* in what you do, others probably will.

12. Without tremendous blunders you will never achieve tremendous successes.

Runthrough Rehearsals

The time will come when the director will want to run the entire play without stop. He wants to see how the whole looks after seeing only its parts. Needless to say, experimentation should stop and final choices emerge. This type of rehearsal allows you to sense your role as a whole, to begin to pace yourself for the demands of a two- or three-hour performance. Rhythm and tempo are most important in these rehearsals. Expect to get notes about cues, pauses, and timing.

Technical Rehearsals

Shortly before opening night, scenery, properties, lighting, and sound will be added to the rehearsals. The goal in these rehearsals is to coordinate the actors with the technical aspects of the production. Continuity is almost impossible. These rehearsals can be tedious but they are extremely important tests of everyone's good humor. Use these rehearsals as extended exercises in concentration. Remain quiet and cooperative.

Dress Rehearsals

This rehearsal adds costume and makeup to the production. Ideally, the dress rehearsal is a performance without an audience. Everything should be as it will be on opening night. The stage manager has by now become a more dominant figure than the director. Do whatever he tells you. You may hear the amateur's consolation, "A bad dress rehearsal means a good show." This saying was undoubtedly coined by a director who misrehearsed his play.

Previews

These are performances of the play for invited or discount audiences before the play officially opens. Previews combine features of dress rehearsals and performances; the company can accomplish last minute changes and adjust the play's rhythm to a live audience.

Reviews of a production occasionally appear at the close of previews. You should welcome reviews. Reviews can be used to develop your confidence. Actors tend to easily dismiss negative reviews as the products of prejudiced or ignorant minds, while welcoming positive ones as the results of objective and sagacious oracles. *Both kinds of reviews need to be ignored.* Your success as an actor does not rest in the hands of another person. As Laurence Olivier is credited with remarking, it is easy to dismiss negative reviews but much harder and more important to dismiss the positive ones. You need to develop your own critical sense of your work; you should be able to dislike a performance even though everyone else raves about it and enjoy a performance which others consider abominable.

The ability to objectively monitor one's own work takes years of experience in the theatre. It is a goal which needs to be fixed at the very start of your career. Until that time you can minimize a critic's opportunity to devastate your ego by practicing the basic craft of acting. The distinguished critic John Simon wishes actors would attend more to their craft:

> My point is that craft—to say nothing of art—is way beyond the reach of hordes of practitioners, even though it, unlike art, is teachable and learnable, at least in theory. I do not wish to be unduly dictatorial, but I do wonder why the practice of medicine and law, for example, should legally require the passing of rigorous examinations, whereas acting, like some evangelical ministries, is presumed to be the divine right of every self-anointed or greasepainted nincompoop.[5]

A grossly neglected aspect of the actor's craft is the use of the voice. Proficiency in this fundamental tool can take you a long way with many critics:

> One of the big problems with the training of American actors is that they are not taught to speak verse. An even bigger problem is that they are not taught how to speak. Some of the lesser actors . . . you would not have been able to understand even at a medium-noisey cocktail party. But not one of them knows how to enunciate and project properly; unlike the great English actors who could make the telephone book sound like poetic drama, . . . the rest can make Shakespeare sound like the Brooklyn phone book read over a bad connection.[6]

If you can withstand the sharp attacks of the critics, and if you think you might be interested in a career in the theatre, read Robert Cohen's *Acting Professionally* before going any further with such ruminations.

THE ACTOR'S ETHICS

All that many actors could tell you about ethics in the theatre might be Stanislavski's statement about loving the art in yourself rather than yourself in art. The ethical nature of acting is almost forgotten, even though the roots of the activity reside in the deepest spiritual longings of mankind. Great theatrical periods have always had great overviews of their place in the grand scheme of things. Today talk of ethics in the theatre and of morality in art is not fashionable; such talk is usually associated with fanatics bent on censoring everything which does not conform to their own narrow view of the world. Even so, beginning actors should consider their work from an ethical viewpoint.

Tony-award-winning actor Barnard Hughes explains why one should take into account the ethics of work:

> I think that my work should be a reflection of who I am and what I am—and I don't sell that cheaply in the theatre or anywhere else. Being an actor, after all, is a wonderful, useful, contributing way to spend your life and I think myself very fortunate to have stumbled onto this trick.[7]

Acting is indeed a reflection of the actor. Every actor has the choice to accept or to reject a role. Every role you take reflects on your character. But the reflection doesn't stop there: you-as-character are a reflection of your audience. Like a priest celebrating the Mass, you assume a character to undergo, to suffer, to experience in the place of your audience. You represent Man. By taking certain roles in certain plays, you are suggesting to your audience ways of thinking of themselves. The actor-as-character affects the audience's self-image.

The multi-talented Harold Clurman spoke of the theatre as food for the soul of man, just as beef, ice cream, and pizza are food for the body of man. A balanced diet is needed for healthy bodies and souls. Man cannot live on only beef or only ice cream nor on only tragedy or farce. Just as certain foods are "junk," loaded with additives and chemicals which can cause physical illness and death, certain plays are "junk" containing ingredients which can cause spiritual malaise or death. The actor with a sense of ethical purpose can determine for himself which plays he should or will play, not simply on the basis of the benefit they may provide his personal career, but on the basis of the effect their performance may have on his audience.

Money is more readily available for actors interested in financial profit than for actors interested in the ethical basis of their profession. The history of the theatre contains hundreds of tales of talented actors who sold their skills. Harold Clurman saw many actors fall into the financial trap:

> With the actor, who lives through exhibition, the element of vanity is necessarily strong (and to a large degree, justified), but the problem goes beyond that. For even when the actor is willing to submit to the discipline that bids him submerge himself for the general good, the outside world, not understanding his motives, shames him, gibes at him, and assures him that he is a "sucker" to "fall for that stuff." It doesn't believe in the ideology that inspires the group which has set itself up within (and, despite itself, against) the current. The outside world talks in terms of its own experience or indoctrination and instructs the actor to take care of himself first, last, and all the time.[8]

The actor who takes an ethical approach to his work might rather choose to wait on tables or drive a cab honorably than sell his talent to hawk deodorant or candy-coated cereal.

The pressures on the young, talented actor can be great. Acting skill is not valued in and of itself; acting is seen by family, friends, and agents as a way to succeed in show *business:*

> The world was and still is run by people for whom, whether they admit it or not, know it or not, life is printed on dollar bills. They are the people whose impulse and goal is power, the specific symbol of which is possessions and money. . . . For the rest of the world, whether they confess it or not, the impulse and goal are one of love.[9]

And so the choice we found Emerson proposing to us early in this book comes back—love *or* power, not both. Why, then, should a young actor choose his love for the theatre over all that power and money can provide him? The playwright Herb Gardner answers for many:

> Because it's alive. And because the theatre is alive, exactly what is terrible is wonderful, the gamble, the odds. There is no ceiling on the night and no floor either; there is a chance each time the curtain goes up of glory and disaster, the actors and the audience will take each other somewhere, neither knows where for sure. Alive, one time only, that night. It's alive, has been alive for a few thousand years, and is alive tonight, this afternoon. An audience knows it's the last place they can still be heard, they know the actors can hear them, they make a difference; it's not a movie projector and they are not at home with talking furniture, it's custom work. . . . Home is you can tell your secrets. In a theatre, the ones in the dark and the ones under the lights need each other. For a few hours all of us, the audience, the actor, the writer, we are all a little more real together than we ever were apart. That's the ticket; and that's what the ticket's for![10]

As an actor you inherit a great tradition of men and women who revealed the truths of great playwrights/poets/dreamers. The visions were not always clear or popular but the actors answered their calling. Honor that wonderful heritage by heeding Emerson's challenge:

> You will hear every day the maxims of a low prudence. You will hear that the first duty is to get land and money, place and name. "What is this truth you seek? What is this beauty?" men will ask, with derision. If, nevertheless, God have called any of you to explore truth and beauty, be bold, be firm, be true. When you shall say, "As others do, so will I: I renounce, I am sorry for it, my early visions: I must eat the good of the land, and let learning and romantic expectations go, until a more convenient season;"—then dies the man in you; then once more perish the buds of art, and poetry and science, as they have died already in a thousand thousand men.—Why should you renounce your right to traverse the starlit deserts of truth, for the premature comfort of an acre, house and barn? Truth also has its roof and house and board. *Make yourself necessary to the world, and mankind will give you bread.*

NOTES

[1]Vilar, "Murder of the Director."

[2]Richard Schechner, *Environmental Theater* (New York: Hawthorn/Dutton Books, 1973), pp. 174–175.

[3]Funke and Booth, *Actors Talk About Acting*, p. 61.

[4]Translated by Ellen Chances.

[5]John Simon, "Craft and Art," *New York Magazine*, September 1, 1980, p. 45. Copyright © 1980 by News Group Publications, Inc. Reprinted with the permission of *New York Magazine*.

[6]John Simon, "Come Back, Al Pacino! All Is Forgiven," *New York Magazine*, August 25, 1980, p. 68. Copyright © 1980 by News Group Publications, Inc. Reprinted with the permission of *New York Magazine*.

[7]Kalter, *Actors on Acting*, p. 251.

[8]Harold Clurman, *The Fervent Years* (New York: Knopf, 1957), p. 69.

[9]Ibid., p. 273.

[10]Herb Gardner, *A Thousand Clowns. Thieves. The Goodbye People.* (New York: Doubleday) p. xiii.

APPENDICES

Open Scenes

OPEN SCENE 1

A: Anything
B: No
A: Harder
B: I am
A: Where'd (he/she/it) come from
B: You got me   What should we do
A: Do I have to tell you what you have to
B: Allright   But if any trouble comes of this
A: Just get on with it

    Enough that's enough   We've got other things to do
B: I got so carried away I almost forgot
A: Well don't forget   Here   Take this and let's get going
    We've wasted enough time already   Now what have you got
B: It was with (it/her/him)
A: Well get rid of it and let's go
B: Not so fast I'm not sure if we shouldn't
A: I am
B: But what if
A: Never mind get back to what we started
B: It sure changes things

OPEN SCENE 2

A: Good
B: You didn't want to
A: I'm sorry
B: Oh   I'm sorry
A: Now you won't
B: Thanks

B: Where'd (he/she/it) come from
A: So you got it
B: I haven't been there
A: Then why did (he/she/it) come here
B: (He/she/it) wanted to make sure I guess
A: Well (he/she/it) looks—
B: It's stupid
A: Of course it is   Will you sit down
B: Sorry   There's something I want to ask you
A: I understand
B: Please   I know what I said   It isn't necessary for you to—
A: Really
B: I'll try
A: Good Go

OPEN SCENE 3

A: Whenever, then
B: I need more help
A: Never, never
B: I'm going to find the way
A: You you you you
B: Wait a minute
A: In some way or other
B: For example
A: Not so fast
B: Look at the streets
A: It works in the same way
B: Let me
A: You're finished
B: Now the smoothest
A: America
B: Believe me, I know
A: Where did you get that
B: Here

OPEN SCENE 4

A: They made a million
B: Better look
A: Broadway actress
B: Pay attention
A: I want to get out of the house
B: I

A: The University of Alaska
B: I like my children
A: Common error
B: Maybe
A: Ain't it some kinda world
B: 20 percent off
A: That damn prison
B: Mike has got to do something
A: You know I'd rather have you with me
B: I'll explain
A: Please
B: Oh man, I know you do, you say it out
A: Grin
B: Six great projects
A: Squeeze

OPEN SCENE 5

A: This looks like the place
B: Are you sure
A: Sure I'm sure   Can't you see   It has all the signs
B: I guess so . . . but still—
A: Well   look at this
B: Who are you
C: Guess
A: Don't get smart with me   What are you doing here
B: Yeah   we thought you had—
C: Ah   shut up will you   If I had a dollar for all the times I've had to—
A: Allright   allright   Let's get down to business   We were called and we came   So
C: Yeah   yeah   I guess this is what you're after
A: You're not kidding
B: Wait a minute   I'm not so sure
A: Quiet   Of course that's it   Now let me have it and we can all go home
C: Not so fast   There's one condition
A: What condition   You don't mean
C: Yes, that's exactly what I mean
B: I think all of this has just gone too far
A: Shut up and follow orders
C: That's more like it   A real pleasure doing business with you

OPEN SCENE 6

A: How
B: This looks like it

A: Sure
B: Can't you see   What else could it be
A: I guess so but—Well look at this
B: What is it
A: Guess
B: Don't play games   Where did it come from
A: I thought we had decided to—
B: Shut up   There's more in here
A: Forget it   We can never put—
B: I guess this is what you're after
A: You're not kidding
B: Take your time
A: Let me
B: On one condition
A: I think this has gone far enough
B: That's what you think
A: Look out
B: Now what
A: There has to be a better way
B: Not like that
A: Produce the right one
B: Now you've got it

OPEN SCENE 7

A: Thank you
B: Can you describe the ceiling
A: Old and new
B: The spelling is valid
       I'll bet you called him
C: In intimate connection
A: There are dozens of forms
C: Indeed   Mrs. Engine   is it thus with you
B: Tell us something
C: I never said that
A: Mr. Bing was saying what a good idea it was to have this away from the
       supper room
C: You do love trains   don't you
B: So you'd been to a trial
A: Please
B: I can't talk
A: Try and guess why I'm all dressed up
B: Do you know what this is
C: Oh my Lord   my Lord

OPEN SCENE 8

A: Someone has to just listen
B: That'll be fine
A: A new style labor
B: Many of my people are slaughtered each year
A: So ya say
B: Right here
A: Oh didn't he ramble
B: Oh didn't he ramble
A: Oh didn't he
B: Ramble
A: Oh didn't he
B: Come with me
A: Now come back here
B: Boy
A: If my boy could see me now
B: If that don't beat all
A: No blood
B: We were always kind to
A: Not now
B: Yes
A: Just thought I'd check
B: Forget it   It's been chopped off

OPEN SCENE 9

A: Hello
B: Help your baby learn
C: They like fresh meat
B: It's a sparrow hawk
C: Goof proof
A: They're a better teeth cleaner
A: A jury of twelve decent citizens who voted
B: Full strength
A: Fleecy soft
B: Built right in
A: Smells fresh
C: Go forward   Bluebeard
A: I'm an American just the same
B: So   you're interested in truth
C: Put that down

B: So   you're interested in truth
C: Put that down
A: Put that down
A: Nice arms
B: What

Verb List

abandon
abate
abduct
abide
abscond
abolish
abominate
abort
abound
abrade
abridge
abrogate
absolve
absorb
abstain
abuse
accede
accelerate
accept
acclaim
accommodate
accompany
accost
accumulate
achieve
acknowledge
acquaint
acquiesce
acquire
act
activate
adapt
add

address
adhere
adjust
administer
admire
admit
admonish
adopt
adore
adorn
advance
advertise
advise
advocate
affect
affirm
affix
affront
aggravate
agitate
agonize
agree
aid
ail
aim
air
alarm
alienate
alleviate
allocate
allot
allow
allure

alter
amaze
amble
ambush
amend
amplify
amuse
analyze
anchor
anger
anguish
annihilate
announce
annoy
anoint
answer
antagonize
anticipate
ape
apologize
appall
appeal
appear
appease
applaud
apply
apprehend
approach
appropriate
approve
argue
arise
arm

arouse	babble	bathe
arraign	baby	batten
arrange	back	battle
arrest	back away	bawl
arrive	backbite	bay
articulate	back down	beam
ascend	backfire	bean
ask	back off	bear
assail	back out	beat
assault	backpedal	becalm
assemble	backslap	beckon
assert	backtrack	bedazzle
assign	back up	bedevil
assimilate	badger	bedraggle
assist	bad-mouth	befriend
associate	baffle	befuddle
assuage	bag	beg
assume	bail	begin
assure	bait	begrudge
astonish	balance	behold
astound	balk	belabor
atone	ball up	belch
attach	bamboozle	beleaguer
attack	ban	believe
attain	bandage	belittle
attempt	bandy	bellow
attend	bang	belt
attest	bang away	bemoan
attract	bang up	bend
attribute	banish	berate
augment	banter	bereave
augur	bar	beseech
avenge	bare	beset
aver	barf	besiege
avert	bargain	besmear
avoid	barge	besmirch
avouch	bark	bestow
avow	barrel	bet
await	barricade	betray
awake	barter	bewilder
awaken	bash	bewitch
award	bask	bid
ax	baste	bind

bitch
bite
blab
blare
blast
blaze
bleat
bleed
blemish
blend
bless
blind
blink
block
bloody
bloom
blossom
blotch
blow
bludgeon
bluff
blunder
blur
blurt
blush
bluster
boast
bob
bobble
boggle
boil
bolster
bolt
bombard
boom
boost
boot
bop
boss
bother
bounce
bound
bow

box
brace
brag
brand
brave
bray
break
breathe
breeze
bribe
bridge
bridle
brighten
bristle
broach
broadcast
broil
brood
browse
bruise
bubble
buck
budge
bug
bully
bumble
bump
bundle
bungle
burble
burden
burn
burp
bury
bushwhack
bustle
butcher
buttonhole
buy
buzz

cackle
cage

cajole
call
calm
camouflage
campaign
canonize
capitalize
capitulate
capsize
captivate
capture
care
careen
caress
carom
carouse
carry
carry off
carry on
carry out
cascade
cast
castigate
castrate
catapult
catch
catch up
caterwaul
caution
cavort
cease
celebrate
censor
certify
chafe
chain
challenge
champion
change
channel
chant
characterize
charge

charm	coach	concentrate
chase	coast	conclude
chastise	coax	concoct
chat	coddle	concur
chatter	coerce	condemn
cheat	coil	condense
check	collaborate	condescend
checkmate	collapse	condone
cheer	collar	conduct
cherish	collect	confer
chew	color	confide
chide	comb	confine
chill	combine	confirm
chime	come	confiscate
chip in	come across	conflict
choke	come upon	conform
choose	come off	confound
chop	come out	confront
chortle	come to	confuse
christen	comfort	confute
chronicle	command	congest
chuck	commence	congratulate
chuckle	commend	conjure
circle	commit	connect
cite	commute	connive
claim	compare	conquer
clamp down	compel	consent
clam up	compete	consider
clap	compile	console
clarify	complain	conspire
clasp	complete	constrain
classify	complicate	construct
claw	comply	consult
clean	comport	consume
clean up	compose	contact
clear	compound	contain
cleave	comprehend	contaminate
clench	compress	contemplate
climb	compromise	contend
clinch	compute	contest
cling	con	continue
clobber	conceal	contort
clown	concede	contract
club	conceive	contradict

contrast
contribute
contrive
control
convene
converge
convert
convey
convict
convince
convulse
coo
cool
cooperate
coordinate
cope
cop out
copy
corral
correct
correlate
corroborate
corrupt
counsel
count
counter
counteract
counter-attack
counterfeit
cover
cower
crack
crack down
crackle
cradle
cram
cramp
crane
crank
crank out
crash
crave
crawl
creak

create
credit
creep
crimp
cringe
cripple
crisscross
criticize
creak
cross
crossexamine
crouch
crow
crowd
crown
cruise
crumble
crumple
crunch
crusade
crush
cry
cuddle
cudgel
cue
cuff
cultivate
curb
cure
curse
curtail
curve
cushion
cut
cut out
cut up

dab
dabble
dally
dam
damn
dance
dare

darken
dart
dash
daub
dawdle
dawn
daydream
dazzle
deaden
deafen
deal
debase
debate
debauch
debilitate
debunk
decapitate
decay
decelerate
decide
deck
declaim
declare
decline
decommission
decompose
decompress
decontaminate
decorate
decoy
decrease
decree
decry
dedicate
deduce
deduct
deem
deemphasize
deepen
deescalate
deface
defame
defeat
defend

defer	desecrate	dip
defile	desert	direct
define	design	disable
deflate	designate	disagree
deflect	desire	disappear
defraud	desist	disappoint
defuse	despair	disapprove
defy	despise	disarm
degenerate	destroy	disavow
degrade	detach	disburse
deify	detail	discard
deign	detect	discern
delay	deter	discharge
delegate	deteriorate	discipline
delete	determine	disclaim
deliberate	detest	disclose
delight	detour	disconcert
delineate	detract	disconnect
deliver	detain	discount
delude	devastate	discourage
delve	develop	discover
demand	deviate	discredit
demean	devil	discriminate
demolish	devise	discuss
demonstrate	devote	disdain
demoralize	devour	disenchant
demote	diagnose	disgorge
denigrate	diagram	disgrace
denounce	dial	disgruntle
deny	dicker	disguise
depart	dictate	disgust
depend	die	dish
depict	differ	dishearten
deplete	differentiate	dishevel
deplore	dig	dishonor
deploy	digest	dish out
deport	dig in	disillusion
deprecate	dignify	disintegrate
depress	digress	dislike
deprive	dillydally	dislodge
derail	dilute	dismantle
deride	dim	dismiss
descend	diminish	dismount
describe	dine	disobey

disorganize
disorient
disown
disparage
dispatch
dispel
dispense
disperse
display
displease
disprove
dispute
disqualify
disrobe
disrupt
dissect
dissolve
dissuade
distance
distill
distinguish
distort
distract
distress
distribute
distrust
disturb
dive
diverge
divert
divest
divide
divine
divulge
do
do away
dodge
dog
do in
dole
doll up
dominate
domineer
donate

doodle
dote
double
double cross
double up
doubt
doze
drag
drain
dramatize
drape
draw
drawl
draw out
draw up
dread
dream
dream up
dredge
dress down
drift
drill
drink
drip
drive
drone
drool
droop
drop
drop back
drop behind
drop in
drop off
drop out
drown
drub
drum
drum up
dry
dub
duck
duel
dumbfound
dump

dupe
duplicate
dwell
dwindle

earn
ease
eat
ebb
echo
edge
educate
effect
effervesce
effuse
egg
eject
eke
elaborate
elapse
elbow
elect
electrify
elongate
elucidate
elude
embarrass
embody
embrace
emcee
emend
emerge
emit
emote
emphasize
employ
empty
emulate
enchant
encircle
enclose
encompass
encounter
encourage

encroach
encumber
end
endanger
endear
endeavor
endorse
endure
energize
enfold
enforce
engage
engineer
engross
engulf
enhance
enjoy
enlarge
enlighten
enlist
enrage
enrapture
enrich
entangle
enter
entertain
enthrall
enthuse
entice
entrap
entreat
entrust
enumerate
enunciate
envelop
envisage
envy
equalize
equate
equip
equivocate
eradicate
erase
erect

erode
err
erupt
escalate
escape
escort
establish
estimate
evade
evaluate
evict
evoke
evolve
exacerbate
exact
exaggerate
exalt
exasperate
exceed
excel
exchange
excite
exclaim
exclude
excuse
exemplify
exercise
exert
exhale
exhaust
exhibit
exhort
exile
exit
expect
expedite
expel
experience
experiment
expire
explain
explode
exploit
explore

expose
extemporize
extend
extol
exude
exult
eye

fabricate
face
fade
fail
faint
fake
fall
fall flat
fall for
fall short
fall back
falsify
falter
fan
fantasize
fascinate
fasten
fast talk
fatigue
fear
feel
feign
fetch
fib
fiddle
fidget
fight
figure
fill in
finagle
find
finger
finish
fix
fizzle
flail

flame

flap

flash

flatten

flatter

flaunt

flee

flinch

fling

flip

flirt

flit

float

flock

flop

flounder

flow

flower

flub

fluctuate

fluff

fluster

flutter

fly

foam

focus

foil

fold

follow

fondle

fool

forbear

forbid

force

forebode

forego

foresee

foreshorten

forestall

forfeit

forget

forgive

forgo

form

formulate

foresake

fortify

foster

foul

foul up

frame

free

freeload

freeze

fret

frighten

frisk

fritter

frolic

frown

frustrate

fry

fudge

fuel

fulfill

fumble

fume

furnish

further

fuss

gab

gabble

gag

gain

gall

gallivant

gallop

galvanize

gambol

gang

gape

garble

gargle

garnish

gasp

gather

gauge

gawk

gaze

generalize

generate

gesticulate

gesture

get along

get by

gibe

giggle

gild

gird

give

give in

give out

give up

glamorize

glance

glare

glaze

gleam

glide

glimmer

glisten

glitter

gloat

glorify

gloss

glow

glower

gnash

gnaw

go

go at

go back on

go down the line

go for

go one better

go over

go to bat for

goad

gobble

goof

go on

go out	hallucinate	henpeck
go over	halt	herd
gossip	ham	hesitate
gouge	hammer	hide
grab	hamper	highlight
grade	hand	hinder
grant	handcuff	hint
grapple	handicap	hire
grasp	handle	hiss
grate	handpick	hit
gratify	hang	hoard
grease	hang in	hobble
greet	hang on	hobnob
grieve	hang up	hock
grill	harangue	hog
grimace	harass	hoist
grin	harbor	hold
grind	harden	hold forth
grip	harken	hold to
gripe	harm	hold with
groan	harness	hold out
grope	harp	holler
grouch	hassle	honk
group	hasten	honor
grouse	hatch	hoodwink
grow	hate	hook
growl	haul	hoot
grub	haunt	hop
grudge	have at	hope
grumble	have done with	host
grunt	have to do with	hound
guarantee	hawk	hover
guard	heap	howl
guess	hear	huddle
guide	heat	hug
gull	heave	hum
gulp	heckle	humble
gurgle	hedge	humiliate
gush	heed	humor
	heighten	hunger
hack	heist	hunt
haggle	help	hurl
hail	hem	hurry

hurt
hush
hustle
hypnotize

idealize
identify
ignite
ignore
illuminate
illustrate
imagine
imitate
immerge
immerse
immobilize
impair
impart
impersonate
impinge
implant
implement
implicate
implore
imply
importune
impose
impress
improve
improvise
impugn
impute
incapacitate
incense
inch
incite
include
inconvenience
incorporate
increase
incriminate
indicate
individualize

infatuate
infect
infer
infest
infiltrate
inflame
inflate
inflect
inflict
influence
inform
infringe
infuriate
ingratiate
inhibit
initiate
inject
injure
inquire
insert
insinuate
insist
inspect
inspire
install
instigate
instill
instruct
insulate
insult
insure
integrate
intellectualize
intend
intensify
intercede
intercept
interest
interfere
interject
intermingle
interpret
interrogate

interrupt
intersect
intervene
interview
intimate
intimidate
intone
intoxicate
intrench
intrigue
introduce
intrude
intrust
intwine
inundate
invade
invalidate
inveigle
invent
invert
invest
investigate
invigorate
invite
invoke
involve
irk
irritate
itch
itemize

jab
jabber
jangle
jeer
jeopardize
jerk
jest
jibe
jiggle
jilt
jimmy
jingle

jitter	lavish	lose
join	lay	lounge
joke	lead	love
jolly	leak	lumber
jolt	lean	lump
josh	leap	lunge
jostle	learn	lure
jot	leave	lurk
judge	lecture	lust
juggle	leer	
jumble	lend	madden
jump	lengthen	magnetize
junk	lessen	magnify
justify	let	maim
juxtapose	level	make
	libel	malign
keep	liberate	mall
kibitz	lick	manage
kick	lie	mangle
kid	lift	manipulate
kidnap	lighten	maneuver
kill	like	manufacture
kiss	liken	mar
knee	limit	march
kneel	limp	mark
knife	linger	marry
knock	link	mash
know	lisp	mask
knuckle	list	massacre
	listen	massage
label	live	master
labor	liven	match
lack	load	mature
lag	loaf	maximize
lambaste	loan	mean
lament	locate	measure
languish	lock	meddle
lap	loiter	mediate
lapse	loll	meet
lash	long	melt
last	look	memorize
laud	loom	menace
laugh	loosen	mend
launch	lope	mention

merge
merit
merrymake
mess
milk
mill
mime
mimic
mince
mind
mine
mingle
minimize
mirror
misadvise
misallege
misapply
misbehave
miscalculate
misconstrue
miscue
misdescribe
misdirect
misread
misgive
misguide
misinform
misinstruct
misinterpret
misjudge
mislay
mislead
mismanage
mismatch
misplace
mispronounce
misquote
misread
misreport
misrepresent
miss
misstate
misstep
mistake

mistrust
misunderstand
misuse
mix
moan
mock
moderate
modify
modulate
moisten
mold
molest
mollify
monitor
mop
moralize
mortify
motion
motivate
mount
mourn
mouth
move
mug
mull
multiply
mumble
murder
muscle
muse
muster
mutilate
muzzle
mystify

nag
nail
name
narrate
near
neck
need
needle
negate

neglect
negotiate
nestle
neutralize
nibble
nip
nod
nominate
nose
note
notice
notify
nourish
nudge
nurse
nurture
nuzzle

obey
obfuscate
object
obligate
oblige
obliterate
observe
obstruct
obtain
occupy
offend
offer
officiate
offset
ogle
omit
ooze
open
operate
oppose
oppress
optimize
orate
orbit
ordain
order

organize	pad	pet
ostracize	paddle	petition
oust	paint	petrify
outfit	pair	phrase
outlast	palpitate	pick
outline	pamper	picture
out maneuver	pan	pierce
out match	pander	pile
outshine	panic	pin
outstrip	pant	pinch
outwit	parade	pinpoint
overact	paraphrase	pitch
overcome	pardon	pity
overdo	parrot	place
overemphasize	part	plan
overestimate	participate	plant
overextend	pass	plaster
overflow	paste	play
overhear	patch	plead
overlap	patronize	please
overlook	pattern	pledge
overpower	pause	plot
overpraise	paw	plow
overprotect	pay	pluck
overrate	peck	plug
overreach	peek	plumb
override	peel	plunder
overrule	pelt	poach
overrun	penalize	pocket
oversell	penetrate	point
overshadow	perceive	poison
oversimplify	perfect	poke
overstate	perform	police
overstep	perk	polish
overthrow	permit	ponder
overturn	perpetrate	pool
overwhelm	perplex	poop
overwork	persecute	pop
owe	persist	puppet
own	personalize	portray
	persuade	pose
pace	perturb	possess
pacify	pervert	pounce
pack	pester	pound

pout
practice
pray
preach
precipitate
predetermine
predict
preempt
preface
prefer
prejudge
prepare
present
preserve
preside
press
presume
presuppose
pretend
prevent
prick
prime
prize
probe
proceed
procure
prod
produce
profess
profit
progress
prohibit
project
prolong
promise
promote
prompt
pronounce
prop
propel
propose
prosecute
protect
protest

protrude
prove
provoke
prowl
prune
pry
psychoanalyze
publicize
puff
pull
pulsate
pulverize
pump
punch
punctuate
puncture
punt
purchase
pursue
push
put
puzzle

qualify
quench
quibble
quit
quiver
quote

radiate
rag
raise
rake
ramble
rank
rankle
ransack
rap
rate
ratify
rationalize
rattle
rave

ravish
raze
react
read
readjust
realize
reap
rearrange
rebel
rebound
rebuild
rebut
recall
recap
recapitulate
recapture
recast
recede
receive
reciprocate
recite
reckon
reclaim
recline
recognize
recoil
recollect
recommend
recommit
recompense
reconcile
recondition
reconstruct
reconvey
recount
recoup
recover
recreate
recriminate
recruit
rectify
recuperate
recycle
redeem

redistribute
redo
redouble
redress
reduce
reenter
reexamine
refer
refine
reflect
reform
refrain
refund
refuse
regain
regale
regard
regress
regret
rehash
rehearse
reiterate
reject
rejoice
rejoin
rejuvenate
relapse
relate
relax
release
relegate
relent
relieve
relinquish
relive
relocate
remain
remake
remark
remember
remind
reminisce
remove
render

renew
reopen
reorganize
repair
repay
repeal
repeat
repel
rephrase
replace
replay
replenish
reply
repossess
reprieve
reprimand
reproduce
reprove
repudiate
repulse
repute
request
require
requite
rescind
rescue
resent
reserve
resign
resist
resolve
resonate
resort
resound
restate
restore
restrain
restrict
resume
resurge
resuscitate
retain
retake
retard

retell
retire
retort
retouch
retract
retreat
retrench
retrieve
revamp
reveal
revel
revenge
revere
revert
review
revise
revitalize
revive
revoke
revolve
rewind
rework
rhapsodize
ricochet
rid
ride
rifle
rig
rile
ring
rip
ripple
rise
roar
roast
rob
rock
roister
roll
rollick
romanticize
romp
root
rot

roughen

rouse

rout

rumble

ruminate

rummage

rumple

run

rupture

rush

rustle

sack

sag

salivate

salute

salvage

sashay

satisfy

saturate

saunter

save

scamper

scan

scare

scatter

scavenge

scintillate

scoff

scold

scoot

scorch

scour

scram

scramble

scrap

scrape

scratch

scrawl

scream

scrimp

scrounge

scrunch

scrutinize

scuffle

scurry

search

seclude

second-guess

secrete

sedate

seduce

see

seek

seem

seep

seethe

seize

select

sell

send

sequester

serve

set

settle

sever

sew

sharpen

shatter

shave

shift

shimmer

shine

shiver

shoot

shortchange

shove

show

shrink

shrivel

shrug

shudder

shuffle

shut

sidestep

sidetrack

sigh

signal

simmer

simper

simplify

simulate

sing

sink

sip

sit

sizzle

skim

skulk

slam

slant

slash

slay

slide

slip

slither

slubber

slog

slosh

slouch

slug

slump

slur

slurp

smack

smash

smear

smell

smirk

smolder

smother

smuggle

snap

snarl

snatch

sneak

sneeze

sniff

sniffle

snitch

snoop

snooze

snort

snuggle

soar

socialize

sock

softsoap

soil

solemnize

solicit

solidify

solve

soothe

sound

spend

spar

sparkle

squeak

squeal

squeeze

squelch

squint

squirm

squirt

squish

stab

stage manage

stagger

stagnate

stalk

stammer

stamp

stand

stare

start

startle

stash

stay

steal

steer

stem

stew

stifle

stimulate

sting

stink

stipulate

stir

stop

stow

straddle

strafe

straggle

straightarm

strain

straiten

strangle

stray

strengthen

stretch

stride

strike

strip

struggle

strut

stumble

stun

stupify

stutter

subdue

subjugate

submit

subscribe

subside

substantiate

subvert

succeed

succumb

suck

suffer

suffocate

suggest

sulk

summarize

supplicate

supply

support

suppose

suppress

surge

surmise

surmount

surpass

surprise

surrender

survey

survive

suspect

suspend

sustain

swagger

swallow

swap

swarm

swear

sweat

sweep

swell

swelter

swerve

swim

swindle

swing

swirl

swish

swoon

sympathize

synchronize

take

talk

tamper

tan

tangle

tantalize

tap

tarnish

tattle

taunt

tear

teem

teeter

teethe

temper
tempt
tend
terminate
terrify
terrorize
testify
thank
thaw
think
thrash
threaten
thrive
throb
throw
thrust
thwack
thwart
tickle
tighten
tilt
tingle
tip
tiptoe
tire
titilate
toast
toddle
toil
tolerate
tootle
topple
toss
tote
totter
touch
toughen
tousle
tout
tow
trail
tramp
trample
transact

transcend
transfer
transgress
translate
transmit
transport
transpose
traumatize
travel
tread
treat
tremble
trespass
triumph
trump
trounce
truck
trudge
try
tuck
tug
tumble
turn
tussle
tweak
tweet
tweeze
twist
twirl
twitter
two-time
typify
tyrannize

umpire
unarm
unbalance
unbelt
unbend
unbind
unbolt
unbuckle
unburden
unbutton

uncage
uncap
unchain
unclasp
unclench
unclothe
uncover
underact
undercut
underestimate
undergo
undermine
underplay
underrate
underscore
undersell
understand
understate
undervalue
underwrite
undo
undress
undulate
unearth
unfasten
unfold
unglue
unhand
unhinge
unhitch
unhook
unify
unite
unlatch
unleash
unload
unlock
unmask
unnerve
unpack
unpin
unravel
unriddle
unrobe

unroll
unscrew
unseal
unseat
unsettle
unshackle
unsnap
unsnarl
unstick
untie
unveil
unwind
unwrap
upbraid
upend
uphold
uplift
upset
upturn
use
usurp
utilize

vacate
vacillate
validate
vamoose
vandalize
vanish
vanquish
vary
vault
vaunt
veer
vegetate
vend
ventriloquize
verify
vex
vibrate
victimize
vie
view

vindicate
violate
visit
visualize
vocalize
voice
volley
volunteer
vote
vouch
vow
vulgarize

wad
waddle
wade
waffle
wag
wager
waggle
wagon
wail
wait
waive
wake
walk
wallop
wallow
waltz
wander
wane
wangle
want
war
warble
warm
warn
warp
warrant
wash
waste
watch

wattle
wave
waver
waylay
weaken
wear
weary
weasel
weather
weave
wed
wedge
weed
weep
weigh
welcome
welsh
wet
whack
wham
whang
wheedle
wheel
wheeze
whelp
whet
whiff
whiffle
while
whimper
whine
whinny
whip
whir
whisk
whisper
whistle
whitewash
whiz
whoop
whoosh
whop
whore

widen

wield

wiggle

wile

will

wilt

win

wince

wind

windowshop

wine

wing

wink

wipe

wire

wish

withdraw

wither

withhold

withstand

witness

wobble

wolf

womanize

wonder

word

work

worm

worry

worsen

worship

wound

wrack

wrangle

wrap

wreak

wreathe

wreck

wrench

wrestle

wriggle

wring

write

writhe

yak

yammer

yank

yap

yawn

yawp

yearn

yell

yelp

yield

yodel

yowl

zap

zigzag

zing

zip

zoom

Open Pantomimes

OPEN PANTOMIME 1

A enters up left
crosses to center
five second pause
crosses up left to close a door
backs right
crosses to down right chair
removes coat
stands on chair
smiles
five second pause
crosses up left to open a door
falls

OPEN PANTOMIME 2

A is on sofa down left
crawls stage right to a chair
rises
crosses to center
looks at object on the floor
crosses up left to a door
jumps
crosses to down left chair
sits
smiles

OPEN PANTOMIME 3

A lies on floor down center
sits up

lies down
stands up
sits down
laughs
rises
crosses up center
stands on table
stands on one leg
jumps off table toward up left door
backs right

OPEN PANTOMIME 4

A enters up left
B rises from sofa
A crosses to center
B hides behind sofa
A crosses up left to a door
B crosses to center
A crosses down right to chair
B looks at object on floor
A removes his coat
B crosses to up left door
A stands on a chair
B jumps three times
A smiles
B crosses to A
A puts hand on B's shoulder
B smiles

OPEN PANTOMIME 5

A enters up left
B lies on floor down center
A crosses to center
B sits up
A sits down
B crosses up left to close a door
A laughs
B backs right
A rises
B stands on table

A removes coat to hand it to B
B jumps off table toward up left door
A falls
B backs right

OPEN PANTOMIME 6

A lies on sofa down left
B lies on floor center
A rises
   crosses to center
   sits
B kisses A
A slaps B
B laughs
A rises
   crosses up right
B laughs
A looks at object on floor
B rises
   crosses to A
A crosses up left to a door
B nods
A crosses to sofa down left
B smiles
A sits on sofa

Articulation

VOWELS

A vowel is a sound made by the vibrations of the vocal cords with an open mouth free from obstruction. The alphabet contains five or six characters considered vowels. However, A, E, I, O, U, and Y may be pronounced in a variety of ways. The alphabet does not provide you with a sure guide to the spoken sound of vowels. Another alphabet, concerned with speech sounds rather than with writing and spelling, can help. The International Phonetic Alphabet has a symbol for each speech sound and each sound has only one symbol. The advantage of this alphabet is that it allows you to think and write in terms of sounds rather than in terms of spelling. It stimulates the development of a good ear, helps eliminate dialects, catches mispronunciations, and encourages clear enunciation.

The International Phonetic Alphabet

Vowels

Symbol	Examples of Sound
u	you, flew, fruit, who, you, shoe, rule, tooth, true, through, pool, wooed, Lulu
U	put, full, could, wood, good, woman, look
o	go, omit, tone, show, oasis, home, obey, toe, blow
ɔ	all, jaw, law, broad, talk, gone, caught, Paul, laud, awful
ɒ	wander, sorry, watch, not, got, long, off, laurel, doll
ɑ	calm, father, hard, far, amen, arm, sergeant, balm, tot, shah
æ	and, hang, gas, glad, plaid, sang, back, marry, tan, cat
ʌ	flood, truck, must, does, custom, above, upon, mud, one, nothing, bun, rough, come
ə	*about*, sof*a*, fam*ou*s, cap*a*ble
a	dance, half, class, aunt, path

ɛ	set, let, then, said, ever, yet, lecture, many, steady, tell, Thames, merry
3	serve
e	make, rate, shape, cake, gape, play, chaos, they, gauge, vacation, prostrate
I	symbol, pity, busy, fit, guild, women, ship, sieve, pin, did
i	siege, east, bee, speech, eat, weed, police, machine, ski, receive, peat

Symbol	Guide to Pronunciation
[u]	Place the back of your tongue near the soft palate. Your lips are round and tense, protruding with the front of your tongue depressed.
[U]	Relax your tongue and lips from [u]. Your lips are less round and your mouth more open as your jaw drops.
[o]	Drop your jaw and lower tongue from [U]. Your lips protrude and round a bit with your tongue in a middle-high position.
[ɔ]	Lower your tongue, unround your lips a bit, and somewhat relax your tongue and lips. Your jaw drops a bit.
[ɒ]	Your tongue muscles relax and you drop the back of your tongue and jaw from the [ɔ] position. Your lips are open to make a larger circle than [ɔ].
[ɑ]	Your tongue is low, flat and relaxed. Lower your jaw to its lowest point. Spread your lips far apart and unround them.
[æ]	Your tongue is almost flat and relaxed on the floor of your mouth with a slight raising of the front part. Your mouth widens from the [ɛ] position.
[ʌ]	Raise the middle of your tongue from [ɑ]. Your jaw rises somewhat while your lips remain as for [ɑ].
[ə]	Relax your tongue with the tip toward your hard palate. This sounds like an unaccented version of [ʌ].
[a]	This is an Eastern seacoast or New England sound. The vowel sound lies midway between [æ] and [ɑ]. The front of your tongue rises from [ɑ] and moves forward slightly. Your mouth closes as your jaw rises.
[ɛ]	Widen your lips and move your tongue forward from the [ə] position.
[3]	Place the front of the tongue higher than the back. Lower the jaw and open your lips as in [ə].
[e]	Move your tongue up and forward from [ɛ]. Your jaw becomes more closed and your lips tense a bit. Avoid excessive nasality with this vowel.
[I]	Raise the front of your tongue from [e] and move it forward. Your tongue tenses and your teeth become closer. Spread your lips a bit further.
[i]	Raise the front of your tongue almost to your hard palate. Your tongue tenses and your lips are slightly apart. Your jaw nearly closes.

EXERCISES

1. Sing a familiar tune such as "Row, Row, Row, Your Boat" or "Farmer in the Dell" using only a variety of vowel sounds.

2. Plan and articulate vowel sounds for *Jabberwocky*. Put the phonetic symbols above the sounds.

3. Put a jaw prop (a piece of cork about ¼" thick and 1¼" in diameter) in your mouth between your upper and lower molars to keep maximum resonance space. Practice the vowels of the Phonetic Alphabet with the prop to experience the lip and tongue movements characteristic of each. Keep your jaw free of tension. Repeat the vowels without the prop keeping your jaw wide. Check your tongue placement with Figure 3-3.

4. Play a practice selection with the jaw prop. Attend to the lip and tongue movements for the vowels. Articulate the selection without a prop.

Diphthongs

Symbol	Examples of Sound
aI	sky, by, while, aisle, I, time, height
ɔI	ahoy, boy, oil, void, loyal, voice
aU	cloud, how, now, kraut, bough, town, loud, sound

Symbol	Guide to Pronunciation
[aI]	Your tongue begins in the [a] or [ɑ] position—relaxed tongue, low in the mouth, lips unrounded, jaw dropped—and glides to the [I] position—with the front of your tongue raised high and forward.
[ɔI]	Begin this sound from the [ɔ] position and glide with your tongue raised far forward to the [I] position.
[aU]	Your tongue is relaxed and low; your lips are unrounded as in [ɑ]. Glide to [U] with the back of your tongue raised and your lips rounded.

EXERCISES

1. Review *Jabberwocky* paying attention to diphthongs.

2. Practice the diphthongs with and without a jaw prop, noting your lip and tongue movements.

3. Review the practice selection used for the vowels this time attending to diphthongs.

CONSONANTS

Consonants break, divide, or separate the stream of vowel sounds; consonants obstruct the breath in some part of the mouth or throat. Vocal obstructions are of two types—voiced and voiceless. If you place your fingers on your larynx as you pronounce a voiceless consonant, no vibrations are felt. Only voiced consonants vibrate. Further classification of consonants separates them according to the part of the mouth or nasal passage in operation during their formation. The Phonetic Alphabet can guide us again.

Consonants

Symbol	Voiced	Voiceless	Type	Example
t		X	plosive	tend, item, hat
d	X		plosive	dew, idea, hid
p		X	plosive	pat, open, pit
b	X		plosive	bat, robber, mob
k		X	plosive	cat, liquor, kick
g	X		plosive	gay, haggard, bag
h		X	fricative	held, heap, holiday
f		X	fricative	for, enough, caliph
v	X		fricative	very, vacuum, sav-ior
s		X	fricative	sap, scene, sass
z	X		fricative	xylophone, has
m	X		nasal	melt, amid, hem
n	X		nasal	nose, inner, son
l	X		glide	lady, holy, Paul
r	X		glide	ran, ride, scissor
w	X		glide	won, quiet, wit
ɵ		X	fricative	thesis, bath
ð	X		fricative	this, bathe
ʃ		X	fricative	show, machine
ʒ	X		fricative	beige, casual
tʃ		X	affricative	cello, church
dʒ	X		affricative	jewel, soldier
ŋ	X		nasal	singer, long
j	X		glide	youth, beyond
hw		X	glide	while, where

Symbols	Guide to Pronunciation
Plosives.	A current of air is stopped completely and then is released with a mild ex*plos*ion of breath.
[t--d]	Place the tip of your tongue against the upper gum ridge; the sides of your tongue touche the inner edges of your teeth, blocking the air passage momentarily. By lowering the tongue tip, release your breath suddenly with a small ex*plos*ion.
[p--b]	Close your lips tightly so that your breath mounts under pressure. By suddenly parting your lips, ex*plo*de the pressurized air.
[k--g]	Raise the back of your tongue to your velum, shutting off the air passage. Build up pressure so that the breath ex*plo*des out when you suddenly lower your tongue.
Fricatives.	The breath of air is narrowed or squeezed to prolong a fricative sound.
[f--v]	Raise your lower lip against the edges of your upper front teeth. Force air out between your lower lip and upper teeth.
[s-z]	Place your tongue tip against the lower gums while raising the sides of your tongue to touch the inner edges of your upper

	back teeth. Force air out along the groove of your tongue and over the edges of your front teeth.
[θ-ð]	Protrude your tongue with a flat tip between your upper and lower teeth. Force the air between your tongue and upper teeth.
[ʃ--ʒ]	Touch the edges of your upper teeth with the sides of your tongue. Almost close your teeth. Make the air flow out through the wide ridge in the middle of your tongue. Your protruded lips are almost rounded.
[h]	Put the tip of your tongue against your lower gum ridge and explode some air.
Affricatives.	A combination of movements for plosive and fricative sounds as the tongue shifts from blocking to squeezing the air.
[tʃ--dʒ]	Press the tip of your tongue firmly against your upper gum ridge, assuming an arched position for [s]. Lower the tip of your tongue and your breath explodes as for [t--d].
Glides.	The breath has neither a free passage nor a completely blocked entry. The tongue glides from the vowel's characteristic starting position to utter the sound.
[l]	Hold the top of your tongue lightly against your upper gum ridge. Voiced breath escapes over the relaxed sides of your tongue as it glides to the vowel sound position.
[r]	Raise your tongue sides toward your teeth and your tongue tip toward the palate behind your upper gum ridge. Protrude your lips, begin vocalization and glide your tongue to the position for the vowel sound which follows.
[w]	Protrude your rounded lips with the back of your tongue raised to pronounce [u]. As the sound begins, glide your lips and tongue into position for the subsequent vowel.
[j]	Raise your tongue to the [i] position. As the sound begins, glide your lips and tongue into the position of the following vowel.
[hw]	Begin to pronounce [w] but slide immediately to a voiceless [h].
Nasals.	Vocalized breath passes into the nasal cavity rather than into the mouth. The mouth is blocked by the lowered soft palate.
[m]	Assume the position for [p--b] but lower your soft palate to direct the sound through your nasal passages.
[n]	Assume the position for [t--d] but lower your soft palate to direct the sound through your nasal passages.
[ŋ]	Assume the position for [k--g] but lower your soft palate to direct the sound through your nasal passages.

EXERCISES

1. Practice nasal consonants to develop full uninterrupted frontal resonance.

a. m - mi - ma - mu

b. n - ni - na - nu

c. ŋ - ŋi - ŋa - ŋu

2. Practice voiced fricative consonants to develop full uninterrupted resonance.

a. v - va - vi - vu
b. z - za - zi - zu
c. ð - ða - ðo - ði
d. ʒ - ʒa - ʒi - ʒu

(These are phonetic vowel symbols)

3. Practice initial and final consonant sounds with these phonetic vowel signs.

a. pap, bab, tapt, taspt, pat, dad, stad, stast, zapt, pasts, kak, gag, pakt, paskt, tat, hat, tasθ, tasθs, ta θs, faf, vaf, mam, nan, nang, blap, plap, drap, thrab, krab, shrap, klast, grapt, glasts, sprak, brag, strakt, traskt, frat

b. pip, bib, tipt, tispt, tipt, did, stid, stist, zipt, pists, kik, gig, pikt, piskt, tit, hit, tisθ, tis θs, tiθs, fif, vif, mim, nin, ning, blip, plip, drip, thrib, krib, shrip, klist, gript, glists, sprik, brig, strikt, triskt, frit

c. pup, bub, tupt, tuspt, tupt, dud, stud, stust, zupt, pusts, kuk, gug, pukt, puskt, tut, hut, tusθ, tus θs, tu θs, fuf, vuf, mum, nun, nung, blup, plup, drup, thrub, krub, shrup, klust, grupt, glusts, spruk, brug, sturkt, truskt, frut

4. Practice the following consonants to limber articulation muscles. Accent marks establish a rhythm.

a. tá ta ta, tá ta ta, etc.
b. dá da da, dá da da, etc.
c. pá pa pa, pá pa pa, etc.
d. bá ba ba, bá ba ba, etc.
e. ká ka ka, ká ka ka, etc.
f. gá ga ga, gá ga ga, etc.
g. há ha ha, há ha ha, etc.
h. fá fa fa, fá fa fa, etc.
i. vá va va, vá va va, etc.
j. sá sa sa, sá sa sa, etc.
k. zá za za, zá za za, etc.
l. má ma ma, má ma ma, etc.
m. ná na na, ná na na, etc.
n. lá la la, lá la la, etc.
o. wá wa wa, wá wa wa, etc.
p. θá θa θa, θá θa θa, etc.
q. ðá ða ða, ðá ða ða, etc.
r. ʃá ʃa ʃa, ʃá ʃa ʃa, etc.
s. ʒá ʒa ʒa, ʒá ʒa ʒa, etc.
u. tʃá tʃa tʃa, tʃá tʃa tʃa, etc.
v. dʒá dʒa dʒa, dʒá dʒa dʒa, etc.
w. ŋá ŋa ŋa, ŋá ŋa ŋa, etc.

x.   já ja ja, já ja ja, etc.

y.   hwá hwa hwa, hwá hwa hwa, etc.

Repeat this exercise with the vowels *u, o, e,* and *i.*

5. Review and play *Jabberwocky* in light of your new facility with consonants. Translate the poem into phonetic symbols.

6. Review and play the tongue twisters examined in Chapter 1, attending to consonant production. Translate the tongue twisters into phonetic symbols.

7. Prepare and play the poems "Nephelidia" or "I am the Very Model of A Modern Major General." Concentrate on consonant production. Translate either poem into phonetic symbols.

8. Overly precise articulation is as unsatisfactory as sloppy articulation. Use a pronouncing dictionary such as Kenyon and Knott's *A Pronouncing Dictionary of American English* to find the correct pronunciation for the following words.

sailor	a	barbarous
garden	Wednesday	literature
parliament	clothes	future
often	waistcoat	desperate
the	postscript	calmly
issue	nature	postpone
February	misery	naive
business	grievous	mischievous
ordinance	asked	vegetable

Translate the words into the phonetic pronunciation you think correct before looking up the answers.

Bibliography

A student of acting should find the following books interesting and useful in developing his craft. The list ranges from standard expositions of the Stanislavski approach to acting, to American teachers' adaptations of the Russian method, to actors' reminiscences, to psychological and sociological works, to more general theatre books dealing with the actor's place in the theatre. Many of these books have been cited in the text; others will become more important as you study the theatre in other courses. Each will help you develop your own unique view of acting.

THE STUDY OF ACTING

BARKER, CLIVE. *Theatre Games.* New York: Drama Book Specialists, (Publishers), 1977.

BENEDETTI, ROBERT. *The Actor at Work,* rev. ed. Englewood Cliffs, N.J.: Prentice-Hall, 1976.

BLUNT, JERRY. *The Composite Art of Acting.* New York: Macmillan, 1966.

BOLESLAVSKY, RICHARD. *Acting: The First Six Lessons.* New York: Theatre Arts Books, 1966.

BOWSKILL, DEREK. *Acting: An Introduction.* Englewood Cliffs, N.J.: Prentice-Hall, 1977.

CALVERT, LOUIS. *Problems of the Actor.* New York: Henry Holt, 1918.

CHEKHOV, MICHAEL. *To the Actor on the Technique of Acting.* New York: Harper & Row, 1953.

COHEN, ROBERT. *Acting Power.* Palo Alto, Calif.: Mayfield Publishing Company, 1978.

————. *Acting Professionally.* Palo Alto, Calif.: Mayfield Publishing Company, 1975.

COLE, TOBY, ed. *Acting: A Handbook of the Stanislavski Method.* New York: Crown Publishers, 1971.

GROTOWSKI, JERZY. *Towards a Poor Theatre.* New York: Simon and Schuster, 1969.

GUTHRIE, TYRONE. *Tyrone Guthrie On Acting.* New York: Viking, 1971.

HAGEN, UTA. *Respect for Acting.* New York: Macmillan, 1973.

HAYMAN, RONALD. *Techniques of Acting.* New York: Holt, Rinehart & Winston, 1969.

LINKLATER, KRISTEN.   *Freeing the Natural Voice.* New York: Dramabook Specialists, Publishers, 1976.

LEWIS, ROBERT.   *Advice to the Players.* New York: Harper & Row, 1980.

———.   *Method or Madness?* London: Heinemann, 1960.

MAROWITZ, CHARLES.   *The Act of Being: Towards a Theory of Acting.* New York: Taplinger Publishing Company, 1978.

———.   *Stanislavski and the Method.* New York: The Citadel Press, 1964.

PENROD, JAMES.   *Movement for the Performing Artist.* Palo Alto, Calif.: National Press Books, 1974.

ROLFE, BARI.   *Behind the Mask.* Oakland, Calif.: Persona Books, 1977.

SHURTLEFF, MICHAEL and GORDON HUNT.   *Audition: Everything an Actor Needs to Get the Part.* New York: Walker, 1978.

SPOLIN, VIOLA.   *Improvisation for the Theatre.* Evanston, Ill.: Northwestern University Press, 1963.

STANISLAVSKI, CONSTANTIN.   *An Actor Prepares.* New York: Theatre Arts Books, 1966.

———.   *Building a Character.* New York: Theatre Arts Books, 1949.

———.   *Creating a Role.* New York: Theatre Arts Books, 1961.

TURNER, J. CLIFFORD.   *Voice and Speech in the Theatre,* revised Malcolm Morrison. London: Pitman Publishing House, 1977.

ACTORS TALK ABOUT ACTING

BURTON, HAL.   *Great Acting.* New York: Bonanza Books, 1967.

COLE, TOBY and HELEN KRICH CHINOY.   *Actors on Acting.* New York: Crown Publishers, 1965.

FUNKE, LEWIS and JOHN E. BOOTH.   *Actors Talk About Acting.* New York: Avon Books, 1961.

KALTER, JOANMARIE.   *Actors on Acting.* New York: Sterling Publishing Company, 1978.

ROSS, LILLIAN and HELEN ROSS.   *The Player.* New York: Simon and Schuster, 1962.

HUMAN BEHAVIOR AND GROUP DYNAMICS

ALLPORT, GORDON W.   *Personality: A Psychological Interpretation.* New York: Holt, Rinehart & Winston, 1937.

ARNOLD, MAGDA.   *Emotion and Personality.* 2 Vols. New York: Columbia University Press, 1960.

BERNE, ERIC.   *Games People Play.* New York: Grove Press, 1964.

GOFFMAN, ERVING.   *Frame Analysis.* New York: Harper & Row, 1974.

———.   *The Presentation of Self in Everyday Life.* New York: Doubleday, 1959.

MASLOW, ABRAHAM.   *Motivation and Personality.* New York: Harper & Row, 1954.

———.   *Toward a Psychology of Being.* New York: D. Van Nostrand, 1968.

POLSTER, ERVING and MIRIAM.   *Gestalt Therapy Integrated.* New York: Vintage Books, 1973.

STEINER, CLAUDE.   *Scripts People Live.* New York: Grove Press, 1974.

THEATRE BOOKS

BARRAULT, JEAN-LOUIS.   *The Theatre of Jean-Louis Barrault.* New York: Hill and Wang, 1959.

BECKERMAN, BERNARD.   *Dynamics of Drama: Theory and Method of Analysis.* New York: Drama Book Specialists (Publishers), 1979.

BERMEL, ALBERT.   *Contradictory Characters.* New York: Dutton, 1973.

BRAUN, EDWARD, ed. and trans.   *Meyerhold on Theatre.* New York: Hill and Wang, 1969.

COLE, DAVID.   *The Theatrical Event.* Middletown, Conn.: Wesleyan University Press, 1975.

HEFFNER, HUBERT C., SAMUEL SELDEN, and HUNTON D. SELLMAN.   *Modern Theatre Practice,* 5th ed. Englewood Cliffs, N.J.: Prentice-Hall, 1973.

ST. DENIS, MICHEL.   *Theatre: The Rediscovery of Style.* New York: Theatre Arts Books, 1960.

SCHECHNER, RICHARD.   *Environmental Theater.* New York: Hawthorn Books, 1973.

SONTAG, SUSAN, ed.   *Selected Writings of Antonin Artaud.* New York: Farrar, Straus & Giroux, 1976.

WILLET, JOHN, ed.   *Brecht on Theatre.* New York: Hill and Wang, 1964.

ZORN, JOHN W., ed.   *The Essential Delsarte.* Metuchen, N.J.: Scarecrow Press, 1968.

Index